# THE
# green
## GARDENER'S GUIDE
### JOE LAMP'L

SIMPLE, SIGNIFICANT ACTIONS TO
PROTECT & PRESERVE OUR PLANET

Published by Cool Springs Press
101 Forrest Crossing Boulevard
Suite 100
Franklin, Tennessee 37064

Cataloging-in-Publication Data application in process

ISBN-13: 978-1-59186-426-4

First Printing 2008
Printed in Canada
10 9 8 7 6 5 4 3 2 1

Managing Editor: Michael McKinley

Cover and Interior Design: Marc Pewitt

Indexer: Janel Leatherman

**www.greengardenersguide.com**

Visit the Cool Springs Press Web site at **www.coolspringspress.net**

For more information about Joe Lamp'l, visit **www.joegardener.com**

This book is printed on 100% recycled paper. ♻

# THE
# green
## GARDENER'S GUIDE
### JOE LAMP'L

## SIMPLE, SIGNIFICANT ACTIONS TO
## PROTECT & PRESERVE OUR PLANET

COOL
SPRINGS
PRESS
Franklin, Tennessee

# DEDICATION

This book is dedicated to the past, the present, and the future.

To Rachel Carson, author of *Silent Spring*, the book that is often credited with first launching the environmental movement and awakening our ecological consciousness.

To all the men and women today whose hard work around the world helps us recognize that our environmental crisis is a global issue and who are doing something about it.

But mostly to my children, Rachel and Amy, and to all the children who, I pray, will think and live so that their actions will never be part of the problem but rather the solution.

*Treat the earth well: it was not given to you by your parents, it was loaned to you by your children. We do not inherit the earth from our ancestor. We borrow it from our children.*

ANCIENT NATIVE AMERICAN PROVERB

# ACKNOWLEDGEMENTS

No sooner had I said I wouldn't be doing another book any time in the foreseeable future, than I find myself writing this one. And I'm so glad I did. Because of the many hours poured into the research and writing, it would have been impossible to complete such a book without a dedicated team behind the scenes carefully putting all the pieces into place.

Many times there was an abundance of statistical information to support a particular topic. In those instances, deciding what not to include was the biggest challenge. Other times, it was difficult if not impossible to quantify any information in a way that appeared to be a definitive number. Yet, in the end, through the tireless work of a few key people, *The Green Gardener's Guide* evolved into what I hope you will find to be a book that is not only enjoyable to read but also enlightens you with some interesting facts and stirs your soul as you green your garden.

My sincere appreciation goes to the following very important people because when I say yes to a book project, I know I am deeply involving them as well.

First, to my family: while I managed to burn the candle at both ends, I surfaced too briefly each day to spend time with you Becky, Rachel and Amy. And while I worked away on this project, the three of you patiently waited and gave me the time that I needed to complete this work on time.

To my business partner and loyal friend, Courtenay Vanderbilt: it's safe to say without your help, this book would not exist today (nor might I for that matter). In addition to being my eyes and ears and the voice of reason, you are the master at managing the details. While I might look to the sky to see the big picture, you keep one eye to the ground to keep me from stumbling along the journey. You allowed me the time simply to write, while you thoughtfully refined my words, protected my time, watched my back, and ran a company. We make a great team, but you are the true hero!

Thanks to Michael McKinley, managing editor, quarterback, and playmaker. You laid out a roadmap that was so clear, even I couldn't fail. Thank you for your tenacity and stubbornness because when it was all said and done, your eye for the big picture and your contribution to the little things provided the palette I needed. Thanks also for putting together such a crack team: Veronica Fowler--thanks for jumping in late and providing your assistance. You saved me several weeks and lots of hair. And to Randy Schultz, Diane Jesse Nelson, and Jim Clark for doing much of the research that was so important to bring the book's message home. You really came up with some amazing information!

To Shannon Whitehead, copy editor, for poring through every word of this manuscript and sanding off the rough edges in record time. You had your work cut out for you on this project, but thank you for not being so brutal as you polished my words while keeping my voice . . . not an easy thing to do!

To Cindy "the glue" Games, thanks for keeping a cool head when mine was not. You are a joy to work with and always the key link in the chain holding it all together. Words can't describe what an integral part you were in making this book happen in the time allotted.

# TABLE OF CONTENTS

## Chapter One: Gardening to Make a Difference
*Page 10*

The powerful impact that gardening and landscape enthusiasts throughout the world can have on the environment is astonishing. By changing a few small habits, gardeners can save billions of gallons of water every year, keep millions of pounds of toxic chemicals out of our drinking water, significantly reduce fossil fuel consumption and its related toxic and greenhouse gas emissions, and protect biodiversity, habitat, and healthy ecosystems. Best of all, we can do all this while making the world a more beautiful place!

## Chapter Two: Conserving Water in the Garden
*Page 20*

The depletion of fresh, clean drinking water is approaching a worldwide crisis. On average, outdoor irrigation accounts for about 30% of our overall household water consumption, but that number can skyrocket if we're not paying attention to conservation. Even for gardeners who are already careful with their use of water, there is often more than can be done to reduce water use while still enjoying a beautiful and productive garden.

## Chapter Three: Reducing Garden Chemicals to Protect Our Water
*Page 64*

Millions of pounds of pest controls, fertilizers, and other environmentally damaging chemicals we use outdoors make their way into our water supply every year. The best way to lessen their impact is to reduce our use of chemicals in the first place and then use them more responsibly.

## Chapter Four: Landscaping to Control Runoff
*Page 164*

Eroding soil is the single biggest cause of chemical water pollution, and a lot of it comes from our gardens and home landscapes. Besides reducing our use of chemicals in the first place, the most important way we can keep them from polluting water is to prevent them from moving out of our garden. The way we care for our soil has a big impact on how much gets carried away when it rains or when we irrigate.

## Chapter Five: Turning Waste into Gardening Gold
*Page 200*

Yard waste taxes landfill capacity, and unlike our home compost piles, generates large volumes of methane gas, which is twenty times more damaging to our atmosphere than carbon dioxide emissions. The good news is *that* trash is the best thing we can keep at home to use in our own yards. In its finished state, it's called 'black gold' to gardeners and we can't get enough of it.

## Chapter Six: Consuming Less Energy in the Landscape
*Page 232*

It's amazing how many landscaping techniques not only beautify the outdoors, but also help to reduce fossil fuel consumption and improve air quality in the process. By properly siting trees and shrubs we can significantly reduce the heating and cooling needs of our homes. By reducing our use of two-cycle and four-cycle engines, we can help to decrease the use of gasoline and the air pollution it causes. And that's just the beginning. From efficient outdoor lighting to reducing the heating needs of swimming pools, there are many ways we can lessen energy use outdoors.

## Chapter Seven: Gardening to Protect the Ecosystem
*Page 276*

Nature creates a biologically diverse environment that supports habitats for beneficial insects, supports native birds and wildlife, and promotes healthy soil. By recognizing sensitive habitats right in our own back yards and understanding how they connect to the larger ecosystem, we can work to protect habitat and ecosystems even outside of our personal landscapes. And by choosing carefully what garden plants and products we purchase, and where we buy them, gardeners can play a significant role in protecting endangered species and habitats around the world.

## Chapter Eight: Taking It Over the Fence
*Page 312*

Good things will start at home by putting into practice what you already know and by the insights you glean from this book. But it can't end there. You can make the most difference when you take what you know and believe, and share it with your neighbors, your community, and beyond. This chapter provides a number of ideas for taking our gardener's love of nature "over the garden fence" and into the wide world beyond.

## Notes
*Page 336*

## List of Actions
*Page 353*

## Index
*Page 358*

# CHAPTER ONE

# GARDENING TO MAKE A DIFFERENCE

A day rarely goes by that we don't hear some reference to *going green, climate change, greenhouse gases, carbon neutral, eco-friendly, environmental footprint*, or *global warming*. How did these buzz words weave themselves into the fabric of our everyday lives, seemingly overnight? And why didn't we hear more about them as recently as even a few years ago?

The fact is, these terms have been in use for decades, but they were rarely given the attention they deserved at the time. It has taken mounting environmental and weather-related events at home and around the world, credible predictions of dire consequences, and the global attention brought by politicians, scientists, celebrities, respected citizens, and even a Noble Laureate to not only give these terms new meaning but also to create a sense of urgency and call to action.

No longer are *climate change* and *global warming* empty words that we can't relate to. Glossed over for decades, these words now have a face, a voice, and pictures that bring to life the meaning behind them. For many, those words now cause us to take note. For some, they stir our soul. And on occasion, we are even motivated to do something about it.

## Why should we care?

Our unique perspective as gardeners has allowed us personally to witness the environmental impact in recent years more than ever. As we create natural environments in our own little spot on the planet, we glean insights into a bigger picture. The changing conditions present themselves in many ways: Higher than average temperatures are causing plants to leaf out and bloom earlier than ever. Birds and butterflies are breeding and migrating earlier as well. Many wildlife species are being found at higher elevations and farther north than in previous years.

Perhaps you have noticed that heat zone maps are being redrawn as more recent historical data confirms that the warmer zones of the south are migrating north. The newest revisions to the 2006 arborday.org Hardiness Zone map reflect such changes.

Yet gradual changes in temperature from one year to the next may not seem all that significant to you and me. But in the delicate balance of nature, even slight changes can have severe implications. As temperatures increase, exotic, invasive plants will find new ground, out-competing and overtaking native species and destroying fragile ecosystems in the process.

In the same manner, invasive and exotic pests will find new territory as those regions become warmer through climate change. Areas previously unthreatened by certain destructive pests could soon be faced with severe infestations and habitat destruction.

Climate change is exacerbating weather extremes not only in our gardens but also around the world. As the atmosphere heats up, it throws off our entire planet's climate system. Today, storms are more frequent, intense, and destructive.

You have likely experienced in recent seasons conditions ranging from excessive rain and potential flooding to severe drought and outdoor watering bans. Droughts followed by heavy rainfall lead to flash floods and major water quality issues.

Even in cases of normal rainfalls, as runoff moves across our yards, gardens, driveways, and sidewalks, it picks up fertilizers and pesticides, heavy metals, and other pollutants that, unfortunately for the most part, we gardeners have put there. Ultimately this runoff of silt and contaminants finds its way into our streams, rivers, and lakes.

## Contributions we make as gardeners to the problem

In a book written for gardeners, why am I telling you all of this? Because *as* gardeners, environmental stewardship is our responsibility. But all too often it is taken for granted. At the very least, the extreme conditions brought about by seemingly innocent actions on our part are creating stressful environmental conditions, not only locally but also collectively around the world.

There are over ninety million American households participating in some form of gardening activity. It may be as simple as enjoying a few potted plants on a balcony, or it could involve managing a full blown vegetable and perennial garden on an expansive landscape. But no matter what the level of involvement, billions of dollars are spent each year to stock our gardens and keep them looking lush and beautiful. Quite often the products used for this purpose are the very things that are polluting our planet.

It's quite ironic when you think about it. As a group, we're the very ones creating so much beauty by planting gardens and landscapes that promote the health of vigorous plants, lush lawns, and healthy trees. For some weekend warriors, this weekly ritual is more work than pleasure. The less time spent working in the yard, the better. Products designed to save time and effort in their yards are staples in their shed or garage.

For other more passionate gardeners, time in the yard is a labor of love as they care and coddle all things growing in their outdoor sanctuary. These gardeners often purchase and use products perceived to bring their garden even one step closer to perfection.

But as we mow our lawns, trim our hedges, whack our weeds, and blow our leaves, the equipment we use is pumping pollution into the air. The chemicals we use to fertilize our plants and kill pests and weeds are killing more than we ever imagined. Much of the water we use to irrigate our lawns and plants is being wasted as it runs off our property into nearby watersheds. Unfortunately, this runoff takes with it many of the chemicals and pesticides applied earlier to our yards and gardens.

According to the Environmental Protection Agency, fifty-four million Americans beautify their lawns and landscapes each weekend, specifically by mowing their yards. In the process, we're burning up eight hundred million gallons of gasoline. As bad as that sounds, consider that using one gasoline-powered mower for just one hour pollutes as much as forty late model cars. Oh yes . . . and weed eaters and leaf blowers are even worse.

In our quest for the perfect yard, garden, or landscape, we have an arsenal of chemicals at our disposal to pump nutrients into our plants and wage war on even the threat of any offending pest. Accustomed to excess, we believe that if some is good, more is better. So we blanket our plants and lawns with any chemical that will kill something or make it grow better, without regard to the consequences of our actions.

In most cases, simply using a chemical is not the crime; rather it's how and when we use it. Responsible application by users would prevent a lot of the environmental consequences we see today. Unfortunately, in our busy lives, we rush to mix chemicals up and throw them down, ignoring specific and readily available instructions for both processes. Consequently, many beneficial insects are unnecessarily killed, aquatic life is destroyed, the soil food web is damaged, and harmful chemicals are washed into our creeks, rivers, and lakes.

As we busily go about hosing down our gardens and lawns, we fail to pay attention to just how much water we are using in spite of an ever shrinking supply. We have taken water for granted and are now just beginning to pay the price. The good news is that simple changes in this area can make a big difference.

Outside the house, there are easy ways we can capture and retain the water coming off our roofs and driveways so that it can be used whenever needed, and in spite of any existing watering ban. From inside, much of the water we waste comes from heating it up for our bath or shower or from rinsing food in the kitchen sink. These thousands of gallons per household can be saved and reused in the garden as well.

## Contributions we can make to the solution

As gardeners, we have a tremendous opportunity to affect and improve the health of our environment at home and beyond. First we must face the truth: gardeners are some of the biggest users of products that pollute our environment. We're also some of the biggest consumers of precious natural resources like water. Also true is that, from where we stand today, we have a tremendous opportunity to protect and preserve the health of our planet in the future.

Even beyond reducing the amount of chemicals and resources we apply, and then using them more responsibly, we have other opportunities. *How* we landscape can not only provide beautiful vistas for all to enjoy; it can also help conserve valuable resources like water and energy, reduce emissions from greenhouse gases, and slash the need for chemicals that pollute our soil and water.

On the surface, "green gardening" may sound like a radical change, but it's not. In fact, in many ways, gardening and landscaping with environmental stewardship in mind can greatly reduce the amount of time and maintenance required. I'll show you this through specific examples in subsequent chapters.

We *can* still have beautiful gardens and landscapes while being more responsible in our choices of how we make them so.

## How to use this book

As you read this book, you will find a number of meaningful tips to help you garden more successfully while becoming a better steward of our environment. We'll address eco-friendly ways to reduce water usage, pollution of soil and water, erosion, runoff, and solid waste. We'll also cover ways gardeners can protect and conserve air quality as well as nonrenewable energy consumption, biodiversity, and ecosystems.

Finally, we'll look over the garden fence and explore ways gardeners can take this work to the next level, moving beyond our own gardens and out to where our efforts can have an even broader reach.

Each chapter provides a number of simple and significant actions we can do to protect and preserve our planet. Each action contains a specific step you can take as you make a difference.

In discussing environmental solutions for today, for each action I have tried to include real world, practical, and oftentimes anecdotal experiences from my lifetime of gardening and from my constant pursuit of environmental stewardship.

Sprinkled throughout each action description are boxes labeled *Did You Know,* which share specific data and interesting facts on the real-world impact of current negative environmental practices and how some of these habits have been changed for the better. Narrowing all the available statistics down to just a few statements was a challenge. Unfortunately, the environmental impact from man's carelessness with nature's resources is far-reaching and well documented.

In each action description you'll find a box labeled *The Impact of Gardening Green,* designed to help you understand just what you can accomplish by taking a stand and acting. The magnitude of the numbers may seem hard to comprehend at times. You may even feel overwhelmed as just one small gardener on this big planet. But you're not alone. I and countless others are there with you, doing exactly the same things you are to make a difference. I'll be working hard not only in my own garden but in my efforts to get this message to millions more. But I need your help. The suggestions that follow in the chapters ahead vary in their level of simplicity for getting started and following through. Yet all are significant in their own right and have a global impact when we work together.

To help get you off to a fast start, consider the following list of *10 simple actions* from this book that you can do right now. In other words, if you do nothing else, do these. They are easy steps, and they will make a difference. In the following chapters, you'll find each action described in greater detail, including the impact you'll have on the environment by doing them. Maybe that will help you see that every small bit truly does add up if we all play a part. So here's my choice for a fast and effective start:

# 10 SIMPLE ACTIONS FOR A FAST START TO POSITIVELY IMPACT OUR PLANET

**Use rain barrels to capture roof runoff. (See page 32.)** You'll reduce runoff and quickly capture precious water for thirsty plants during times of drought.

**Fix leaky faucets. (See page 37.)** Wait till you see the numbers, but drop by drop, it really does add up.

**Water only when you need to and no more than your plants need. (See page 23.)** We tend to overwater. Plants don't need as much as we think to survive. Toughen up plants and save a valuable resource in the process.

**Compost for healthy, living soil. (See page 73.)** Simply the best and most significant soil amendment you can add, compost provides valuable nutrients, promotes pest and disease resistance, and improves soil. It's also free when you make your own. Compost keeps yard debris and kitchen scraps out of the landfill, too. Read even more about that in Chapter 5.

**Use natural sources of nutrients. (See page 79.)** Rather than using synthetic fertilizers, feed the soil and let the soil feed the plants. Natural and organic nutrients promote healthy, living soil. They're also more environmentally friendly.

**Grow the right plant in the right place. (See page 83.)** When planted in the right place, plants are healthier and have less pest and disease issues.

**Catch problems early. (See page 94.)** Proactive, early detection makes controlling pests and diseases much easier and more environmentally friendly.

**Get a soil test before you add fertilizers and other amendments. (See page 138.)** When you know what your soil needs before planting, you create a healthier environment for them to grow. It translates to fewer chemicals, less water, and less work later.

**Use bagged soil and mulch that is certified. (See page 154.)** Mulch is the solution to so many gardening problems. But make sure your mulch is free of dangerous chemicals. There's no place for contaminated mulch in an eco-friendly garden.

**Buy locally (compost, mulch, topsoil, and plants). (See page 250.)** The number of miles that products have to travel to market can wipe out the good things we are trying to accomplish.

In addition to these ten tips, I wanted to list the top ten actions from this book that would make the *greatest impact*. Yet, as I looked over each one, I realized that though their impact may differ in degree, *each one is important*. So instead of trying to quantify the specific global impact of certain actions, I decided to list the ten most significant **concepts** I would like you to consider for creating an eco-friendly garden that impacts the planet in a positive and significant way. All are supported by actions that speak to these issues with plenty of relevant information to encourage and inspire you in our journey.

# THE TEN MOST SIGNIFICANT CONCEPTS FOR CREATING AN ECO-FRIENDLY GARDEN

1. Garden to reduce water usage.
2. Garden to reduce pollution of soil and water.
3. Keep plants healthy to reduce the need for pesticides and chemicals.
4. Practice Integrated Pest Management.
5. If using chemicals, apply them safely, responsibly, and effectively.
6. Landscape to reduce soil erosion and runoff.
7. Garden to reduce waste through recycling and composting.
8. Garden to reduce nonrenewable energy consumption and protect air quality.
9. Landscape to protect biodiversity and ecosystems.
10. Plant the seeds of change beyond the boundaries of our gardens.

So there you have it, *ten actions* to give you a fast start and *ten concepts* that delve into a much bigger world. Explore the pages ahead to learn more about many important eco-friendly actions you can take to create a healthier garden and a healing planet. Along the way, I hope you'll take comfort in knowing that as you seek new ways to become "greener," I will be doing so as well. I'm certainly not yet able to accomplish all the tips I've laid out for us . . . but I'm working on it. I hope you will, too.

*In the spring at the end of the day you should smell like dirt.*

MARGARET ATWOOD

# CHAPTER TWO

# CONSERVING WATER IN THE GARDEN

Earth is sometimes referred to as the "water planet" because so much of it is covered by water. In fact, many of us learned in elementary school that about three-fourths of the earth's surface is covered by it. "Wow," we would say as our teachers held up a globe or referred to the giant map on the wall.

Unfortunately what we usually didn't hear was the sentence that should have followed: Even with all that water, 99 percent is unavailable to us as usable water—97 percent is salt water, and 2 percent is frozen (for now) in glaciers and polar ice caps. That leaves a miniscule 1 percent of all the water on earth for us to use for drinking; bathing; washing food, clothes, dishes, and cars; and watering our gardens, lawns, and landscapes. It sounds like a lot of demand for such a small reserve, and it is.

Perhaps if we had been told how precious this limited resource was then, we would have been doing more along the way to preserve and protect this finite supply. We didn't realize then that a global water crisis was looming, and it is here today. Water is the most important natural resource issue across the world, in countries both rich and poor.

The amount of fresh water on our planet is indeed a limited resource. It remains the same even though global populations continue to explode, and demand for water soars. Surface water is being harvested at unprecedented rates, taxing the ability of groundwater levels and aquifers to recharge worldwide.

For some of us, a water crisis is hard to imagine, as we recall widespread flooding or days of relentless rain. For others, the realities of drought seem all too real, as many homeowners today face total bans on *all* outdoor watering.

In spite of the variability at times between excessive rains and extreme drought, the fact remains that global climate change, unsustainable groundwater levels, and continued competition for fresh water will present ongoing challenges to each of us. Indeed, we face a global crisis with local implications.

But when confronted with the impending depletion of such a precious resource as water, we gardeners are not without our own resources— our own creative and significant solutions. The tips that follow are just some of the ways we can start making a difference right away.

Some ideas are tangible, simple ways to save water so often wasted from leaks and unnecessary usage. Other tips just focus on watering properly. So much is lost to evaporation and excessive application that minor changes and new techniques will translate to literally thousands of gallons saved per yard each year.

> DID YOU KNOW THAT...
>
> ❀ Between 1950 and 2000, when the U.S. population doubled, the public demand for water more than tripled.[1]
>
> ❀ The average American now uses about 100 gallons of water every day—enough to fill 1,600 drinking glasses. And of those 100 gallons, at least 25 to 29 gallons per person per day goes to watering lawns, plants, and gardens. (Some estimates put the average amount of landscape use at 40 to 50 gallons per person per day, or as much as 50 percent of all residential water consumption!)[2]
>
> ❀ The EPA estimates at least half of all the water we use on our landscapes and gardens is wasted. That is to say, if we all stopped wasting water in our gardens and landscapes right now, we could save 3.25 billion gallons of water per day, which translates to about 1.2 *trillion* gallons of water each year![3]

Knowing just how much is enough when it comes to watering your lawn and landscape will allow you to use less while achieving the same great results as before. Specific tips will give you ideas on how to know when you reach that point of "enough."

Other solutions will encourage you to harvest and use runoff water, both from outside your house via your roof and downspouts, and from several sources inside.

Homeowners often use as much as 50 percent of their total water consumption outside to keep lawns green and landscapes and gardens lush. Many municipalities consider this outdoor water use unnecessary and thereby impose total outdoor bans. Although I disagree with such a blanket indictment, it *is* up to us to conserve water and use it responsibly whenever possible. By doing so, collectively we'll save billions of gallons of water each year, reducing runoff and erosion as well. That's not a bad place to start.

# Supply only the water your plants need—know when to water and how much.

*Get to know your plants—they'll tell you when to water.*

## Using less water by not watering too often

You may not be aware that more plants die of too much water than of not enough. We are literally killing them with kindness through overwatering, and it's simply not necessary. The problem is, most of us don't realize when our plants have received sufficient moisture, so we overcompensate. Most of us don't have sandy or well drained soil, where overwatering is rarely a problem. On the contrary, the majority of gardeners have soil that is more likely to drain slowly, sometimes *much* too slowly.

When we overwater, the soil becomes saturated, forcing out vital oxygen and literally drowning our plants. Although it is essential to provide ample water to new plants as they become established, once that is achieved, the water you apply should be reduced significantly.

After plants are established in the landscape, they should require supplemental water *only* in the absence of rainfall. When it comes to watering, the least demanding plants are ones native to the area where you live. They are the ones that survive in nature with only the water that Mother Earth provides. Take a note from her and you'll spend far less time, water, and money keeping your plants alive.

A good rule of thumb for many plants is, in the absence of rain, provide one inch of supplemental water each week, or whatever is necessary to make up the difference. Of course this rule will vary from new seedlings to established, hardy natives. In fact, providing the ideal amounts for individual plants is beyond the scope of this tip, but you get the idea.

## Using rain gauges

A rain gauge is a simple tool that shows just how much water has reached the soil surface. It's also a great way to know how much irrigation is needed to supplement what Mother Nature has provided without guessing or overwatering.

Rain gauges are readily available at nurseries and garden centers. They can be as simple as a small tube or container on a stake (costing only a few dollars) to electronic devices that can cost a few hundred dollars. These more expensive units relay a wireless signal to a monitoring station inside your house. Either way, be sure the gauge is free from any overhead obstructions that might affect the measurement, and empty the gauge after each rain. Even if you are trying to get a cumulative reading for a period of time, evaporation can affect your results. It's best to record the amounts individually and frequently, then add them to get the total per week.

In situations where you are attempting to record rainfall in a woodland garden or under a canopy of trees, it is a good idea to install a rain gauge even though the leaves may obstruct the results. This is the best way to give you a good idea of the amount of rainfall actually reaching the ground, beneath the canopy. In this case, it may be possible that plants and understory trees did not receive as much water as plants outside the canopy of the larger trees. Make note of any deficiencies, and supplement your watering accordingly.

Here's one final note on that point. Because you are more likely to find understory trees and shrubs in an environment sheltered from sunlight and evaporation, they may *not* require supplemental irrigation even when they receive less water. The cooler conditions and the reduced evaporation may compensate for any reduction in water reaching the surface there.

## Listen to your plants; they're talking to you.

As simple as it sounds, pay attention to what your plants and trees are telling you. Unfortunately, a plant that is underwatered or overwatered can show the same symptoms: limp droopy foliage, yellowing, and a lack of luster in the foliage. Similar symptoms can also occur in plants suffering from pests and diseases.

Since opposite causes may yield the same visual clues, you will have to do a bit of deductive reasoning. Given what you know, is it more likely that the plant has been getting too much water or not enough?

Just in case you're still not certain, and in the spirit of simplicity, here are a few easy ways to know for sure:

### *The finger test*
Remember when you were a child and you stuck you finger in your mouth to wet it and then held it up in the air to feel which way the wind was blowing? That wet finger came in pretty handy, didn't it? And the good news is that it can also be a good guide to let you know if your plants need more water, too.

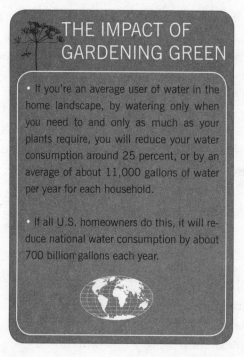

**THE IMPACT OF GARDENING GREEN**

• If you're an average user of water in the home landscape, by watering only when you need to and only as much as your plants require, you will reduce your water consumption around 25 percent, or by an average of about 11,000 gallons of water per year for each household.

• If all U.S. homeowners do this, it will reduce national water consumption by about 700 billion gallons each year.

Most of the time, you simply cannot tell what the moisture conditions are below the surface simply by looking. In fact, it's impossible if the soil under your plants is covered by mulch. Although not the most scientific approach, that pointer finger of yours can be a good indicator of the moisture conditions in the soil at the root level.

Poke your finger into the soil around the base of the plant, down to the second knuckle. Pull it back out and take a look at your finger. If it's clean (relatively speaking), the soil is dry and in need of water. If your finger came back up with soil stuck to it, then there is sufficient moisture in the soil and no supplemental irrigation is necessary at this time. I know this method seems quite simplistic, and it is. That's the beauty of it, along with the fact that it's a pretty good indicator. I use this technique often with reliable results.

### The dig test

Another easy and practical method of preventing overwatering is to conduct a dig test. Don't worry—no studying is required. Before watering, simply make note of the moisture level of your soil, six to twelve inches below the surface (the target depth). Ideally, the soil will be dry at this point. Your goal is to determine how long it takes for your irrigation system, whether it's a soaker hose, drip irrigation, watering wand, or overhead system, to soak the soil to the target depth.

THE **green** GARDENER'S GUIDE

Assuming that the soil is dry when you start, commence the irrigation process and make note of the time. Several minutes later, depending on the flow rate of your system, turn off the irrigation and dig down to the target depth. If the soil is saturated at this point, you know that you need that amount of time *or less* to achieve your target irrigation volume. Conversely, if it is still dry at the target level, you need to operate your irrigation system a bit longer.

By repeating this process, eventually you'll determine the optimal time needed to get moisture down to the target level. The beauty of the dig test is that once you determine the amount of time needed (assuming no major changes to your soil), you never have to waste water again by allowing the system to run longer than needed.

Remember, the time determined in the above example assumes the soil started out dry. Once your soil maintains a consistent moisture level, it will take less time to keep it there. Note this as well and reduce the amount of time you water to maintain optimum levels.

# Water deeply and less often.

*Keep plants growing strong—encourage roots to explore deeper into the soil.*

In many ways, plants are like some people I know. They don't work any harder than they have to! Consequently, if all the moisture needed is right near the surface, plants won't use extra energy and nutrients to grow roots deeper into the soil where moisture levels are consistently higher.

This is why the key is to water infrequently but deeply. *Reducing* the overall amount of water to plants (and especially lawns) keeps them growing stronger. Deep watering encourages deep roots, and roots that are encouraged to explore farther into the soil to find sustenance have better access to moisture when the area closer to the surface dries out. This upper layer *always* dries out first because soil at or near the surface warms faster and is subject to evaporation and the drying effects of wind.

> **DID YOU KNOW THAT. . .**
>
> ❀ The roots of turf watered deeply every third day are usually at least 4 to 6 inches deep—but the roots of grass watered briefly every day grow only about 1½ inches deep. The deeper the roots, the more likely turf will be able to withstand droughts and reduced irrigation.[1]
>
> ❀ A study of water users in Southern California found that water applied deeply but ½ to ⅓ as often produced turf with roots more than 3 times as deep—and resulted in a 72 percent drop in water bills![2]

When a gardener waters every day but for only brief periods, water rarely soaks deeply enough into the soil to encourage roots to grow there. In order for roots that are growing only near the surface to stay healthy and alive, continued frequent watering is *required* to provide them with sufficient moisture. The "pampered" plants never have to develop an extensive root system reaching farther down to find water.

But what happens if you go on vacation and forget to set your irrigation timers, or the batteries fail, or your neighbor forgets to water your lawn or plants? In periods of drought or inconsistent irrigation, plants with deeper roots can still receive adequate moisture in many cases because the roots are where the water is.

Now, deep watering doesn't mean turning on the sprinkler and leaving it on while you go and play a quick nine holes! The surface layer of most soils becomes quickly saturated after watering for only a few minutes, and then all the water applied from that point on runs off and is wasted. Research shows that the most efficient and effective way to get water down deep is to water an area for a short time until the upper surface is saturated—say, ten minutes for most soils (less if it's on a slope)—then stop and let that water soak in for thirty minutes to an hour, and then water again for a few minutes more. This allows the water to be deeply absorbed into the soil while reducing runoff, and ultimately lets you go much longer between watering.

## THE IMPACT OF GARDENING GREEN

- By watering deeply but only 1/3 as often, the average homeowner will reduce his or her landscape water usage by 30 percent, which translates to about 13,000 gallons of water saved per year for every household.

- If everyone does this, it will reduce national water consumption by 820 billion gallons per year!

With the exception of container gardens that tend to dry out daily, brief but daily irrigation is an inefficient use of time and water.

# Water at the right time of the day.

*The time of day that you water can have a significant effect
on the water's efficiency.*

The hotter it is, the more water is lost to evaporation. Add wind to the equation and even more water is vaporized in the atmosphere before it ever reaches the ground. Depending on your irrigation system and the timing of *when* you water, as much as half the water can be lost to drift and evaporation, especially when using overhead sprinklers.

> **DID YOU KNOW THAT...**
>
> ❀ As much as 30 percent of water used to irrigate landscapes in the middle of the day is lost to evaporation.[1]
>
> ❀ Direct evaporation from sprinklers can account for a 50 percent or greater loss of water in a desert climate.[2]

## THE IMPACT OF GARDENING GREEN

• By watering very early in the morning or at night rather than in the heat of the day, the average homeowner will reduce water usage by 25 percent, and by twice that amount in desert climates. This translates to an average water savings of 11,000 gallons per year, per household.

• If everyone in the U.S. does this, we will save 700 billion gallons of water per year.

If you water at night, or very early in the morning, temperatures are cooler and winds are calmer. Late at night or very early in the morning is also the best time to use soaker hoses or drip irrigation. The coolness during darkness along with the calm skies allows soils to soak up the maximum amount of water, without the influence of drying winds or evaporative sunlight.

# Mulch, mulch, mulch!

*Mulch is an important tool for a gardener in more ways than one.
As a way to conserve water, it can't be beat.*

Mulch is one of the most versatile additions to any garden. It has many uses which will be covered throughout this book, but from the standpoint of water conservation, it is a star. A three- to five-inch layer of mulch will

> DID YOU KNOW THAT...
>
> ❀ In summer, just 2 inches of mulch cuts water loss by 20 percent and lowers temperature in the top 4 inches of soil by 10 degrees.[1]

provide an insulating blanket that greatly reduces surface evaporation, slows runoff, moderates soil temperatures on hot days, and lowers the moisture requirements of the plants. It also dramatically cuts down on weed production, lowering the demand and competition for nutrients and water.

Mulch can be organic, such as leaves, straw, compost, or bark. It can even be gravel or plastic. In all cases, the mulch holds the moisture in place, in the ground, right where it is needed most.

## THE IMPACT OF GARDENING GREEN

• By keeping a 2-inch layer of mulch on garden beds during the growing season, the average homeowner will reduce water usage by 5 to 10 percent (depending on how much of your landscape is occupied by beds rather than lawn). This translates to 4,400 gallons of water saved per year.

• If every household in the U.S. does this, it will save the nation 277 billion gallons of water per year.

# Use rain barrels.

*Harvesting rainwater from your roof is convenient and free.*

Rain barrels are an easy way to harvest rainwater from your roof. They provide a convenient (and free) supply of water whenever you need it or when water restrictions make your normal sources unavailable. In fact, you might be surprised to know just how much water can be harvested from the roof of even a modest-sized home.

**DID YOU KNOW THAT...**

❋ For every one inch of rain that falls on a catchment area of 1,000 square feet (the size of a typical roof), approximately 600 gallons of water can be harvested.[1]

❋ Many North American cities are sponsoring rain barrel programs. Check with your municipal water authority to find out about the one nearest you.

❋ When the city of Toronto sponsored a rain barrel program involving 150 single family homes, 56 percent of the participants reported that they had emptied the barrel more than once a week to water their yards, saving 55 to 65 gallons per barrel.[2]

Ready-made rain barrels are available from a wide range of sources, including gardening catalogs, Internet sources, and some garden centers and home improvement stores. Barrels can also be recycled and easily adapted for rainwater harvesting as a do-it-yourself project. However, if you take this route, you should consider the barrel's original use before deciding to use it to harvest and store water that will eventually go into your garden and landscape.

When installing rain barrels, there are a few things you should know to get the most benefit from them. First, don't have all gutters leading to just one or two downspouts. Rain barrels under these will fill rapidly, often resulting in overflow. Instead, have multiple downspouts inserted where *you* want them. (Many times installers will place them where it is convenient for them.)

Having rain barrels under multiple downspouts will increase the opportunity for collecting the maximum amount of water possible from your roof while reducing the risk of excess overflow, potentially leading to stormwater control problems.

Downspouts that lead directly into the rain barrel can contain a lot of debris. What doesn't get filtered out will end up in your rain barrel, ultimately affecting what comes out of the barrel spigot and limiting flow. Direct connections also allow an entry for mosquitoes. A good solution to both problems is to install an inlet drain to stop large debris and a mosquito screen as a barrier to entry.

Safety is also a concern with water barrels. If the cover is flimsy, a child could fall through if he or she happened to stand on top of it. All rain barrels should be childproof. In addition, the outlets from the barrels should be too small to let animals in.

Flow rate from your rain barrel is affected by two things: gravity and elevation. Gravity provides a constant water pressure, and elevation is the key to increasing that pressure.

Whether you are making your own rain barrel or purchasing one that is ready-made, be sure the outlet is placed at the very bottom of the barrel. Otherwise too much water can accumulate in the barrel below the outlet and become stagnant and putrid.

Even with covers and screens, water collected in a rain barrel will have debris in it from pollen, dust, etc. This is harmless to your plants but can eventually affect and clog watering emitters. Installing an in-line filter will help keep the lines clear. Check and clean it periodically to provide the best flow rate over time.

Water is typically collected from the rain barrel by way of the spigot at the bottom. A watering can provides a quick fill and total portability. In other cases, you may want to connect a hose for directing the

## HOW TO SHOP FOR A RAIN BARREL[3]

*If you are shopping for a rain barrel, here are some tips to keep in mind:*

❀ **The barrels should have spin weld fittings.** This fitting is the only kind that can be guaranteed leakproof; the fitting and the tank are welded together.

❀ **The barrels should not have unique hardware.** Hardware needs to be easily replaceable, so as not to render your barrel unusable. Hardware should all be common sizes so that they are easy to find and inexpensive.

❀ **The barrels should be able to connect to more tanks.** This allows for a greater holding capacity and helps you to avoid overflows that require hard-to-find hoses or expensive linking kits.

❀ **The barrels should complement your home.** Unsightly containers that detract from the appearance of your home may lower the value of your home when it's time to sell. On the other hand, attractive water collection systems can add to your home's value and appeal.

❀ **The barrels should have a guarantee and warranty.** Rain barrels should be made to allow for the system to last season after season without needing to replace significant parts or entire tanks. The company should also offer information about the set up, care, and use of its product.

❀ **The barrels should be affordable, but not unreasonably inexpensive.** A high quality rain barrel is made by seamless rotational molding, spin weld fittings, UV stable resin, and time. It is an expensive process and is not the same as a garbage can or milk jug.

❀ **The barrel suppliers should provide information on shipping.** Shipping costs can easily escalate the cost of purchasing the barrel. Inquire about rebates in your area. Many cities around the country are offering rebates to encourage water conservation and storm water control.

Source: Arid Solutions, Inc.

water to a more concentrated area. (Although I am a strong advocate of using soaker hoses, they may not always be the best solution when attached to a rain barrel. The porosity of these hoses varies, and there may not be enough water pressure for soakers to function properly all the way down the line.)

Many people express concern over how to fill a rain barrel when it's not raining. Don't let that discourage you; make use of opportunities to harvest water from inside your house. You would be amazed to know how much water is wasted from inside the typical house every day for ordinary household routines. In the kitchen as we work at the kitchen sink, washing vegetables and rinsing our hands and in the bathroom, we waste gallons of water every day as the water runs down the drain while we wait for the water to get hot.

Seize these precious opportunities! Keep a pitcher in the kitchen sink to catch "slightly used water" before it goes down the drain and keep a bucket near your bathtub or shower. Even the dehumidifier bucket can be a valuable source of water.

All of these sources and more can provide valuable "non-rainwater." When the pitcher or buckets are full, pour them into your rain barrel. As the summer progresses and you are harvesting those lovely tomatoes or herbs, rinse them over a pitcher (or bowl) and put that water into your rain barrel for watering the very same plants! The water is still just fine for the garden, and it serves as a closed circle of use.

## THE IMPACT OF GARDENING GREEN

• If you install just one 65-gallon rain barrel that fills, and you use the water on your garden once every 2 weeks through a 20-week growing season, you will save 650 gallons of water each year. If you install 2 of these barrels, you will save 1,300 gallons of water each year. If you install 10 of these barrels (enough to harvest all the water from a 1-inch rain off the roof of a typical home) you will save 6,500 gallons of water each year.

• If every household in the U.S. installs just one rain barrel and uses it to water their garden once every 2 weeks throughout the growing season, it will save 41 billion gallons of water each year.

Rainwater is a wonderful, organic source of water that is relatively free of chemicals. A natural complement to this form of pure irrigation is to fortify it with nutrients going onto your plants or into the soil. Techniques that utilize brewing compost or worm castings in barrels or buckets are known as making "compost tea" or "vermicompost tea," respectively.

*No occupation is so delightful to me as the cultivation of the earth . . . I am still devoted to the garden.*

THOMAS JEFFERSON

# Fix leaky faucets and hoses.

*All those drips and drops add up to savings if you stop them.*

Drop by drop, it all adds up. One drip per second equates to about 260 gallons a month! So it makes sense to *stop the drops* wherever we can. With the exception of an irrigation system, the biggest opportunity outdoors to do that comes from the hose bib or spigot, or with the hose itself.

It seems that some amount of water leakage is the norm rather than the exception. But it doesn't have to be. Take time to inspect all your outdoor faucets and connections. Before calling a plumber, there are a few simple repairs you can make yourself, and all the parts are easy to find and inexpensive as well.

Start with the spigot. When you turn it on, does it leak? If so, is it from the handle? If you answered yes to that, simply remove the handle. It's held in place by a screw or nut. Remove the packing nut and the rubber gasket or washer inside. Over time, these rubber parts become hard and brittle. When they crack, that's when the leaks start to happen.

Take the parts with you to your neighborhood hardware store so you can purchase the appropriate replacements. You can also buy Teflon® packing tape, which looks like thick string; it works well as a replacement.

> **DID YOU KNOW THAT...**
>
> ❀ At the rate of 1 drip per second, a leaky hose bib wastes 8.64 gallons of water per day. Letting that hose bib leak for an entire month wastes almost 260 gallons of fresh, drinking-quality water.[1]

If the water is leaking from the hose connection, it's simply a matter of replacing the rubber washer inside the hose coupling. A replacement pack is inexpensive, so have some extras on hand. You'll use them all eventually. It's one of the fastest and easiest plumbing fixes I know.

Replacement parts are also available if the leak is coming from one of the hose ends. Know what diameter hose you have so when you purchase the replacement parts, you have the right size. Most hoses for home use are either one-half or five-eighths inch. If you don't know the exact measurement, cut the end off before you go and take it with you.

Hoses can eventually develop holes or cracks in the rubber too. Replacement hoses are expensive. Before you go out and buy a new one, try fixing the hose first. Once you've identified the leak, cut out that area and remove it. You'll then join the two ends together with a repair kit that you can purchase at any home improvement or hardware store. Again, be sure to get the right size, based on the diameter of your hose (one-half or five-eighths inches usually).

When making the repair, be sure the connections are good and snug and that the screws are tight. In a matter of minutes and for only a few dollars, you've likely fixed your leak problem, saved a lot of water, and avoided the unnecessary expense of hiring a plumber or buying an entire replacement hose.

## THE IMPACT OF GARDENING GREEN

• If you fix just one leaky hose bib or faucet that you might have ignored for a month, and that leak was occurring at the rate of 1 drop per second, you will save 260 gallons of water each month.

• If just 10 percent of the single-family homes in the U.S. have one hose bib that leaks a drop per second, and all those leaky hose bibs are fixed, that will save 55 million gallons of water in one day! If just half of those leaks are fixed that would have otherwise been allowed to go on for a month, fixing them will save 1.65 billion gallons of water!

# Don't use water in place of a broom or blower.

*It's amazing how much water goes down the drain when we clean our walks and driveways with a hose.*

It's tempting to blast that loose dirt and debris back into the lawn and garden with a stiff spray of water from the hose. But avoid the temptation, opting for the old standby broom instead. Besides saving precious water, broom power is good for you and leaves zero footprints on the environment.

> DID YOU KNOW THAT...
>
> ❀ A hose with a pressure nozzle typically emits 4 to 5 gallons of water per minute.

If you opt for using a blower instead of water, then consider a battery powered, rechargeable version rather than a gas powered model. It's an acceptable and commendable compromise to the gas-powered alternative and for some, is easier on the body than the broom.

## THE IMPACT OF GARDENING GREEN

• If it normally takes you 20 minutes to hose down your driveway, you're using up to 100 gallons of water each time you do it. If you use a broom for this weekly task, you'll use *zero* gallons.

• For every 100,000 homeowners who switch from hosing down their driveways to sweeping them clean, we'll save 10 million gallons of water per week.

• If every household in the U.S. does this, the nation will save 126 billion gallons of water every year.

# Don't leave your hose running while unattended.

*Even for short periods of time, a running hose wastes hundreds of gallons of water.*

This seems so utterly obvious that it's a no-brainer, but I can't tell you how many times I've seen water flooding down the gutter at curbside while a neighbor leaves his or her hose running. It's easy to make that careless mistake—I know, I've been there. The phone rings, or the baby cries, and boom! There goes the hose, thrown down into the gutter or on the driveway, gushing out gallons of water every minute while you run and deal with the emergency.

> DID YOU KNOW THAT. . .
>
> ❀ A hose without a nozzle shutoff can gush 10 gallons of water every minute.[1]

I realize that some situations require fast action, and it's not always possible to take the time to walk over and turn off the spigot first. That's why I always buy nozzles, watering wands, and other hose fixtures that have a shut-off valve right on the handle. They make it easy to temporarily turn off the flow of water. Some nozzles even have spring-loaded automatic shutoffs—let the nozzle go and it shuts off automatically. Now that's easy!

THE IMPACT OF GARDENING GREEN

• Not leaving your hose running for 10 minutes will save you 100 gallons of water.

# Program your irrigation system to apply the right amount of water.

*Measure its output to know just how much is enough.*

How much water is enough to keep our lawns and landscapes looking great without overdoing it? Experts tell us that lawns need an average of one inch of water per week from all sources. This includes rainfall and supplemental irrigation to make up the deficiency. That's true for lawns and most plants.

But how much is an inch?

For an overhead irrigation system, whether it's one portable sprinkler or an in-ground system, place tuna, cat food or other similarly sized cans around your yard in strategic areas where your irrigation system waters the lawn or garden. When the can has one inch of water in it, you've added an inch of water to *that* area.

This can test may take longer than you think. Trust the can, though. Your soil isn't getting an inch of water until that can has an inch of water in it. Keep in mind that some parts of the surface area under the irrigation flow will receive more or less than other areas, so place several

> **DID YOU KNOW THAT...**
>
> ❀ Most lawns need, at most, 1 inch of water per week. And that's even in the hottest summer months.
>
> ❀ A residential irrigation system applying 1 inch of water to an average-size, 5,000-square-foot lawn delivers a total of 3,000 gallons of water.
>
> ❀ Studies show that most people water more than twice as much as their lawns need to be healthy and look good—an average of 2 to 2 ½ inches of water every week.[1]

cans out in different parts of the irrigation path as a test. If possible, try to fine-tune your system or adjust your spray pattern so all areas are receiving about the same amount each week. You'll be surprised to find how much water coverage may vary from even a single sprinkler head.

Here's an example of how to adjust your timing for just the right amount: Place several cans in a line heading out from the sprinkler. Turn the water on for a specific amount of time, say thirty minutes. Then measure the amount of water in each can. The one farthest away will likely have the least amount of water. This is where you will have the most need to overlap your sprinkler system. Determine how long to water to achieve one inch of coverage. If there is one-fourth inch of water after half an hour, then you will need to water for two hours total.

## THE IMPACT OF GARDENING GREEN

• If you have an average-size lawn of 5,000 square feet and you reduce the amount of water you apply by half—from 2 inches to one inch per week—you'll save 3,000 gallons of water every week. That's 78,000 gallons over one growing season!

• If just 100,000 households in the U.S. do this, it will save the nation 7.8 billion gallons of water per year.

# Include a rain sensor in an automatic irrigation system.

*This is one of the easiest ways to conserve a precious natural resource.*

We've all seen it. It's pouring as we drive by a house where the irrigation system is dutifully doing its job. Thank the timer for that. Unfortunately, a brain is not part of the standard equipment on an irrigation system. But doesn't it just drive you crazy? Talk about wasting water!

Fortunately, this scenario doesn't have to be the rule, nor should it ever be. For a small extra cost, rain sensors can be included or added to many in-ground automatic irrigation systems. These sensors are typically mounted on or near the gutters and are designed to detect rainfall. The sensors are designed to override the cycle of an automatic irrigation system when adequate rainfall has been received. If the system happens to be operating at the same time the rain falls, the sensor shuts the irrigation system off.

DID YOU KNOW THAT...

✿ Studies show that installing a rain sensor device in an automatic irrigation system in areas with frequent rainfall can reduce water use by as much as 30 percent.[1]

## THE IMPACT OF GARDENING GREEN

• If your landscape is a typical size (5,000 square feet) and you water the correct amount (one inch per week), every time your rain sensor overrides an irrigation cycle you will save up to 3,000 gallons of water. In average precipitation climates, this can amount to a savings of 20,000 gallons of water or more through the growing season.

• If just 100,000 homeowners with automatic irrigation systems install a rain sensor and each saves 20,000 gallons of water through the growing season, it will save 2 billion gallons of water each year.

Many sensors must accumulate a certain amount of water before overriding the system to shut off. That can waste one-fourth to one-half inch of water. However, current technology is available that overrides an operating irrigation system at the first indication of rain. It's well worth having this water-saving option.

*A man does not plant a tree for himself; he plants it for posterity.*

ALEXANDER SMITH

# Install an integrated weather monitoring system.

*This high-tech system is becoming increasingly available and valuable throughout the country, and it can really cut down on water use!*

Overwatering is all too common, not only when we do so by hand but especially when using automated irrigation systems. In the past, even the most conservative applications didn't account for current soil moisture or provide a way to measure ever-changing climate conditions. Fortunately, more precise and appropriate irrigation practices are now available to homeowners that take into consideration real-time, local weather data to determine if and when irrigation is appropriate.

By going way beyond simply detecting active rainfall, these monitoring devices combine the integration of local weather information along with the amount of water loss from evaporation from the soil and transpiration (the loss of water from plant leaves) from plants. The combined term is *evapotranspiration*, or ET. Both evaporation and transpiration are affected greatly by the ever-changing weather. Essentially, ET

> ### DID YOU KNOW THAT...
>
> ❀ A study in Austin, Texas, revealed that the typical residential water customer was using twice as much water for landscape irrigation as local conditions (measured by evapotranspiration rates) required. Sure enough, after on-site irrigation evaluations, the average home reduced outdoor water use by 37.5 percent the next month.[1]
>
> ❀ Similarly, homeowners in an Irvine, California, study were found to be using about 1½ times as much water on their landscapes as was needed based on local ET rates.[2]
>
> ❀ A subsequent two-year study in Irvine, California, showed water savings of 22 percent using "smart" irrigation technology. A similar study in the Las Vegas, Nevada, area showed overall water savings of 20 percent. And a two-year study in Santa Barbara, California, resulted in an average of 26 percent water savings—with the highest savings at 59 percent![3]

monitors take the guesswork out of when and how much to water.

The ET device receives current local weather updates hourly via radio signals from area weather monitoring stations. This information includes current data on temperature, humidity, wind, rain, and solar radiation. It then uses this information to activate an irrigation system only as needed. These easy-to-install devices work with virtually any existing irrigation controller.

The newest "smart" irrigation controllers consist of an irrigation controller linked to a network of local weather stations via pager technology. This allows ET data to be sent to the units on a periodic basis. The controller then adjusts the irrigation schedule as appropriate in order to insure the correct applications for the specific plant types in each zone of the system.

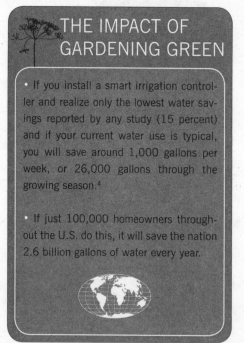

THE IMPACT OF
GARDENING GREEN

• If you install a smart irrigation controller and realize only the lowest water savings reported by any study (15 percent) and if your current water use is typical, you will save around 1,000 gallons per week, or 26,000 gallons through the growing season.[4]

• If just 100,000 homeowners throughout the U.S. do this, it will save the nation 2.6 billion gallons of water every year.

ET technology is setting a new standard in weather-based control of irrigation while providing a significant way to reduce unnecessary watering. Since precise landscape water management is essential to a healthy lawn and garden, ET management is a valuable tool that aides in water conservation. The only drawback to date is that it is not yet available for use in all parts of the country.

# Irrigate deeply using the two-step "cycle-and-soak" process.

*Avoid applying water faster than it can be absorbed.*

There's nothing more aggravating than trying to do everything right when it comes to water conservation in our home landscapes, only to see water still running off our property when we irrigate. That's a sign that water is being applied faster than it can be absorbed. This usually happens on slopes or with soil that is compacted or high in clay. But it doesn't mean the water must go to waste. It just means you "cycle and soak" instead.

Irrigation systems on automatic timers are set based on how long we want the water to run in a given zone. We're told to give our lawns an inch of water each week, so we allow the system to run for the duration it takes for that to happen. But what we don't realize is that heavy clay or compacted soil can only absorb so much water

> ### DID YOU KNOW THAT...
>
> ❀ Most soils underlying turf can hold water for 10 to 15 minutes of sprinkler run time and then they become saturated; longer irrigation periods on lawns that have any slope will cause runoff as soon as soil saturation has been reached.[1]
>
> ❀ Watering cycles for lawn grass and landscaped areas should usually last no more than 15 to 30 minutes. A level area of light sandy soil or sandy loam under turf can typically absorb 1 inch of water per hour. (Sloped areas can often absorb just ½ inch an hour.) So if sprinklers are applying water at a rate of 2 inches per hour, that flat plot of lawn is going to become saturated after 30 minutes. And after about 15 minutes, water will start running off a sloped lawn.[2]

at a time. The rest is wasted as runoff. In order for all the water to be fully utilized, set your run cycles by splitting the time in half or even thirds. Then have the system move on to the next zone.

For example, if the original time set for the zone in question was thirty minutes, divide it into two sessions of fifteen minutes each or even three ten-minute sessions. Programmable timers today can easily handle this type of starting and stopping adjustment for effective cycle and soak irrigation.

And to really know how long a cycle should last, start the system and note how long it takes before the water starts to run off. That's the maximum amount of time the water should run before switching off and moving on to the next zone.

Presumably, by the time the system cycles back around to the split zone, the water already applied will have had time to soak into the soil with new capacity to receive additional water.

## THE IMPACT OF GARDENING GREEN

• Because the two-step watering process of cycle-and-soak gets water down deep, you'll need to water less often and use less water when you do. Some studies show that by using this technique, homeowners need to water their lawn $1/3$ as often and can reduce their water consumption by as much as 70 percent—all while enjoying healthier lawns and plants.[3]

• By watering deeply with the two-step process, but only $1/3$ as often, the homeowner with an irrigation system will reduce landscape water usage by 30 percent (a conservative estimate). For homeowners with an average-size lawn of 5,000 square feet, that savings amounts to about 18,000 gallons of water per year.

• If just 100,000 households in the U.S. do this, it will reduce national water consumption by nearly 2 billion gallons per year.

# Program your irrigation system for seasonal needs.

*Your plants need less water in the cooler months of spring and fall.*

As plants and lawns go from active growth into dormancy and back again, their need for water changes. Plants use approximately 40 percent less water in the cool seasons of spring and fall when compared to the peak demands of summer. According to studies, water set at a constant rate through the entire watering season can use about 30 percent more water than is actually needed to keep plants and lawns healthy during the 24-week irrigation season.

> **DID YOU KNOW THAT...**
>
> ❀ When the City of Albuquerque studied the actual water needs of landscapes, it found that a traditional, lawn-dominated landscape needed 5.74 inches of water in July. But only 90 percent of that amount was needed in August, 62 percent was needed in September, and just 35 percent of that peak water amount was needed in October.[1]

As the season changes to fall, gradually set back your watering output so that by late fall, irrigation amounts have been reduced by 40 percent. As temperatures warm up again next spring, gradually increase the irrigation output back to 100 percent by July.

## THE IMPACT OF GARDENING GREEN

• By reducing irrigation in spring and fall, you can save 30 percent of the water you use on your landscape. For the average household with a 5,000-square-foot lawn, this amounts to about 18,000 gallons of water per year.[2]

# Maintain your irrigation system.

*Ensure irrigation water goes where you want it to and not down the drain.*

Efficient irrigation involves more than just making sure you're watering at the right time and with the right method. It also means making regular inspections of your system to ensure that it is operating properly and is leak-free. Consistent inspections, tune-ups, and repairs can yield substantial water savings.

Over time, even the best irrigation systems will succumb to cultural and environmental pressures (normal wear and tear, lawn mowers, foot traffic, and of course the car or delivery truck that drives over them). Generally, most irrigation problems are easy to identify and repair. But without regular inspections, thousands of gallons of wasted water may have already been lost.

## Identifying leaks

Sometimes irrigation leaks are obvious. You either see water spewing out of the ground or you step into a soggy puddle, even though it hasn't rained in weeks. That's when you can safely assume you have an irrigation-related leak. But in the cases where you don't see a problem but suspect one, try this:

First, look for the water meter. It may be located near the street, under a metal or plastic cover. Remove the cover, clean off the meter, and observe the gauges. When water is running, these gauges will spin. Conversely, when all the water is off, the numbers or dials on the meter will not move at all. If you're lucky, your meter will even have a small "leak detector" dial. It spins and records the low volume water use that is common with many leaks.

Next, turn off all the water inside and outside of the house. Check the meter again. If the gauges or dials are still, there is no leak. However, if there is movement, you have a leak and you must now determine if it is inside or outside. Locate and close the main shut-off valve going into the house. Check the meter again. If there is no movement, the leak is inside. However, if it is moving, the leak is outside.

Now you need to rule out the possibility of a leak in the main supply line to the house. Simply close the valve that supplies water to your irrigation system. If the meter is still moving, the leak is not in your irrigation system. But if the meter is still, you know that somewhere in your irrigation lines, there is a leak.

Walk the lines and look and listen for a problem. Many times the leak can be heard or felt before it is seen. You may even have a copy of the installation plan if you had your system installed. This indicates the lines, head locations, and valve boxes.

DID YOU KNOW THAT...

❀ Most irrigation system leaks are hard to detect because they're underground. But even a tiny leak can waste a lot of water. A one-thirtysecond-inch hole in a water line with 60 pounds of pressure can waste 6,300 gallons of water a month—that's 75,600 gallons a year![1]

❀ A study of irrigation systems at 100 homes in Orange County, California, found that 36 percent of the irrigation systems had leaks and 66 percent had inefficiency problems such as overspray and clogged or blocked heads. Virtually every home had some level of inefficiency in the irrigation system.[2]

❀ The Las Vegas Valley Water District estimates that up to 30 percent of the water used in the landscape by homeowners in the Las Vegas, Nevada, area is wasted due to leaks in irrigation systems. If every one of the 286,000 single family homes served by the Las Vegas Valley Water District eliminated this water waste, more than 27 billion gallons could be saved every year.[3]

## Leaking rotor or sprinkler head

If water is constantly seeping from the head, the problem is in the control box valve. The leaky valve will need to be replaced. You can either replace the worn diaphragms in the solenoid valves, or in the case of a sealed unit, you will need to replace the entire valve.

Water that gushes up at the head location when the system is operating indicates a leak there. Turn the system off and unscrew the head. Inspect the cylinder for any obvious signs of problems. Replacement parts are readily available once you locate a store or dealer that carries your brand. As a side note, it's a good idea to have spare parts on hand. It never fails; systems usually break when going to the store is either inconvenient or not an option.

It may be that the risers or swing pipes under the head are damaged or a seal in the coupling has been breached. At this point, it will take a little detective work and a bit of digging, but the problem will become apparent as you scan the area. In addition to having spare parts for your irrigation heads, be sure to have extra pieces of PVC pipe, risers, 90-degree fittings, fresh primer, glue, and a PVC cutter. Once the repair is made, allow ample time for the glue to dry, then test the system again.

One note of caution. This may not be your only leak, especially if you have not checked your system in a while. So while you're dirty and have your equipment close at hand, be sure to thoroughly inspect the rest of your lines and heads as well.

 THE IMPACT OF GARDENING GREEN

- If you fix just one small leak (a one-thirtysecond-inch hole) in an irrigation line that would otherwise have gone unnoticed, you will save 75,000 gallons of water every year.

- If just 100,000 homeowners in the U.S. do this, it will save the nation 7.5 billion gallons of water every year.

- If every homeowner in the U.S. with an irrigation system fixes all leaks regularly as soon as they occurred, it will save the nation's water supply more than 250 billion gallons of water every year.

## Other irrigation system problems

Another common problem leading to wasted water is a clogged nozzle. Again, nozzles can easily be unscrewed and inspected. Most of the time they can be cleaned with a blast of water or a thin piece of metal. You can suspect a clogged nozzle if the spray pattern is warped, the volume is reduced, or if areas of your yard or garden appear to be dry from lack of moisture in the zone in question.

An easy fix and one that will save you a lot of water is to readjust heads that overspray and are misdirected so the water goes where it's supposed to. That means not on the driveway, sidewalk, street, or your neighbor's yard!

Tilted heads should be straightened so that water delivered to the ground is even from side to side. Sunken heads that have been overgrown by surrounding vegetation confine the water to a very small area around the head. Similarly obstructed heads prevent water from getting to its intended target zone. The result is overwatering near the obstruction and insufficient water beyond it.

# Convert to soaker hoses or drip irrigation where feasible.

*This is the ideal way to deliver water to a specific area.*

Watering directly at the soil level is the most efficient way to irrigate, for two reasons. First, it cuts down on wasted water tremendously. Water is delivered directly to the soil. Because water is not shot into the air before falling back to earth, all water is utilized right where the plant needs it most—at the roots. With this method, there's no drift or evaporation. Furthermore, the water isn't deflected away or suspended on the foliage where it is exposed to wind and sun, the two biggest culprits of rapid evaporation.

DID YOU KNOW THAT...

❀ Drip systems in nonturf areas can save from 25 to 75 percent of the amount of water used by in-ground sprinkler systems, depending upon the local climate and the types of plants being irrigated. Most studies show savings in excess of 50 percent.[1]

❀ Drip systems are much more efficient than conventional sprinklers because virtually no water is lost to wind, runoff, or evaporation.[2]

Second, by watering at the soil level, the foliage stays dry. Keeping foliage dry is an important step in minimizing plant diseases. That's an important point when it comes to water conservation because a healthy plant requires fewer resources to keep growing strong. That includes water! Drip irrigation, also, known as *microirrigation* or *trickle irrigation*, is a popular system for applying water at or just under the soil level.

It may not be as appropriate for lawn areas, but for the most precise and efficient watering of individual plants (such as trees, shrubs, groundcovers, perennials, vegetables, and containers), drip irrigation is the ideal way to go. In fact, it's so efficient that many water municipalities exempt landscapes watered with drip irrigation from restrictions during drought. The concept has been used since ancient times when buried clay pots were filled with water and the water gradually seeped into the soil.

Although modern technology has provided improvements to the original design, the concept is still the same. A plastic supply line is connected to the water supply. Along the line, microtubes (¼-inch, flexible spaghetti-like tubing) are inserted into the supply line, and emitter tips are attached to the ends of the microtubes. The emitters allow the water to drip from the end. Based on the emitter tip selected, the rate of flow can vary from a few ounces to several gallons per hour while using much less water than conventional impact sprinklers.

Drip irrigation parts and accessories are readily available at garden centers and home improvement stores, as well as online and in catalogs. They can be purchased piecemeal or in kits.

## Installing a system

The basic equipment needed for the typical home system makes installation quick and easy. Connect the flexible plastic supply line to the spigot, just as you would with an ordinary garden hose. Run the supply line along the path that will deliver the water to the area needed. Once you have enough length laid out, cut the end, and then bend it back and secure to crimp.

Next, determine where along the supply line you want to insert the microtubes that will supply the water to the base of your plants. Kits come with a puncture tool that makes the hole in the supply line you'll need to insert the microtubing. You can also buy it separately. Connect the desired emitter to the end of the microtube, and you're finished.

## THE IMPACT OF GARDENING GREEN

- Convert your above-ground irrigation system for trees, shrubs, and perennials to drip irrigation and you'll save around 50 percent of your water use. For the homeowner with an average landscape of 2,500 square feet of trees, shrubs, and perennials, this amounts to a water savings of about 18,000 gallons of water per year.

- If just 100,000 homeowners in the U.S. do this, it will save the nation nearly 1.8 billion gallons of water every year. If all 10 million homeowners in the U.S. with above-ground irrigation systems do this, it will save us 180 billion gallons of water each year!

In permanent systems, a *backflow prevention device* is installed at the beginning of the line to prevent contaminated water from being sucked back into the water source should a reverse flow situation occur.

Drip irrigation is ideal for container gardening as well. Run the microtubing up the back side of the container so it's out of sight, and lay it in the container. Larger containers will often get two or more emitter lines. In either case, attach an automatic timer to the system for a carefree, low-cost, highly efficient watering system.

## Pros and cons versus conventional irrigation

Drip irrigation is not a replacement for conventional overhead watering. However, it certainly can be used most efficiently in place of overhead watering if your goal is to target certain areas. Moisture levels can be more consistently maintained and soil erosion is minimized.

Note that micro-irrigation lines are subject to occasional clogging, so periodically inspecting the lines and system will ensure more efficient operation. Also note that because the supply line and micro-tubes are along the soil surface, care should be taken for maintenance of plants around the system.

# Use plants that need less water—Xeriscape™.

*These fundamental design principles not only save water but also provide for a beautiful landscape.*

## Xeriscape principles

Putting the right plant in the right place is one of my favorite mantras for sound gardening practices. There are many important benefits to this simple concept. Not only does it cut down on pests and disease problems, but in this case, it also reduces the amount of water required. One of the best ways to significantly reduce watering needs in the garden is to seek out and install plants that don't require any supplemental irrigation. The concept is often referred to as "Xeriscaping™" (pronounced zera-scape).

More specifically, *Xeriscaping*™ is a word that was coined in 1978 by Denver Water, the water department of Denver, Colorado. The term combines the Greek word *xeros* meaning dry, with *landscape*. The concept was developed to emphasize plants whose natural requirements are appropriate to the local climate. Attention is also given to minimize the loss of water from runoff and evaporation. In a nutshell, the concept of Xeriscaping promotes techniques that improve landscapes while reducing the need for water, maintenance, and other resources.

> **DID YOU KNOW THAT…**
>
> ❀ Converting just a 20-foot by 20-foot patch of grass to Xeriscape can save as much as 22,000 gallons of water a year.[1]
>
> ❀ Replacing a single heavy-water-use tree, shrub, or flower with a low-water-use plant can save up to 550 gallons of water each year.[2]

❀ In the Southwest, low-water-use plants such as blue grama grass and desert willow trees use 73.4 percent less water than high-water use plants such as Kentucky bluegrass. Converting a 5,000-square-foot traditional landscape to Xeriscape in Albuquerque can save *at least* 50 percent of landscape water—and sometimes as much as 75 percent (depending upon the types of plants chosen). That's a potential savings of 74,680 gallons per year per home.[3]

Contrary to popular belief, Xeriscaping doesn't mean using plants that can live *without* water, or even using *only* drought-tolerant ones. More simply, it means grouping plants according to their water needs (hydrozoning) and using plants that are better adapted to the local area—specifically choosing native plants whenever possible. Since they survive and usually thrive with only the water supplied by Mother Nature, it stands to reason that you shouldn't have to water these plants, once they are established, any more than she does.

A *Xeriscape* is not a specific look or even any set group of plants. It's actually a combination of seven common-sense gardening principles, all with the result of saving water without giving up a lush-looking and beautiful landscape.

## Fundamental landscape design principles

**Plan and design for water conservation and beauty from the start.** Get to know your property in regard to light requirements, slope and terrain, soil conditions, orientation to the sun, traffic areas, and any other unique factors.

The landscape plan serves as a blueprint for the design and construction of your Xeriscape. Group plants according to similar needs, such as water and light requirements. One of the keys to a successful Xeriscape is keeping plants with different watering requirements separate!

**Create practical turf areas.** There is not a mandate to get rid of all your grass. (Although that would not be a bad thing since lawns are the single largest consumer of water in our landscapes.) However, rather than carpet the yard with turf, give thought to where it is really needed. It can serve a very important function in the home landscape by providing a recreational area.

Where turf is important, be sure to choose the most appropriate variety for the site. Some grass types hold up well to foot traffic, but they require considerably more water than less foot-tolerant grass choices that are more drought resistant. When a lawn is necessary but foot traffic may be lighter, seek a more drought-hardy variety instead and have the best of both worlds.

Where a lawn area is not essential, consider alternatives such as native groundcovers or drought-hardy plants.

**Select and group plants appropriately.** Plants have different requirements when it comes to light, water, and soil. For them to look their best, they should be planted where all those requirements are met.

One of the most important goals in a Xeriscape plan is to make sure irrigation is handled as efficiently as possible. A key way to make this happen is to group plants with similar watering needs together. In this way, you're not overwatering

> DID YOU KNOW THAT . . .
>
> ❀ Converting a 10,000-square-foot lawn-dominated landscape to a "Florida Water Wise Landscape" (consisting of 35 percent lawn and 65 percent bedding plants and shrubs watered using micro-irrigation) reduced landscape water use by 28.3 percent. That's an annual savings of 168,507 gallons for a typical home every year.[4]
>
> ❀ In Denver, converting a typical yard of 4,346 square feet of landscaping (consisting of 90 percent Kentucky bluegrass) to Xeriscape (35 percent buffalograss lawn with the remainder for the landscape consisting of xeric shrubs) can cut water use by 47 percent, saving 33,513 gallons per year.[5]

drought-tolerant plants just to hit the moisture-loving ones. In addition, when plants receive the appropriate amount of water, they are healthier, requiring less from us to maintain a healthy landscape.

**Improve the soil.** Soil that has been amended with organic material will help to retain moisture and improve drainage. Although it sounds contradictory, it's not. Organic amendments are a gift to gardeners, and what they do for improving soil quality is the essence of creating a successful Xeriscape.

Soil that drains well reduces the chances of runoff and evaporation. Soil that retains moisture requires less water. So either way, improving the soil is an important part of Xeriscaping, and it's one of the most important things you can do to create a healthy environment for your plants to thrive.

Improving the soil with organic matter is simply a matter of incorporating several inches of compost, aged manure, shredded leaves, mushroom compost, or topsoil (preferably all of the above) into the soil to a depth of six to twelve inches. A turning fork works well for this.

**Mulch.** Oh the miracles of mulch! It does so much—suppressing weeds, moderating soil temperatures, protecting plants from soil-borne diseases, and especially retaining soil moisture. All of these benefits epitomize the ideals of a successful Xeriscape. Mulch even adds a finished, aesthetically pleasing look to any garden bed.

Apply a layer of mulch about three to five inches thick, depending on the type. Mulch can come from natural material such as bark, straw, leaves, or grass clippings. One of the goals when I use mulch is to incorporate it into my garden beds after it breaks down (remember what we discussed above about improving the soil?).

**Use efficient irrigation.** The details of watering efficiently have been addressed in separate tips earlier in this chapter, but it's so important to the concept of Xeriscaping that it bears repeating.

Minimize the use of overhead watering. Sprinkler systems that use rotating or oscillating heads force water into the air under pressure. Some of the water falls back to the lawn and garden, but much is lost to evaporation. Keep irrigation water as close to the ground as possible. *On* the ground if you can, through soaker hoses and drip irrigation systems. These methods are the most efficient for watering flowers, vegetables, shrubs, and trees.

Know the output volume delivered by your irrigation heads in a given amount of time. This way you can avoid the costly mistake of overwatering. Use the can test described earlier for an easy way to measure this.

Design your irrigation system or sprinklers to water each zone for only the time appropriate for the watering requirements of the plants growing there. This assumes of course that you followed earlier instructions and grouped your plants by similar watering requirements.

Adjust the automatic timer on your watering system to take into consideration the changing needs of your plants as they become established and as the seasons change. For example, watering needs are drastically reduced from peak demands in midsummer to late fall.

Monitor your sprinklers and systems to be sure they are operating properly and are not leaking. Both problems can contribute to a tremendous amount of wasted water.

Maintain the landscape. A properly maintained landscape does require a bit of proactive participation on your part. But the long-term benefits are significant in the amount of water and other resources saved by having a healthy environment. The ideal Xeriscape provides more than just water savings. The rewards include a beautiful, low maintenance garden—if you keep up with the following:

*Pruning:* It promotes vigorous growth and removes dead and diseased wood and foliage.

*Deadheading:* This cuts down on unwanted volunteers, which often show up in inappropriate places, contrary to our grouping strategy. Deadheading also improves the overall look of the garden by removing spent seed heads.

*Mowing:* Maintaining grass at the proper height allows lawns to photosynthesize and grow deeper roots, and it helps crowd out competing weeds. When cutting, never remove more than a third of the grass blade, and make sure your mower blade is sharp to avoid tearing the grass, exposing it to possible pests and diseases.

*Aerating:* Areas that are subject to a lot of foot traffic can become compacted quickly. Even the forces of nature, especially rain, can compact untrodden earth. But when it comes to lawns, roots should be given an environment to grow deep in non-compacted soil. The easiest way to temporarily alleviate compacted soil is to aerate it. Typically, this is accomplished with a rented machine called an aerator, but it can also be accomplished with a hand operated tool . . . if you have the time and energy.

*Fertilization:* For lawns, be sure to grasscycle. That term means to allow the grass clippings to return to the earth rather than bagging them. It will reduce your annual fertilizer needs by about 30 percent. For trees, shrubs, vegetables, and flowers, continue to incorporate compost into your soil for a healthy way to add nutrients and improve your soil's health.

*Pest control:* My favorite form of pest control is "proactive patrol." Early detection is the best way to catch a problem before it gets out of hand, and allows options for the most benign and eco-friendly remedies.

Xeriscaping, as you've learned, is more than just planting a drought-tolerant garden. Beauty, by no means, need be sacrificed in a xeric landscape. When the previously mentioned steps are followed, a Xeriscape garden can look every bit as good as other gardens *and* save valuable resources in the process.

## THE IMPACT OF GARDENING GREEN

- Convert just one 20-foot by 20-foot piece of lawn to Xeriscape, and you'll save 22,000 gallons of water each year.

- If every single-family household in the U.S. does this, it will save the nation 1.4 *trillion* gallons of water each year!

- If just 100,000 homeowners in the U.S. with a lawn-dominated, automatically irrigated landscape of 10,000 square feet convert it to Xeriscape (35 percent lawn, 65 percent xerophytic trees and shrubs) and reduce their water use by just 30 percent, it will reduce the nation's water use by 4.5 billion gallons every year.

# CHAPTER THREE

# REDUCING GARDEN CHEMICALS TO PROTECT OUR WATER

My awareness of the need to be more environmentally conscious in my own garden was an evolution. I didn't grow up with an organic gardening mentality. I was just fascinated by everything about plants. In my enthusiasm for growing them, I wanted to help them look their best. So I'd dust and spray with insecticides, soak them in fungicide, and layer on the fertilizer—with no rhyme or reason as to when or why.

I've come a long way since then. Having a better understanding of how plants grow and the interdependence they have with nature—both above *and* below ground—has opened my eyes to a whole new world. As a result, I will forever care for them with this new view.

My journey began years ago as I sought ways to learn more about plants and how to grow them to perfection. I assumed that part of the recipe for success included all the things I had been doing, proactively reaching for the bottle and bag anytime I perceived an impending problem.

Even though I thought the plants in my garden looked good, the gardens of more seasoned gardeners always seemed to be more vivacious. My curiosity led me to ask one specific question of them: "What was the *one thing* they attributed most to the success of their garden?"

Much to my surprise, the gardeners I respected the most weren't doing any of the things I was doing. The way they approached their lush and healthy gardens was much simpler and less time consuming than I ever imagined. From one successful gardener to the next, the question was always the same—and so was the answer.

"Put the right plant in the right place" was the mantra I heard time and time again. It's a simple concept really. My awakening led me to realize that in my pursuit of having the perfect garden and landscape, I was actually destroying its natural biodiversity. When plants are allowed to grow in their intended environment, they are strong, healthy, beautiful, and resistant to the problems I was trying fix with chemicals.

DID YOU KNOW THAT. . .

❀ More than 102 million pounds of toxic pesticides are applied to lawns and gardens in the U.S., by more than 78 million households. Herbicides account for the highest usage of pesticides with over 70 million pounds applied on lawns and gardens per year.[1]

❀ Suburban lawns and gardens use more pesticides per acre on average (6.5 lbs) than agriculture (2.7 lbs).[2]

I wanted to know more. Surely that wasn't the *only* thing these experts were doing to make such a difference. And no, it wasn't. They were spending plenty of time in their gardens, but not with a bag or bottle in hand. Their hours were often spent with a cup of coffee or a glass of wine, leisurely strolling and enjoying their healthy and self-sustaining gardens.

Their proactive approaches led them out into their gardens just as much, and while they enjoyed the fruits of their labor, they would inspect their gardens, noting changes and catching potential problems early and proactively, not *reactively* after it was a bigger problem requiring more high-impact measures.

❀ Of 30 commonly used lawn pesticides, 19 have studies pointing toward carcinogens, 13 are linked with birth defects, 21 with reproductive effects, 15 with neurotoxicity, 26 with liver or kidney damage, and 11 have the potential to disrupt the endocrine (hormonal) system.[3]

❀ Of 30 commonly used lawn pesticides, 16 are toxic to birds, 24 are toxic to fish and aquatic organisms, and 11 are toxic to bees.[4]

❀ More than half of the 30 commonly used lawn pesticides are detected in groundwater. More than ¾ have the potential to leach.[5]

There's even a term used to describe this form of proactive behavior that's embraced by gardeners, university horticulturists, entomologists, and plant pathologists around the world: *integrated pest management* (IPM). This practice encourages scouting, tolerance, and proper timing when control measures are necessary. If chemical solutions are utilized, they are applied only in the last phase, giving care and attention to appropriate and responsible application.

The tips and ideas in this chapter will dig deeper into these vital concepts. They will help you understand more about the benefits of putting the right plant in the right place, enjoying your garden more while working less, and best of all, creating a more eco-friendly garden in the process. I wish I'd had this chapter to refer to when I was seeking enlightenment. Enjoy!

# Protect soil flora and fauna.

*Soil undisturbed by chemicals is teeming with life, microscopic organisms that work symbiotically with each other.*

Did you ever wonder why good healthy soil smells so wonderful? You can thank *actinomycetes* for that. They're living microorganisms that help stabilize decaying organic matter and are responsible for giving soil that heavenly earthy smell.

In Rachel Carson's classic book, *Silent Spring*, she describes in prophetic detail how soil undisturbed by man or chemicals is teeming with life, microscopic organisms that work symbiotically with each other and with the plants and roots to provide an efficient and highly sophisticated infrastructure. Col-

> DID YOU KNOW THAT...
>
> ❀ A teaspoonful of healthy soil contains about 4 billion living organisms.[1]
>
> ❀ A single gram of fertile soil has 5,000 to 7,000 different bacterial species and more than 10,000 fungal colonies.[2]
>
> ❀ Between 5 and 10 tons of animal life can live in 1 acre of soil.

lectively, these microorganisms allow flora and fauna above and below the ground to thrive naturally.

How strange that even just a decade ago, many gardeners and even industry professionals thought that having bacteria, fungi, and protozoa in the soil was a bad thing! Although there are certainly good and bad versions of each, we now know that there are many *very good* living organisms in soil that has not been tainted by overuse of chemicals.

Only since the invention of the electron microscope in 1931 have soil scientists been able to fully study and understand the symbiotic relationships within the soil. We have since learned that a single teaspoon of garden soil can contain over a billion bacteria. We discovered that plants attract bacteria and fungi to their roots so that protozoa and nematodes would eat these single-celled organisms. Then they would excrete the excess nitrogen in a form useable by plants right in the rhizosphere, which would then feed the plant! Ten years ago this was really news.

We now know that most flowering perennials and conifers, as well as most tree fruits, ornamental trees, and shrubs, do far better in soils dominated by fungi. Lawn grasses, vegetable row crops, and flowering annuals, on the other hand, grow best in soils where bacteria dominate. The bottom line is that all plants do better in soil that is alive with beneficial soil microbes. Yet until recently, we didn't realize just how much we were doing through conventional gardening practices to promote a soil environment that was anything but alive.

The implication of these facts soon became clear. Using high-salt, dehydrating, chemical fertilizers kills fungi and bacteria at the base of the soil food web and impacts larger members as well. Applying herbicides, pesticides, nematicides, fungicides, and all the other "icides" are practices that hurt the natural order. Why were we using these things? Who fertilizes and "icides" the Redwood, and how did they get to be 380 feet tall and live five hundred years without any help from us?

In our eco-friendly garden, our best asset is healthy soil. That means feeding the billions of beneficial microbes and other subterranean creatures the diet they need to thrive and multiply.

Appropriate moisture in the soil is a major contributor to a healthy soil food web (that complicated but elegant linking of food chains), and the lack of it is a major reason for its decline. Just as avoiding excessive use of salt-based synthetic fertilizers is important to minimize dehydration, the addition of moisture when necessary is equally important. In the absence of appropriate moisture, even though utilizing mulches, cover crops, etc., it may be necessary to irrigate on occasion, even in areas currently void of plants and trees. Although soil organisms can reestablish eventually once conditions are right, it's best to protect existing healthy soil rather than attempt to reestablish lifeless dirt.

What all of this new science means is that we have to make an adjustment to the way we work and play in our yards, gardens, and landscapes. It is incumbent upon us to take into account the real science of the soil and to consider the consequences of not doing so. No longer can we afford to negatively impact the soil food web, from the single-celled organisms all the way up to man.

We live in a new era, from how we communicate to how we garden. It is up to each one of us to embrace the tools that have recently been made available through science to reduce and even eliminate the footprint we have created. As you move away from feeding your plants to feeding the soil, you will be encouraged to know that gardening actually becomes easier. The natural balance in a healthy soil food web makes for healthier plants that look great and are more pest- and disease-resistant, too.[3]

## THE IMPACT OF GARDENING GREEN

• When you take care to protect the life in your soil, you reduce the use of the pesticides and synthetic nutrients that pollute our surface water, groundwater, and the water supply.

• As you 1) reduce your use of pesticides and synthetic nutrients by finding healthy alternatives (see the rest of this chapter), 2) maintain high levels of organic matter in your soil, and 3) maintain proper levels of soil moisture, you encourage the complex web of life in your soil—a plant-supporting network of organisms that ranges from beneficial bacteria, mycorrhizae, and other microbes to beneficial insects and earthworms. This in turn will help increase pest and disease resistance in your plants and maintain naturally optimal levels of nutrients in your soil, which will reduce the need for you to use pesticides and synthetic nutrients in the first place.

# Build healthy soil by adding organic matter.

*For enjoying a healthy garden, there may not be a more important tip in this entire book.*

Whenever you see any information on improving soil, it always stresses the importance of adding organic matter. The natural benefit of rich organic soil will be a reserve of vital nutrients and improved soil quality overall.

DID YOU KNOW THAT...

❀ Organic matter in the soil helps hold nutrients and water for plant use. In sandy soils, organic matter holds over 10 times more water and nutrients than the sand.[1]

❀ In clay soils, organic matter improves soil structure by binding mineral soil particles together to form aggregates. This creates greater pore space among the aggregated particles, providing optimal conditions for root growth. The increased pore space improves both soil drainage and water-holding capacity, and improves soil aeration.[2]

❀ Organic matter in the soil promotes the healthy biological activity of the soil—a complex web of life ranging from microbes to earthworms.

Think of soil rich in organic matter as a savings account for your plants. The nutrients are released back to your plants much like a steady income. The more you need, the more you get. The nutrients found in organic matter stay in the soil much longer than water-soluble synthetics, which rapidly leach through the soil.

Now visualize someone who has just been given a lot of money all at once. Rather than putting it in the bank, they spend it all immediately. It feels good temporarily, but when it's gone, it's gone.

There are no reserves to draw on over time. That's how I think of water-soluble inorganic fertilizers. They work, but what nutrients aren't absorbed by the roots quickly pass through the soil, leaving behind potentially damaging salts.

Organic matter is, was, or comes from living things. Some of the most common natural amendments found in nature include decomposed plant residue, dead roots, excreted waste from soil-dwelling organisms, and composted bark, manure, leaves, and sticks. When you think of the lush forest of a woodland setting, all that makes up the soil there is a collection of natural amendments over time. The only fertilizer they receive is what is derived naturally from the soil. And yet how the forest flourishes!

In our home landscapes and gardens, we can create the same effect. In addition to the amendments mentioned above, we might use grass clippings, mushroom compost, peat moss, peanut or coco shells, and so much more. Collectively, it may be just good old compost, but whatever it's made of, it contains billions of living beneficial microorganisms and includes vital organically-derived nutrients.

There's a second reason adding organic matter is so import to creating healthy soil. It improves drainage of compacted soils and increases water retention in loose, sandy soils. Amendments incorporated into the soil allow some particulates to bind together while preventing others from creating too large a mass. In total, the organic elements along with the native sand, silt, or clay work in harmony to improve the structure, tilth, and texture of any soil while, at the same time, building up nutrients and reducing the need for supplemental water and fertilizers.

As you build healthy soil in your home garden and landscape, how much you add will depend on the condition of your soil before you start. The amount will vary, but your goal is to add enough so that compacted soil breaks apart and loose soil binds together.

There's no cookie-cutter recipe for proper soil, but here's a good rule to follow: Your goal for adding organic matter to the soil should be to end up with a texture that binds together when squeezed but breaks apart easily when disturbed. Over time, organic matter will continue to break down and decompose so you will need to periodically add more. But as you do, know that your soil is getting better and healthier all the time, and as you continue to feed the soil, your plants will reward your efforts.

## THE IMPACT OF GARDENING GREEN

- Maintaining high levels of organic matter in your soil is one of the most important things you can do to have healthy plants. And healthy plants need less fertilizer, pest controls, and other chemicals.

# Use compost as a soil conditioner and fertilizer.

*There is no store-bought product better for the garden than compost.*

Compost helps add life and fertility to the soil. It improves drainage yet allows soil to retain sufficient moisture. Compost helps create the type of soil structure that is critical for nutrients and water to be absorbed and for roots to spread. It protects plants from certain diseases, moderates pH, feeds earthworms, supports beneficial microorganisms, is known to be a growth stimulant, and even buffers toxins in the soil.

In nature, composting occurs constantly. Plant and animal waste breaks down into soil-like particles over time, with no involvement from us. If you choose to make your own, the simplest compost piles are just that, piles of yard waste and kitchen scraps. There are no fancy systems, containers, bins, or compartments to facilitate the process. Although a simple pile will suffice to make perfectly usable compost, more elaborate systems can be built or purchased to contain the mix and help speed up the decomposition process.

> DID YOU KNOW THAT...
>
> ❀ Comparison studies of soil amendments show that plots amended with yard waste compost consistently yield healthier, more productive plants and have more available nutrients in the soil (nitrogen, phosphoric oxide, and potash) than plots treated with synthetic fertilizer.[1]
>
> ❀ Compost can be used as a substitute for fertilizer because microorganisms in compost are able to fix nitrogen into a form that can be used by plants. Compost releases nutrients over time, and the nutrients in compost can adequately supply plants with the nutrients they need for proper establishment and growth.[2]
>
> ❀ The slow release of nutrients in compost is less likely to impact groundwater through leaching than quickly-available synthetic fertilizers.[3]

Compost structures come in many shapes and sizes. Your choice will depend on the space and materials you have available. Structures can be made of woven wire, snow fencing, old wooden pallets, concrete blocks or bricks, or a fifty-five-gallon barrel. Successful composting can even be accomplished in a modified garbage can. Structures can also be made with single or multiple compartments. Once you've decided what structure is right for you, position your compost bin near a water source and make sure the bottom has adequate drainage.

DID YOU KNOW THAT...

❀ Compost helps keep soil pH at optimum levels for nutrient availability.[4]

❀ Compost increases the soil's organic matter content.

❀ Using compost suppresses some plant diseases, such as fusarium crown and root rot in tomato, brown rot in peaches, fusarium end rot in onions, and numerous fungal diseases of turfgrass.[5]

There are a few essential elements necessary for compost to occur. They are water, air, heat, carbon (brown stuff, like dead leaves and twigs), and nitrogen (green stuff, like grass clippings or vegetable and salad scraps).

To start a compost pile, you don't need anything fancy. A simple accumulation of green waste (10 to 25 percent) and brown waste (75 to 90 percent) will get you going. Although mixing the compost pile is not required for compost to form, you can greatly speed up the decomposition process by turning the pile every week or so. Each time the pile is turned, oxygen is introduced, which will increase the rate of breakdown. Add water periodically to keep the pile at the moisture level of a damp sponge. You will be well on your way to making compost. Depending on the variables, you should be able to have usable compost in about four months to one year.

You can add many items to your compost pile or bin, but whatever you add, make the pieces as small as possible for faster breakdown. Almost anything from the yard or garden can be added, but avoid adding diseased plants. The disease pathogens may not be killed in the composting process, and you can end up introducing diseases to your soil. I also choose not to include weeds in the mix. The seeds can persist for a very long time, and they may survive the composting process only to be spread to other areas of your garden as you add new compost.

When adding household products, the biggest items to avoid are meat, fish, bones, dairy products, and pet wastes. They can attract outdoor pests and can harbor many types of bacteria and disease.

Compost will be ready to use when it's dark brown, earthy-smelling, and crumbly. The result is undoubtedly the best soil food and conditioner available—recycling at its best!

## THE IMPACT OF GARDENING GREEN

• Because adding compost to the soil increases soil fertility and the ability of plants to resist insect pests and diseases, including soil-borne fungal diseases, a regular program of adding compost to your soil is an important part of reducing your need to use fungicides and synthetic nutrients.

# Let earthworms do the work for *really* healthy soil.

*When it comes to manure and compost, there's one combination*
*that works so well, it has its own name: vermicompost.*

Worms are quite resourceful, both in what they do *to* our soil and what they do *in* our soil. Let's address the benefits of the worms themselves first. We all know that worms are the epitome of soil-dwelling creatures. As they move about near the surface and underground, they do great things to decompose organic matter. The tunnels they leave behind while mining for sustenance aerate the soil while at the same time improving drainage (especially in clay and compacted soil).

> DID YOU KNOW THAT...
>
> ❀ Extensive research by Ohio State, Cornell University, U.C. Davis, and other horticultural institutions have shown that worm castings improve plant size as well as the bloom quantity, quality, and color for flowers, and they result in significant yield increases *plus* improvements in taste and appearance for fruits and vegetables.[1]
>
> ❀ One study found that a sample of soil with 4 percent organic matter from worm castings contained 246 pounds of nitrogen per 1000 square feet, while the surrounding soil contained 161 pounds of nitrogen per 1000 square feet.[2]
>
> ❀ Ohio State research showed that the optimum ratio of worm castings to native soil is 10 to 20 percent.[3]

And that's not even the best part. Worms consume massive amounts of organic matter on and in the soil. As this material passes through the worm's gut, the output or castings are more nutrient rich than before. In fact, vermicastings are 50 percent higher in organic matter than soil that has not moved through the worms.

Moreover, the castings of worms are as much as seven times richer in phosphate, ten times higher in potash, five times higher in nitrogen, three times higher in usable magnesium, and one and a half times higher in calcium. Those same castings also increase soil aggregation and water-holding capacity of poorly drained soils. Want more? Worm castings are also know to suppress various plant diseases in soil.

Although it takes thousands of worms to make a noticeable quantity of castings suitable for the garden, a little goes a long way. Using it sparingly can still give great results. Worm castings can be purchased at retail outlets in bags or containers, and some commercial operations will sell and deliver bulk quantities.

### THE IMPACT OF GARDENING GREEN

- Adding vermicompost to your soil is an effective way to maintain soil fertility and reduce your need to use synthetic nutrients. It will also suppress soil-borne plant diseases and reduce your need to use fungicides.

At home, it's fun to raise your own worms and harvest the castings. The entire system only takes a couple of feet of floor or shelf space and you can easily raise them indoors. Other than needing food a couple of times each week, they thrive on neglect. The most common and readily available worms for composting are Red Wigglers, or Red Earthworms. They are particularly fond of kitchen scraps, compost, and manure piles. They are also readily available from bait shops or mail order and internet sources.

You can purchase pre-made vermicomposting bins, but it is easy to make your own. A plastic storage bin with a tight-fitting lid is ideal. Aeration is important, so be sure to add some holes along the top or side. I include a few holes for drainage since worms need the proper moisture in their bedding to survive. Width is more important than height. A bin that is eight inches by two feet by two feet is a good size to start with.

Once you have the container, you'll need the appropriate bedding for your worms. It can consist of shredded newspaper strips, cardboard, leaves, compost or manure, and more. A fluffy mix of several ingredients is ideal, but whatever you add, make sure it can absorb water. The overall moisture level you want to establish and maintain is about that of a damp sponge.

Now that the bedding is nice and moist, add the one thousand or so worms you purchased, roughly a pound. The worms will quickly make their way below the surface since they shy away from light. Add kitchen scraps (except for meat and dairy) several times each week. Some people like to bury the food in the bedding. Or, you can lay it on top and the worms will surface to consume it. Smaller pieces allow the worms to consume the scraps more quickly. Coffee grounds, banana peels, lettuce, and vegetables are among their favorites (although they are not very picky).

You'll start to see results in a few weeks, but be patient. Although worms are voracious eaters (you can even hear them at work), it will take time to accumulate enough castings to harvest. At that time, it is also a good idea to change out the bedding. Otherwise, the worms will eventually stop producing and die off on their own. A bin of fresh bedding every four months or so will generate a higher worm population.

In spite of the many wonderful benefits worms and their castings provide to naturally cultivate and fertilize our yards and gardens, humans remain both directly and indirectly their biggest foe. Rototilling destroys worm burrows and can cut earthworms so badly that they never regenerate. Chemical fertilizers high in salts as well as some pesticides are harmful to them.

You'll know you're doing your part to promote a worm-friendly environment when their populations are noticeable in your soil. Their presence in high numbers means a healthy amount of organic matter is available as their food source, and the harmful effects of chemical fertilizers high in salts are absent. The reward will be many pounds of nutrient-rich worm castings on the surface and in the soil, along with all the many other benefits worms provide.[4]

# Use natural and organic sources of nutrients.

*Feed the soil first, then let the soil feed the plants.*

Natural products are showing up everywhere, from what we put in our gardens to the clothes we wear on our back. For the homeowner, there is now a myriad of options for what we use to provide nutrients to our outdoor landscapes and even our houseplants.

To set the stage, the most common terms in this arena today are *organic* and *natural*. They're often used interchangeably, but they don't mean exactly the same thing. To simplify the difference, when used in the context of a fertilizer, the term *organic* means a plant nutrient that contains carbon and provides water-insoluble nitrogen. *Natural* simply means a plant, animal, or mineral source.

DID YOU KNOW THAT...

❀ Only about 50 percent of the nitrogen applied in synthetic chemical fertilizers is actually used by plants. The rest is lost to the atmosphere, to runoff, or through leaching.[1]

❀ Runoff from synthetic chemical fertilizers pollutes streams and lakes and causes algae blooms, depleted oxygen, and damage to aquatic life.[2]

Since this isn't a science book, we won't go any further into explaining the differences, but the bottom line is, eco-friendlier consumers want their lawn and garden nutrients to be truly natural and from the earth since these kinds of ingredients seem to be safer and more responsible.

Classic organic or natural fertilizers and amendments include compost and manures of various types. These are some of the oldest and most time-tested choices for improving the conditions of soil naturally.

More recently, compost tea and vermicompost teas have become popular as well.

## Which nutrients are green?

You may be like many people who decide to grow green and expand your gardening horizons, only to find you're as confused as the next guy when it comes to actually knowing what nutrients to buy and still be eco-friendly. The list of questions builds as you stand in front of the organic gardening section, blankly staring at the increasing choices of bagged and bottled products . . .

> DID YOU KNOW THAT. . .
>
> ❀ Unlike quick-release fertilizers, natural organic fertilizers feed plants slowly and evenly over a longer period of time, with less leaching of nutrients (especially nitrogen) into the watershed.[3]
>
> ❀ While most natural organic fertilizers are more gentle to plants than non-organic quick-release fertilizers, some can still burn plants if over-applied, and others (especially fresh manures) can be high in salts.[4]

Before you give up and throw in your recycled towel, allow me to explain some of the differences between organic and synthetic (non-organic) choices, review a few fertilizer basics, and then offer some viable organic or natural alternatives to non-organic products.

### Organic vs. non-organic

All plants receive their nutrients in chemical form. They cannot distinguish between how the nutrient was derived, whether organic or non-organic.

*Organic* nutrients, when referring to plant nutrition, generally refer to any fertilizer that is derived from plant, animal, or mineral origin. It must contain one or more essential nutrients for plant growth along with the presence of carbon. Once applied, organic nutrients must first be broken down and digested by soil microorganisms, which then release these nutrients in a form available to plants.

This digestive process also produces *humus*, a vital ingredient to improving soil structure. Since organically-derived nutrients are very resistant to leaching and contain a very low salt index, the net result is nutrients that remain in the soil until utilized by plants, with less risk of burning or dehydration even in periods of extreme drought or over-application.

*Non-organic* fertilizers (also known as synthetic or manufactured) are produced chemically. In the classic sense, they are developed either to deliver nutrients rapidly, such as those that are water-soluble, or to give nutrients over time, as a controlled release.

Although very effective for providing rapid or prolonged periods of feeding, non-organic fertilizers have a high salt index. The potential risk to plants and the soil food web is burning and dehydration along with the leaching of unabsorbed chemicals into waterways.

### Fertilizer basics

Exactly what you are trying to achieve for your plant's growing success will determine which fertilizer to buy. Any fertilizer package prominently lists three numbers. These are the primary nutrients that are needed in the greatest quantity by plants. These numbers represent the percentage of nitrogen (N), phosphorus (P) and potassium (K) found in each package.

Nitrogen is primarily responsible for the vigorous growth and dark green color in plants. Phosphorus plays a major role in plants' root development and flowering, while potassium is mainly responsible for disease resistance and the overall hardiness of the plant.

### Organic and natural alternatives

Synthetic fertilizers are usually listed simply by these numbers above, since they are manufactured chemicals. Organic and natural alternatives, however, are often listed primarily by what they actually are, such as blood, bone meal, or fish emulsion.

Still, somewhere on that package you'll find those all-important three numbers, which is the key to knowing what role that product will play in your garden. Here is a partial listing of the most commonly available organic and natural fertilizer alternatives, sorted by their role for providing nitrogen, phosphorus, or potassium:

**Nitrogen**: dried blood, blood meal, cottonseed meal, fish emulsion, and seaweed extract

**Phosphorus**: bone meal, rock phosphate

**Potassium**: greensand, sulfate of potash

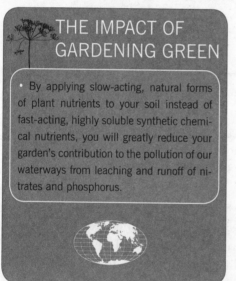

THE IMPACT OF GARDENING GREEN

• By applying slow-acting, natural forms of plant nutrients to your soil instead of fast-acting, highly soluble synthetic chemical nutrients, you will greatly reduce your garden's contribution to the pollution of our waterways from leaching and runoff of nitrates and phosphorus.

In addition to the three primary nutrients, twelve other elements absorbed from the surrounding soil are considered essential for plant growth. Organic and natural soil amendments are a readily available way to provide all of these elements as well.

I rely on multiple natural amendments to ensure I'm feeding the soil, which in turn feeds the plants. I find this to be a safe, effective, and environmentally responsible approach to gardening.

# Grow the right plant in the right place.

*You've just solved most of the challenges around creating a healthy and thriving garden.*

In my role as host of gardening television shows, my travels take me to some of the finest private and public gardens anywhere. It's no surprise that these gardens are meticulously maintained, lush and thriving. They are free of pests, and there are no plant diseases. They are the types of gardens you and I dream about having.

For many years, whenever I visited these places, I always asked the person responsible for taking care of the garden the same first question; "What's the one thing you are doing to keep these plants looking so good?" After getting the same answer time and again, I finally quit asking the question.

## "Put the right plant in the right place."

If I've heard this once, I've heard it a thousand times. And personally I knew it to be true before I ever started inquiring from other expert gardeners. Plants do have an ideal growing environment. Place them in it, and they will reward you with minimal care.

In the eco-friendly garden, placement is an important consideration. Any plant, no matter how small or big, will flourish when planted where it is happiest. And just in case you don't know by now, a happy plant is a healthy plant. We know through scientific observation, healthy plants are less susceptible to pests and diseases. Even when these forces are present, healthier plants are more resistant and resilient when attacked. The bottom line is this: happy, healthy plants rarely need chemical fixes.

Plants that thrive in full sun will never look their best in even partial shade. Plants that prefer shade will become quickly stressed in full sun conditions. Plants that thrive in dry conditions will look terrible in wet soil and vice versa.

When plants don't look their best, they're under stress. Unknowing gardeners try to fix the problem by throwing extra fertilizer, pesticides, and fungicides at the plant, thinking that will take care of it. That's the worst thing you can do! Plants in the right place won't need to be fixed. They'll look great all on their own.

It sounds so simple and really is, as long as you know what the ideal conditions are for that plant or tree. Unfortunately, we too often buy on impulse, never knowing much about the plant or even where we'll place it once we do get around to planting. Here are some tips to help you put the right plant in the right place:

*Know the conditions of your yard or garden.*
Do you know what zone you live in? It's important to know the average minimum and maximum temperatures for your area. Do you have full sun or full shade? In many cases, you'll have some combination. What about soil moisture? Is it constantly damp or as hard as concrete?

To make matters worse, when referring to the soil, there is dry shade, moist shade, dry sun, and moist sun. It's no wonder we sometimes struggle. Unless you get lucky, it's hard to plant the right plant in the right place without knowing all the above.

*Research and read the tag.*
It's so easy to plunk a plant into any old space just to get it out of the driveway and into the ground. But don't do it. This is where the breakdown usually occurs in the home garden. We make the impulse buy, not knowing where we'll ever plant it. Or we buy a plant, not knowing if it will even grow in the place we have in mind.

## HARDY PERENNIALS

*The following are examples of tall perennials hardy to Zone 4 that perform well in shade:*
**Monkshood** *(Aconitum spp.)*
**Black snakeroot** *(Actea racemosa)*
**Goat's beard** *(Aruncus dioicus)*
**Foxglove** *(Digitalis purpurea)*
**Ligularia** *(Ligularia spp.)*
**Ostrich fern** *(Matteuccia struthiopteris)*
**Cinnamon fern** *(Osmunda cinnamomea)*
**Royal fern** *(Osmunda regalis)*
**Rodgersia** *(Rodgersia spp.)*
**Tall meadowrue** *(Thalictrum dasycarpum)*

*The following are examples of perennials hardy to Zone 4 that perform well in wet soils:*
**Sedge** *(Carex spp.)*
**Blue flag iris** *(Iris versicolor)*
**Yellow flag iris** *(Iris pseudocorus)*
**Hyssop** *(Agastache spp.)*
**Jack-in-the-pulpit** *(Arisaema spp.)*
**Cardinal flower** *(Lobelia cardinalis)*
**Great blue lobelia** *(Lobelia siphilitica)*
**Japanese primrose** *(Primula japonica)*
**Hibiscus** *(Hibiscus spp.)*
**Beebalm** *(Monarda spp.)*

*The following are examples of perennials hardy to Zone 4 for dry, alkaline soils:*
**Yarrow** *(Achillea spp.)*
**Rock Cress** *(Aubretia spp.)*
**Mountain bluet** *(Centaurea montana)*
**Jupiter's beard** *(Centranthus spp.)*
**Candytuft** *(Iberis spp.)*
**Thyme** *(Thymus spp.)*
**Wormwood** *(Artemisia spp.)*
**Salvia** *(Salvia spp.)*
**Eulalia grass** *(Miscanthus sinensis)*
**Switch grass** *(Panicum spp.)*

Today there is so much valuable plant information at your fingertips. A simple Internet search with keywords like, "dry shade, groundcover, Zone 7" will quickly produce several Web sites from university extension services, garden forums or discussion rooms, magazine articles, and other authorities. At the very least, all plants should come with a tag that provides preferred growing conditions for sun, shade, and moisture.

The right plant in the right place shouldn't need any supplemental chemicals for pest or disease control, and fertilization can be kept to a minimum. It's an easy rule to follow that really works.

## THE IMPACT OF GARDENING GREEN

• Growing a plant in the right place is essential for that plant's health. Doing so is a crucial step in reducing the need to use chemical nutrients and pesticides.

# Grow tough pest- and disease-resistant plants.

*This can make your gardening life easier and safer for the planet.*

Growing a healthy plant is one of the best natural ways to breed pest and disease resistance into your garden. Strong, vigorously growing plants will have an innate ability to fend off attacks from various disease pathogens and many pests. But if you don't quite have the confidence to rely on this method as your primary defense, there's another way to get a head start. Look for plants that have those defenses built right in!

Finding plants that are naturally pest- and/or disease-resistant makes it possible to eliminate or at least reduce the amount of chemicals used to fight these nuisances. Although not all plants possess the ability to fight off their greatest foes, some plants have developed the genetics to stand up and fend off some of their bigger adversaries.

To be clear, understand that just because a plant is "resistant" does not mean it is pest- or disease-proof. Resistant plants can still be affected; it's just not as likely.

This leads me to my second point: when you do find a plant that is resistant, that quality is specific to a limited number of pests or diseases. A classic example is with tomato plants. When you see VFNT on the tag, it means that plant has genetic breeding that makes it resistant to Verticillium wilt, Fusarium wilt, root-knot nematodes, and tobacco mosaic virus. Even with all that built-in resistance, there are many other pests and diseases that can affect this plant. But since these are some of the most common problems that afflict tomato plants, choosing VFNT plants puts you ahead of the game.

## TOUGH PLANTS

The following are examples of roses that are highly resistant to blackspot and powdery mildew:

Knock Out
Blushing Knock Out
Pink Knock Out
Double Pink Knock Out
The Fairy
Perle d'Or
Belinda's Dream
Else Poulsen '
Carefree Beauty
Sea Foam

The following are examples of disease-resistant tomatoes:

Big Beef VFFNTA Hybrid
Brandywine
Bush Celebrity VFFNTA Hybrid
Bush Early Girl VFFNT Hybrid
Mountain Pride Hybrid
Neptune
Rutgers VFA
Shady Lady VFTA Hybrid
Celebrity
Sunmaster

The following are examples of disease-resistant flowering crabapples:

Bob White
Mary Potter
Molten Lava
Prairifire
Red Jade
Red Jewel
Sargent's Crabapple (Malus sargentii)
Sentinel
Strawberry Parfait
Sugar Tyme

The following are examples of flowers that are resistant to Japanese beetles:

Ageratum (Ageratum spp.)
Columbine (Aquilegia spp.)
Begonia (Begonia spp.)
Coreopsis (Coreopsis spp.)
Coral-bells (Heuchera spp.)
Hosta (Hosta spp.)
Lantan (Lantana spp.)
Showy sedum (Sedum spectabile)
Nasturtium (Tropaeolum majus)
Violet, pansy (Viola spp.)

It is also important to know that just because a plant is resistant now, there's no guarantee it will be that way forever. Pests have an amazing ability to adapt, evolve, and overcome whatever resistance the plant may offer. Changes in the genetics of the pest or host plant can quickly neutralize a plant's resistant qualities.

In a collaborative effort of the scientific and horticultural community, entomologists, plant pathologists, and plant breeders are constantly on the lookout for new sources as they work to develop more resistant plants.

Three basic mechanisms are at work in determining pest and disease resistance. First, a plant may possess chemicals or structures that can impose an adverse effect on a pest. Plants contain an amazing array of chemicals, some of which are toxic to pests. For example, consider the popular botanical insecticides of pyrethrum or rotenone. Even the physical structure of the plant can be a deterrent. Trichomes (or hairs) on the plant can secrete chemicals that present such impediments that the plant is of no interest to the pest.

Second, the plant may possess repelling qualities that make it undesirable for a particular pest or family. It could be simply a matter of color, but chemicals often come into play. Whatever the case, insects will not choose certain plants for feeding or as a host for laying eggs.

Resistance is the third way a plant may demonstrate resilience to pests or diseases. Even though the plant may be damaged by pests or a disease, it is able to withstand and recover from the damage.

Although food crops get much of the attention for their resistant properties due to their inherent value, ornamental crops also offer many of the same protections. Pest and disease resistance in ornamentals, vegetables, and fruits

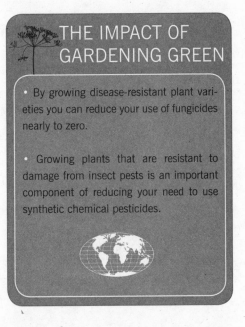

## THE IMPACT OF GARDENING GREEN

• By growing disease-resistant plant varieties you can reduce your use of fungicides nearly to zero.

• Growing plants that are resistant to damage from insect pests is an important component of reducing your need to use synthetic chemical pesticides.

should be a cornerstone in creating your eco-friendly garden.

You can find sources for these plants in gardening and seed catalogs, through your county extension service, and in numerous online publications. And when you are at the nursery, be sure to look on the plant label. Resistance will be noted there.

*Tis my faith that every flower enjoys the air it breathes!*

WILLIAM WORDSWORTH

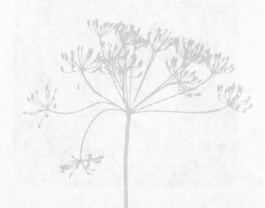

# Reduce chemical use by raising your tolerance for little imperfections.

*Getting to the root of the problem will do more for the long-term success of your garden than throwing chemicals at it.*

If you routinely reach for the herbicide, pesticide, fungicide, or whatever *-icide*, maybe you should ask yourself why? As we learned in a previous tip, the right plant in the right place should be healthy and robust on its own, able to resist many of the conditions that *-icides* are designed to treat.

Fertilizers are chemicals too, and they're definitely not the magic bullet for making your plants look better when stressed by pests, diseases, or improper planting. Although all plants benefit from appropriate nutrients, if you've paid attention to creating healthy soil, feeding the plants shouldn't be so critical that you throw down even more chemicals.

Two of the most important points in this book bear repeating, especially in the context of this topic. Without exception, the best ways you can create an environment that promotes a thriving landscape, beautiful garden, or lush lawn is to first plant the right plant in the right place and, second, feed the soil and let the soil take care of the plant.

The emphasis in both of these concepts is on promoting a healthy plant environment both above and below ground. Time and time again, gardeners and scientist all over the world have seen the positive ways plants and trees respond when fostered in these conditions; the plants are simply healthier and more resistant to pests and diseases.

Remember, even in the best of conditions, plants may come under attack by aggressive pests or disease. But just like you and me, when we're healthier, we recover more quickly and are not affected as severely as when we are out of shape or not taking care of ourselves. Plants respond the same way.

So if you find that your plants show signs of insect damage or disease, ask yourself what you can do to make conditions more conducive to a healthier, happier plant. (Here's a clue; it's probably not to throw more fertilizer at it.) Next, if you're convinced the plant is already in great shape and in the right place, then don't automatically reach for the spray bottle or bag of anything. Instead, monitor the situation and do nothing chemically if you can help it.

In addition, manual controls such as hand-picking pests or blasting them off with a good stiff spray of water will go far. One of the easiest and best things you can do when it comes to insect damage is to let nature take its course. Exercise a little tolerance and allow some damage; it is rarely noticed from a distance. In the meantime, in an eco-friendly garden, nature will take its course. Beneficial insects will move in to fight your battles for you if you allow them enough time.

> DID YOU KNOW THAT. . .
>
> ❀ The U.S. home and garden market spends nearly as much on pesticides as conventional agriculture ($1,288,000,000 compared to $1,326,000,000).[1]
>
> ❀The U.S. home and garden market used 71 million pounds of herbicides, 17 million pounds of insecticides, and 12 million pounds of fungicides in 2001.[2]
>
> ❀ Less than 1 percent of all known insect species are considered to be pests.[3]

If it's a disease issue, remove the affected foliage completely from your garden. That's a good rule to live by even if you are chemically dependent. Removing the problem is a proactive and effective approach to dealing with any disease issue in your garden. Sometimes that requires removing entire plants. And be aware that these should not be composted because the disease pathogens may survive and be spread about the garden later.

One final note of caution: when handling diseased plants, use gloves and avoid touching healthy plants. Otherwise you can spread the disease to unaffected plants simply by touching them.

## THE IMPACT OF GARDENING GREEN

- Learning to live with minor cosmetic damage from pests is an important step toward reducing our use of synthetic herbicides, fungicides, and pesticides.

# Catch problems early.

*By keeping in touch and staying proactive, your
dynamic garden will rarely surprise you.*

Once, I was telling a colleague and respected gardener about
how my garden had been doing so well, in spite of the very strange
weather and conditions experienced that season—conditions perfect
for all types of pests and diseases. As I listed possible reasons for these
positive results, he chimed in, "That's the difference between proactive
and reactive gardening."

The concept made instant sense. I had actually practiced it for years
but had never put it into such practical, logical terms before. The
steps I had taken to ensure a healthy garden were all in an effort to
prevent problems, just as a person might take care of himself or her-
self with diet, exercise, and vitamins.

DID YOU KNOW THAT...

❀ Mature weeds can require twice the rate of herbicide to kill, compared to young newly emerging ones.[1]

❀ Applying organic fungicides early as a preventative measure can keep harsher chemicals out of your garden later.[2]

❀ A few grubs per square foot is not a problem to an otherwise healthy lawn, while 10 or more per square foot can cause turf loss.[3]

I credit this proactive practice to knowing the benefits
of starting off with a healthy
garden and maintaining
vigilance along the way. There
are certainly plenty of
chemicals that can be applied
after the fact, but at what
price? There's no place or reason for that in an eco-friendly
garden.

The best part about being
proactive in your outdoor
environment is that not only are you helping your plants, but you
also get to have fun.

The most important step in the process is simply to observe your garden day to day and note changes. I do this early in the morning with a hot cup of coffee, before the rest of the world wakes up. But even a dash to the car with an eye towards your garden can reveal important information. The concept is simply to pay attention as often as you can.

When you utilize any opportunity you can to "tune in," your dynamic garden will rarely surprise you. And when you do find changes that require your attention, your early detection will make the control methods easier and much safer for you and the garden.

THE IMPACT OF GARDENING GREEN

• Regular daily surveillance during the active growing season allows you to catch problems early. That usually allows you to resolve them with the lowest-impact control and a greatly reduced use of chemicals.

If all of this sounds a lot like IPM (Integrated Pest Management), I'd say you're right; the essence of proactive gardening *is* the first step of IPM—scouting—and there are other similarities, too. This explains why I like IPM so much. Aside from the similarities of the terms, proactive gardening seems to sound much more gardenesque, don't you think?

# Control pests with natural controls first.

*There are some very effective natural control treatments available. Controls for all types of pests in the eco-friendly garden seek to use the least toxic method first.*

Organic pest-control methods are generally less environmentally damaging and less toxic to non-targeted insects, mammals, and aquatic life. Unfortunately, in our time-starved world, many people simply want the most potent, one-application product—no matter what the consequences. But since you're reading this book, I know you understand the costs of such flippancy are great, and you want a more eco-friendly yet effective way.

Pest-control strategies in the eco-friendly garden seek to use the least toxic method first. The good news is, there are some very effective natural control treatments available. With the proper preparation and cultural practices, rarely if ever will you need to go beyond these measures.

The first step in controlling pests, before even applying the most benign treatment, is to create the most hospitable growing environment for your plants. A healthy garden is the single best natural pest-control there is. Healthy plants are less attractive to pests in the first place, and when they are attacked, the plants are better equipped to defend themselves and recover.

Another advantage to the no-spray method of control is that it allows beneficial insects the best opportunity to establish populations in your garden and do the work for you. You may need to exercise a little patience and put up with some cosmetic damage initially, but beneficial insects are incredibly effective at natural pest control.

❀ More and more effective natural pest-control products are being offered commercially to the home gardener every year. They range from microbial insecticides to insecticidal soaps, neem oil, and botanical insecticides.

❀ Effective natural controls for plant diseases are also more available, with new products coming on the market every year. For example, potassium bicarbonate marketed as GreenCure® is safe for organic production and found to be more effective than a previous natural favorite, baking soda combined with horticultural oil, for treating many plant diseases. Sulfur and lime can also be effective against blackspot, powdery mildew, and rust. Vermicompost teas are being offered in home centers to help control plant disease.

With any pest-control treatment, the first step should be to identify the offending pest, and target a control method that affects just it. To keep from throwing out the baby with the bathwater, don't apply a non-selective chemical that kills beneficial insects as well. There are a good number of organic options available, and some are more specific to certain pests than others.

If there's a downside to natural pest-control methods, most people would say that although they can be every bit as effective as synthetic controls over time, they are not as fast-acting initially. To me, that's an acceptable tradeoff—a little patience for a healthier environment! Although there are many natural methods for pest-control, here are some of the most common options:

### Microbial insecticides

These insecticides cause pests to get sick, are very specific to the target pest, and do not harm beneficial insects or poison mammals. One of the most popular choices is Bt *(Bacillus thuringiensis)*. I use this whenever necessary to treat a number of worm larvae from hornworms to cabbage loopers and cutworms. The bacteria in Bt paralyzes the digestive system of the larvae. They stop eating, and within a couple of days, the pests are dead.

### Insecticidal soaps

These soaps utilize the salts and fatty acids within them to target many soft-bodied pests including aphids, whiteflies, mealy bugs, earwigs, thrips, and the early stages of scale. The soaps penetrate the soft outer shell of these and other pests, causing damage to the cell membranes. The membranes then begin to break down, resulting ultimately in dehydration and starvation.

Insecticidal soaps can be phytotoxic (having a tendency to burn) to certain plants, so be sure to test a small area before applying on a larger scale. The other downside is that soaps are non-selective, so they can be toxic to beneficial insects as well. Use them sparingly, as with any pesticide. Insecticidal soaps have not been shown to be toxic to humans and other mammals.

You can make your own insecticidal soap by adding a teaspoon of dishwashing soap (not detergent) and a teaspoon of cooking oil to one quart of water in a spray bottle. Insecticidal soaps are also readily available for purchase at nurseries or in garden centers.

### Insecticidal oils

These oils work by suffocating the pest. The oil coats them with a petroleum-based, horticultural grade liquid, cutting off their oxygen supply. This control method has been around for a long time and is primarily used to kill the eggs and immature stages of insects. These products are very effective because they spread so well and break down quickly. They can and do affect beneficial insects but are less toxic to them than synthetic pesticides.

Oils are often used to control aphids, scale insects, spider mites, mealy bugs, psylla, and some other insects. These oils can harm your plants and trees, primarily by damaging the leaves, so be sure to read the directions that come with the packaging.

Never spray these oils on a hot day, usually not one over 85 degrees, and again, it's best to spray a small area of your plants first. Just spray a test area and wait a few days. If you don't see any damage from the initial spray, commence with a larger application, coating the top and bottom of all leaf surfaces.

### Diatomaceous earth

This product is the fossilized silica shells of algae. Although microscopic in size, they are covered with sharp projections that cut and penetrate the cuticle of an insect. This piercing causes the pest to leak vital body fluids, resulting in dehydration and death. The unique aspect of diatomaceous earth (DE) is that it is not a poison that causes the damage, but the physical abrasiveness of the dust.

DE is effective against soft-bodied pests including aphids, thrips, whiteflies, caterpillars, root maggots, slugs, and snails. However, DE is non-selective and will potentially kill beneficial insects as well.

Apply DE to the soil for ground-dwelling pests and to the foliage for other pests. DE adheres best to moist foliage, so application is best early in the morning, when leaves are wet from dew, or after a rain. Be sure to use natural-grade not pool-grade DE. The latter contains additional chemicals that can be harmful to humans and mammals if inhaled. In either case, it's a good idea to wear a dust mask whenever working with any dusting agent.

### Neem oil

Neem is a broad-spectrum (non-seletive) insecticide, acting as a poison, repellent, and deterrent to feeding. It also sterilizes certain insect species and slows or stops the growth cycle of others. Neem oil is derived from the neem tree, which is native to India. It is applied as a foliar spray or soil drench and is used to kill a wide range of pests, including aphids, thrips, loopers, whiteflies, and mealy bugs.

One unique aspect to this biological agent is its systemic proper-ties. Plants take up the neem extracts through plant foliage and roots, where it is present in the plant tissue. Consequently, neem is also effective against leaf miners, which are usually not affected by other non-systemic foliar sprays.

Generally, neem must be ingested to be toxic and is largely non-toxic to mammals. Although it breaks down quickly, you should spray neem only when necessary and only on plants known to be affect-ed. In this way, you will minimize the damage to beneficial insects.

### Botanical insecticides

There are a number of botanical insecticides, but we are going to focus on the most popular one, *pyrethrin*, an active ingredient extract-ed from the Pyrethrum daisy. Products containing pyrethrin contain compounds that kill on contact. They are considered broad-spectrum (non-selective) and are used to control many chewing and sucking insects. Caution: Do not confuse natural pyrethrin with the synthetic version called Pyrethroid. It is even more toxic to insects.

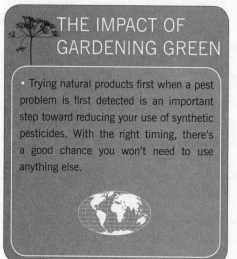

THE IMPACT OF GARDENING GREEN

• Trying natural products first when a pest problem is first detected is an important step toward reducing your use of synthetic pesticides. With the right timing, there's a good chance you won't need to use anything else.

Use caution when applying pyrethrin products as they are toxic to fish and moderately toxic to mammals. They are also harmful to some benefi-cials, including lady beetles.

# Practice good sanitation
# for a healthy garden.

*Clean up for a chemical-free garden.*

Plant disease can only occur when three components are present at the same time: a susceptible host plant, a pathogen capable of causing a disease, and an environment conducive to the disease. This combination is commonly referred to as the *disease triangle*. Based on this triangle, any disease problem can be managed or prevented without ever reaching for chemical controls: eliminate any one of these components, and you eliminate the possibility of the disease from establishing.

One of the most effective ways of controlling diseases naturally in your garden or landscape is through sanitation, a chemical-free way to break the triangular link. The following are some different methods to the approach of sanitation.

The best way to start controlling diseases in your outdoor environment is to prevent their arrival in the first place. *Exclusion* is the term that means keeping unhealthy or diseased plants out of your garden before they ever get there. Although you may not be able to detect every problem in advance, there are some telltale indications when choosing your plants that signal you to leave some of them behind.

First, *look for obvious signs*. Circular spots or rings on the leaves are never good. Discolored foliage nearly always signals a problem—even though the problem could be over or underwatering or improper lighting. Discolored stems at the soil level are another indication of a problem. Whatever the reason for the change in appearance, the plant is under stress and should be left behind.

Also be sure *to inspect the roots*. Healthy roots will be light-colored and pliable. If you find that the roots are brown, slimy, dead, or rancid-smelling, this is a likely case of root disease or nematodes, and the plant should not go home with you.

Now let's move on to what's growing in your garden or landscape. Watch for plants that exhibit disease-related characteristics. Common signs include spotting on foliage or fruit, mosaic patterns in the foliage, wilting, yellowing or other discoloration in the foliage or stem, or melting or wilting in spite of sufficient moisture.

Although other treatment methods may be an option, if you want to play it safe, removal and destruction of the infected plant material is always the safest route. There's even a term for this, *roguing*. I admit that it's extreme and usually reserved for the most potentially damaging cases. But an ounce of prevention is worth a pound of fresh vegetables!

Roguing is an aggressive form of sanitation, one in which the infected material is removed from the garden and destroyed by burning or removal off-site. The material is never added to the compost pile because disease pathogens can survive the decomposition process. To destroy pathogens, temperatures must reach above 120° F (or 49°C) for at least two weeks.

Sanitation doesn't have to be extreme to be effective. It is equally important to eliminate any plant debris from your garden on a regular basis. Non-diseased material can be added to your compost pile. In fall, be especially diligent with your cleanup. Plant diseases will overwinter on material that is not destroyed, only to appear next spring. Removing the host source (dead plants, leaves, and even weeds) will reduce inoculation opportunities of disease pathogens and help to prevent them from building up to damaging levels by next spring.

A dramatic illustration of the consequences of what can happen when you don't practice sanitation is the Irish Potato famine of the 1840s and 1850s. Potatoes left in the field at the end of the season developed late blight, a fungal disease. The pathogens overwintered on the potatoes, and you know the rest of the story. Cleaning up at the end of the season to reduce the amount of overwintering fungus in the soil was a hard lesson learned.

Cleaning your tools and equipment is another important way to reduce the spread of pathogens in your garden or landscape, especially when working around or on infected plants. Disinfect your equipment with a 10 percent solution of common household bleach mixed with water after use or between cuts when working with pruners or loppers.

## THE IMPACT OF GARDENING GREEN

- While good sanitation by itself will not prevent all plant disease, it's an important step toward preventing its occurrence in your garden and toward reducing your need to use synthetic fungicides.

# Water at the right time of day and keep it off the foliage

*This can have a huge effect on reducing the threat of pests and disease.*

Certainly you've seen the guy who waters his lawn at all hours of the day. Perhaps that guy is you. Well, let me let you in on a little secret: the daytime is really not the best time to water.

> **DID YOU KNOW THAT...**
>
> ❀ Soils that are continually wet, especially in the cool seasons of spring and fall, encourage fungal diseases.
>
> ❀ Grass blades that are wet for long periods are more likely to develop fungal diseases.
>
> ❀ Overwatering creates a succulent turf plant that is more attractive to chewing and sucking insects—and also more vulnerable to the damage they cause, both to leaf blades and roots.

We already know from Chapter 2 that irrigating during the day subjects too much water to evaporation. That's a big waste. But in the spirit of IPM (Integrated Pest Management), there's another very important reason: *disease.*

Water is a common and frequent vector for disease pathogens to move from one location to another, namely from the soil to the plant, but that's not the only case. The facts are clear: the longer a plant is allowed to stay wet, the greater the chance of its developing diseases.

We know that plants (including lawns) can naturally become damp during the dew cycle, typically from about 9:00 p.m. to 9:00 a.m., and anytime it rains. We certainly can't do anything about that. But we can control the amount of time we prolong the condition of wet foliage. By not watering overhead after the dew cycle, we do our part to limit the time foliage stays wet.

Of course, lawn irrigation is another story. In addition to the impracticality of not watering from above, as long as it is done between 9:00 p.m. and 9:00 a.m., the risk of contributing to the promotion of disease is minimal.

However, in all other cases, find a way to water at the soil level. Consider using drip irrigation or soaker hoses when possible. Even without drip irrigation, watering wands are an ideal way of directing the flow of water into containers and soil and away from the foliage. You also get the added benefit of targeted watering, utilizing all of it for its intended purpose.

## THE IMPACT OF GARDENING GREEN

- Watering at the correct time of day and with the proper amount is an important part of reducing the need to use fungicides.

# Use beneficial insects, the predatory agents of biological control.

*Without a doubt, nature provides the most amazing, effective, and safe form of pest control.*

Quick, what's the most common beneficial insect? Of course, it's the lady beetle; every small child knows that. But if I were to tell you that flies make the cut, you'd likely find that hard to believe. Trust me; it's not easy even writing those words, but it's true . . . sort of. The common housefly that you and I love to hate isn't in the list. But, its cousins, the Tachinid and Syrphid flies are.

I guess before I go on, you are anxious to know how flies could possibly be beneficial. Well, I'll tell you. It's not pretty, but the larvae are parasites on and in other insects, usually in larvae of moths or butterflies or the larvae of beetles and such. The eggs or larvae of the fly are deposited in a number of ways onto the host. The Tachinid fly larvae begins feeding on essential tissue of the host, ultimately killing it.

Adult Syrphid flies (also known as hover flies or flower flies) are often confused with honeybees or yellow jackets because of their black and yellow abdominal bands. They frequent flowers to feed on pollen and nectar. But as a predatory beneficial, it's the Syrphid larvae that are the stars since they feed on soft-bodied insects. Aphids are a favorite target. A single Syrphid fly larva can consume hundreds of them in a month. See, there *are* good flies out there!

Without a doubt, nature provides the most amazing, effective, and safe form of pest control through predatory, beneficial insects. They're quite resourceful in the garden. In addition to consuming insect pests, parasitic insects may lay their eggs or place larvae on pest hosts, ultimately killing the host, while other insects expedite the breakdown of decaying matter.

Even insects not traditionally thought of as beneficial do no harm and are food for birds and other animals, making them allies in the garden. In fact, of all the insects in the garden, only 3 percent are considered actual pests. The other 97 percent are either neutral or beneficial. Some of the most common beneficial insects are listed here along with their primary role as friend in the garden:

*Lady beetle:* There are many species, but not all are good. Mexican bean beetles for example are lady beetles but are very destructive to plants. The good lady beetles, including their larvae, feed on small, soft-bodied pests such as aphids, mealy bugs, and spider mites.

> ### DID YOU KNOW THAT...
>
> ❀ Less than 1 percent of all known insect species are considered to be pests.[1]
>
> ❀ Less than 3 percent of the insect species commonly found in home gardens and landscapes are considered pests. The rest are harmless to plants or are beneficial predatory species that feed on other insects.

*Ground beetles:* Ground beetles are common too, but they do most of their foraging at night. They consume a wide range of insects and larvae including tent caterpillars, cutworms, maggots, and the eggs of snails and slugs.

*Lacewings:* This insect is appropriately named. Although the body of the adult is only about one-half to one inch long, the large translucent wings dwarf its body. They feed on soft-bodied pests including aphids, thrips, and scale; the larvae even eat caterpillars.

*Dragonflies:* Mosquitoes and gnats are among a dragonfly's favorite food. Their cousin, the more petite damselfly, shares the same good taste in pests. They are most often found around ponds and marshes since they spend most of their pre-adult life underwater.

*Parasitic wasps:* Although there are several species of varying size, they all inject their eggs into host insects or their larvae. The eggs hatch inside the host, and the larvae consume their nourishment through the skin of their host. If you've ever seen a tomato hornworm with what appear to be grains of rice vertically stuck all over its body, you can thank a parasitic wasp for that.

*Yellow jackets:* These insects are aggressive pest predators. They seek out other insects, caterpillars, and larvae to feed their brood. They are known to be aggressive with people too if disturbed, so stay clear and cover those soda cans!

## Attracting beneficials to your garden

Build it and they will come—just don't use insecticides! As long as there are food sources for beneficial insects, they will come and stay. In addition, providing a biodiverse garden with various plants that provide pollen and nectar, water, and assorted hiding places will create ample opportunities to attract and host many predatory insects.

Insecticides, even organic or botanical, can be non-selective and kill beneficials too. Don't use them if you can help it. Let the beneficial insects do the pest control work for you.

## Purchasing beneficials

Even when you've done all you can to attract the good guys, you may want more or perhaps require a specific predatory insect. Numerous online and mail order sources will gladly ship you what you need. You can easily find sources in an Internet search, or contact your county extension agent or local botanical garden for suggestions.

One interesting note if you are considering purchasing lady beetles: commercially available and commonly sold, Convergent lady beetles are a migratory species that have a strong dispersal trait once released in the open. For this reason, many gardeners are disappointed to find out that newly purchased lady beetles fly away shortly after being released in the garden.

## THE IMPACT OF GARDENING GREEN

• By far the most effective way to encourage beneficial insects to help control pest species in your garden is not to kill the ones that already live there. Avoid the use of synthetic chemical pesticides and you not only help reduce the presence of chemicals in the water supply, you also help to build a web of natural pest control in your garden.

# If you're going to use an insecticide, explore biological ones first.

*Use living organisms to combat pests.*

Biological insecticides are living organisms that are used to manage specific pests. They can be a safe and effective way to control insect pests in your lawn and garden. The biggest advantage of using biological controls is that they have extremely low toxicity to all but the target-specific pest, making them safe to humans, pets, wildlife, and other insects. In fact, some biological controls are so specific that they only affect one stage of the life cycle in the targeted pest. The low toxicity also means less risk to watersheds and groundwater. Two of the most commonly used controls in the home garden are listed below.

### *Bacillus thuringiensis (Bt)*

Don't worry about the pronunciation; it's usually referred to as "Bt" anyway. Also, you will find this form of bacteria sold as DiPel, Thuricide, Bactur® and other trade names, but it's still the same ingredient. Bt is specific only to the larvae stages of certain common insects. Some of the most common include hornworms, cabbage worms and loopers, armyworms, earworms, cutworms, European corn borers, and webworms. (This is just a partial listing of affected larvae. The complete listing is extensive.)

Bt is formulated to be applied as a dusting powder, in dry or wettable granules, or

> DID YOU KNOW THAT...
>
> ❀ Bt should be used with care, as it can dramatically reduce the number and variety of moth and butterfly species where it is applied, which in turn can have a severe effect on the populations of birds that feed on the caterpillars.[1]

with sprays and concentrates. When the larval pest ingests Bt, it stops feeding within a few hours and dies within a few days.

If there is a downside to using Bt and other similar biological controls, it is that they are slow-acting. Biological controls do not have a long shelf life and should be used as soon as possible. When stored, they should be kept away from heat and ultraviolet light, where they can break down quickly.

### Milky Spore

Biological control commonly used in the fight against Japanese Beetles is Milky Spore *(Bacillus popillae-Dutky)*. This is a naturally occurring, host-specific bacterium that is lethal to the larvae of Japanese Beetles. You may know these larvae as "grubs."

When this bacterium is applied to the soil in lawns, the grubs will consume it as part of their normal feeding process as they munch away on the roots of grass and other vegetation in the soil. Once consumed, the bacteria eventually kill the grub within seven to twenty-one days. As the grub decomposes, it releases literally billions of new spores which further inoculate the soil to control future generations.

Milky Spore is not a poison. But the bacterium that kills the grub is effective and highly target-specific. It will not harm other beneficials, earthworms, birds, bees, pets, or humans and is safe for use around food crops.

The best control is achieved over a period of several years, once Japanese Beetle populations have built up. Control is also more effective when used on a widespread basis through neighborhood and community efforts. The larger the area of treatment, the better the control. Also, do not apply Milky Spore with other anti-grub insecticides as they can interfere with the population buildup of the bacteria.

## Know what to expect

Unlike non-selective, synthetic pesticides that are broad-spectrum, fast-acting, and highly lethal, biological controls take longer to work and may not provide as dramatic results initially. As with the case of Milky Spore, for example, repeated and widescale use is necessary to have a measurable impact on the general population of the ever-migrating Japanese Beetle.

## THE IMPACT OF GARDENING GREEN

• Using Bt to control caterpillars in your vegetable garden, and Milky Spore to control Japanese Beetle grubs in your lawn is a two-part component of an effective program to reduce your use of synthetic chemicals in your garden and landscape.

# Mulch to control weeds.

*Mulch is a multitasking miracle for the garden.*

I love everything about mulch. If there were ever a workhorse in the garden, I would say compost and mulch are on top of the list . . . or bed in this case. This leads me to the point about using mulch to suppress weeds. When you place a generous layer of mulch on your beds, you are effectively blocking sunlight that otherwise reaches the soil surface and allows seeds to germinate and grow.

DID YOU KNOW THAT. . .

❀ A 3- to 4-inch layer of mulch can significantly reduce weed growth in an area.

Not all weed seeds need light to germinate, but all plants including weeds need it to grow. Weeds that come up each year from seed are referred to as "annual weeds," and mulch is very effective at blocking their germination. Although it's not a sure thing for every weed all the time, mulching should be a standard practice in your garden to reduce the amount of work you'll have to do when it comes to managing weeds later.

Perennial weeds, on the other hand, come back each year from other means. Although seeds are included in the list, rhizomes, stolens, and regrowth from the base of the original plant are the most common sources of these weeds. Since there's not a germination issue in these cases, perennial weeds will often come back with or without mulch.

When mulching, be sure that you apply enough mulch to actually block the sunlight and prevent germination. In general, a three-inch layer should be sufficient. If you apply less, you certainly open up the possibility for inadvertent bare areas. Too much mulch could pose a different problem: the thick layer that blocks the light and prevents germination may also restrict airflow. Mulch should not be so thick as to suffocate the plant roots underneath.

Mulch comes in many varieties. Sometimes the only common denominator of mulch is that it covers the ground. Beyond that, it can be sorted into two categories: organic and inorganic. Organic mulches are natural products like shredded leaves and wood, bark, straw, pine needles, and coco or peanut shells.

Organic mulches will decompose usually within a season and need to be replenished consistently in order to maintain effectiveness as a weed suppresser. On the other hand, incorporating composted mulch into the beds at the end of each season is an excellent way to improve the condition of your soil.

> **DID YOU KNOW THAT...**
>
> ❀ The weeds that do manage to germinate in mulched soil are much easier to pull and remove.
>
> ❀ Studies show that by mulching an area, the average amount of time required to remove weeds is reduced by two-thirds.[1]

Inorganic mulches typically either do not break down or do so slowly. Black plastic is an example of inorganic mulch that will eventually break down and is very effective at weed suppression. Stones, gravel, and even recycled tires can be used. With inorganic mulch, frequent replacement is not necessary. However, it will not improve your soil at the end of the season either.

There will be times that in spite of your best efforts, weeds will start growing from your mulch. Usually the weeds you find growing *in* the mulch (as opposed to through it) will come from seeds transported into your mulch from any number of ways, but usually from wind, birds or other animals. It's a common sight, and they are easy to remove by hand-pulling since they likely haven't been able to root into the soil yet. Try it. You'll be pleasantly surprised to see how easy it is. I wish all weeding were that easy!

## THE IMPACT OF GARDENING GREEN

- By maintaining a 3- to 4-inch layer of mulch, you can virtually eliminate the need to use herbicides in landscapes and garden beds.

*All good work is done the way ants do things: little by little.*

LEFCADIO HEARN

# Use landscape fabric to control weeds.

*Suffocate weeds, but let the soil breathe.*

One of the most obvious benefits of using any physical barrier to weed growth in the eco-friendly garden is the reduced need for chemical herbicides. With this in mind, permeable fabrics for weed suppression are the contemporary replacement to plastic sheeting for one major reason: they allow the exchange of water and gases through the fabric and in most cases, effectively screen weed growth. Plastic mulches, although excellent as a weed barrier, preclude the exchange of water and gases and therefore can lead to adverse consequences for plants and trees growing under it. Soil needs to breathe, so geotextile fabrics are a better alternative. (Mulches also have a difficult time staying in place when used as a covering over the ultra-smooth plastic.)

> **DID YOU KNOW THAT...**
>
> ❀ Recent advances in geotextiles have resulted in landscape fabrics that almost totally suppress weeds while allowing water and air to pass through to the soil below.

But even though these permeable geotextiles are effective at erosion control and useful in weed suppression, they should not be used without an additional layer of mulch protection on top. The damaging rays of the sun's ultraviolet light can break down fabrics quickly. The mulch layer also works to provide additional screening from sunlight and gives a more aesthetically pleasing look to any bed or landscape.

When properly installed, a geotextile fabric can last indefinitely. There are three main types of landscape fabrics, and your needs will determine the best choice:

*Thermally spunbonded* fabric has fibers that are fixed in place. For weed suppression, this is the best choice. Although weeds may germinate above the fabric, typically in the mulch, the roots are unable to penetrate the fabric with any level of significance.

*Woven* fabrics are strong and the best choice when the most durable fabric is needed. But the pattern of the weave provides many opportunities for weeds to penetrate. Weed extraction through this weave can be troublesome since there is little room to manipulate the roots once they grow through the openings in this very tough fabric.

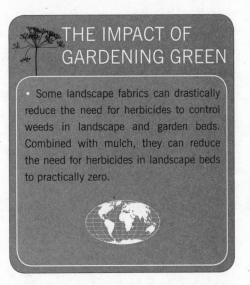

THE IMPACT OF GARDENING GREEN

• Some landscape fabrics can drastically reduce the need for herbicides to control weeds in landscape and garden beds. Combined with mulch, they can reduce the need for herbicides in landscape beds to practically zero.

*Needle-punched* fabric has a very loose weave, and plants can easily grow through it. This fabric is often used with imbedded grass seed and pinned in place for retention and reliable germination rates. Weeds can easily grow up through this fabric just as roots can grow down through it from the mulch above.

*Note: Once landscape fabric is in place, pinned down, and covered with mulch, it is difficult to go back later to access the soil. So be sure to make your soil improvements and amend the soil thoroughly before applying fabric. When planting into the material, simply cut two slits in an 'X' pattern into the fabric with a sharp knife.*

# Use other easy ways to eliminate weeds without chemicals.

*Hand-pulling is natural and effective, but so are these options.*

Call me crazy but I actually enjoy pulling weeds. Manual extraction by hand-pulling has an element of satisfaction that no other weed control method can offer. If you like instant gratification, it's the only way to go. It's also one of the few ways for selective control. But it's not the only one. (You can breathe a sigh of relief now.)

Although highly satisfying, I realize hand-weeding is not always a practical solution to the problem. Time and ambition are usually the two most important assets to taking on a manual project such as this. Furthermore, hand-weeding in any size garden is always helped along after a soaking rain. The soil is soft, and roots easily yield to even the gentlest tug.

When you're ready to manage weeds with organic controls but hand-pulling is not your style, consider some of these other popular alternatives using eco-friendly methods.

*Mowing higher*, or letting the grass grow tall, is one of my favorite non-chemical ways to fight weeds in my lawn. Although there is an upper limit on how tall any variety of grass should be, taller grass has the opportunity to shade out developing and sun-loving weeds before they have a chance to establish. When it is time to mow, remove no more than a third of the total height of your grass. It's better on the lawn and keeps the grass blades tall enough to still shade most weeds.

*Boiling water* works well at killing most weeds with one application. Some weeds, especially those with tap roots such as dandelions, may need multiple applications. Be sure to use extra caution when using boiling water. The risk of burning yourself, children, pets, or others is a real possibility. You might even be wondering about the damage burning water can have to the beneficial microorganisms in the soil—it will kill them as well. However, take comfort in knowing that billions of microbes will fill the void quickly in healthy soil.

> **DID YOU KNOW THAT...**
>
> ❀ More than 90 million pounds of herbicides are applied to residential gardens and landscapes every year.[1]
>
> ❀ 2, 4-D, found in weed and feed and other lawn products, is the herbicide most frequently detected in streams and shallow groundwater from urban lawns.[2]
>
> ❀ Using combination weed-and-feed products is not the most accurate way to control weeds. Unnecessary herbicides are likely to be broadcast onto lawn areas where there are no weeds and into adjacent areas where non-target plants will be damaged. And certain trees growing in lawn areas can also be damaged when their shallow roots take up herbicides.[3]

*Acetic acid (vinegar)* works, but common household vinegar at 5 percent concentration is not effective for mature weeds. Concentrations above 7 percent are needed to manage tougher weeds, and multiple applications may be necessary with tap-rooted weeds such as thistle. Use caution when using acetic acid as it can burn skin and eyes on contact. Approved sources of acetic acid for herbicide use can be found online or at farm supply stores.

*Plant-based ingredients* such as citric oil, clove oil, and garlic are nonselective, post-emergence herbicides also. Use caution as they will injure or kill all vegetation they come in contact with. Tougher weeds usually require multiple applications for complete control. Ready-to-use products are available through organic gardening supply sources online and in some garden centers.

*Flame weeders* are those devices that use the intense heat of a concentrated flame to destroy the cell structure of the plant. Typically powered by a propane canister, these devices are portable and effective. Simply pass the flame over the weed for several seconds. It is not necessary to visibly burn or ignite the weed. A few seconds of intense heat is all that is necessary. The heat will collapse the cell walls and render the plant unable to sustain itself. Because the roots are unaffected, the toughest weeds may require multiple applications. Again, use extreme caution when working with this tool.

Tap-rooted weeds can seem impossible to control no matter what method you are using. Even when the top growth is damaged or destroyed, there is enough energy in the remaining root to regenerate a new plant. If you are hand-weeding, be sure to get the *entire* root! The other methods listed above may need repeated applications to destroy the weed.

Although these control options can be directed precisely onto the target weeds, they may not be considered completely selective. Any misdirection or drift can kill any plant they come in contact with. It's up to you to apply these controls only to the targets.

No matter which method of weed control you prefer, prevention is still the best way to make sure you keep the weeds from spreading next year. Although they can still come into your yard through other means, eliminating weeds on your property before they go to seed will save you many hours of work next year and beyond.

## THE IMPACT OF GARDENING GREEN

- By removing weeds mechanically, you will greatly reduce your need to use herbicides.

# Don't nuke those weeds—
# solarize 'em.

*Solarization also has an interesting advantage
to beneficial organisms in the soil.*

## What is solarization?

Solarizing your soil may sound a bit intimidating at first. But if you'd like a way to control many of the weeds that come up in your garden beds—without the use of chemicals—it's one of the best ways to go.

The premise behind solarization is to heat the soil to a level that destroys the viability of the weed seeds, thus preventing them from germinating. Plastic sheets are placed on top of the soil surface for several weeks to heat the soil to such a high degree that most seeds are rendered unviable. It won't prevent all seeds from germinating, but it's well worth the effort for the eco-friendly garden.

## How does it work?

The most effective way to solarize your soil is to use clear plastic sheeting, laid tightly across your beds. Clear plastic allows more sunlight to pass through to heat the soil. Black plastic is not recommended because it blocks much of the light that helps heat the soil.

> DID YOU KNOW THAT...
>
> ❀ Glyphosate (a broad-spectrum herbicide and the active ingredient of weed killers such as RoundUp) is the second most commonly used herbicide in home gardens and landscapes, next to 2,4-D. It is toxic to fish and other aquatic organisms and is a contaminant of groundwater.[1]

Similarly, thinner plastic works better than thicker plastic. However, don't use plastic so thin that it will easily tear. A thickness of between one to two millimeters is effective and usually strong enough for most home applications.

Under ideal conditions, temperatures under the plastic will heat up to about 140°F (60°C) at the soil surface, 130°F (54°C) two inches below, and almost 100°F (38°C) at eighteen inches deep. The longer the soil is heated, the better the results. Even a few days at these temperatures will kill many of the weed seeds, but leaving the plastic on for four to eight weeks is ideal, especially for hard-to-kill weeds like nutsedge and crabgrass. Leaving it on even longer does not hurt.

## When is it most effective?

For solarization to be most effective, plastic should be applied during the hottest time of year. The summer days from June through August are ideal. Clear skies and calm days also improve conditions since solarization is not as effective on cloudy or windy days.

## Steps to solarization

Along with ideal timing, there are a few additional steps that will help ensure the best possible results. First, break up the soil in the area to be solarized to a depth of six to eight inches. Breaking up any soil clumps will bring weed seeds closer to the surface where they will be exposed to higher temperatures.

Next, rake the bed so that the plastic can rest directly on a smooth soil surface. If the surface is uneven, leaving air pockets under the plastic, solarization will lose its effectiveness. Dig a trench around the outer perimeter beyond the area to be solarized by about two feet if possible. This will hold the plastic in place when it is put down later.

It is also important to wet the soil before laying down the plastic. Field capacity of 70 percent or greater is recommended for effective results. If the soil is too dry, seeds and other pathogens may not be as affected by the higher temperatures.

Another important step at this point is to prepare your bed ahead of time for planting. The less the soil needs to be disturbed after the plastic is removed, the better the control results will be. Although the solarization process will kill many of the seeds, it is most effective closest to the surface. Cultivation of the soil after removal of the plastic will bring up seeds that survived below and are still viable.

Once the soil is cultivated, raked smooth, and watered, lay the plastic tightly across and directly on the soil surface. Extend the plastic into the trench which was dug earlier. Tuck the plastic into the trench and bury it with the excavated soil. This method ensures a tight, heat-trapping seal all the way around the perimeter. An alternative method would be to hold the plastic in place with stones, bricks, or long boards. All of these methods work, but the more heat you can trap under the plastic, the better your results will be.

## Pros and cons

Soil solarization is an effective way to eliminate many of the weed seeds which will germinate in your garden bed. First understand though, you are giving up valuable planting space during a prime growing season. If you can spare the space for a couple of months, the sacrifice will be worth it. Of course, the biggest advantage to this method is that it is a chemical-free way to manage many of the weeds. (It is most effective against annual weeds. Perennial weeds are more difficult to manage since, in addition to propagation from seeds, many parts of the remaining plant can regenerate into new weeds.)

Besides killing weeds, there are other advantages to heating the soil. Studies have found that solarization has an interesting advantage to beneficial organisms in the soil. Ironically, while the high temperatures are fatal to many seeds and they also kill numerous disease pathogens and nematodes residing there, most beneficial organisms actually benefit from solarization.

During solarization, some beneficial microorganism populations are reduced temporarily; others not only survive, they thrive, and many recolonize at even greater rates than before. For example, mycorrhizal fungi may show a population decrease at the higher soil levels but not to the point that their beneficial impact is reduced. Even earthworms don't appear to be harmed by solarization. They simply retreat to lower soil levels where temperatures are more hospitable, leaving behind nutrient-rich burrowing tunnels.

Plants growing in solarized soil have also been observed to grow faster and produce higher and better quality yields. It is thought but not proven that the survival and rapid reestablishment of beneficial microorganisms through the solarization process plays a key role.

With all its positive attributes and its few negative consequences, solarization may be just the ticket for an eco-friendly solution to many of the problems that plague gardeners everywhere.

 THE IMPACT OF GARDENING GREEN

• Solarizing a planting bed will help you to reduce your use of herbicides, particularly broad-spectrum herbicides such as glyphosate.

# Use corn gluten as a natural pre-emergence weed control.

*Corn gluten is the only organic control that gets the spotlight for preventing weeds from even getting started.*

Sooner or later, anyone with a lawn is faced with that inevitable question: how do I prevent all those weeds from coming up? Historically, the standard weapon of choice in the *not* so eco-friendly lawn has been synthetic pre-emergence granules. Weekend warriors would buy a few bags at the local garden supply store and carpet the lawn in fall, late winter, and early spring.

Thankfully, the eco-friendly lawn and garden has a solution to this age-old problem. Corn gluten's discovery as an effective, natural, pre-emergence weed control was, in fact, by accident. **Corn gluten** was initially being tested for reasons entirely unrelated to weed control. But during the testing, it was observed that it had an inhibitory effect on the germination of grasses. Further testing revealed that the corn gluten also had the same effect on other germinating seeds. In 1991, it was patented as a *natural* pre-emergence herbicide.

An added discovered benefit is that corn gluten has a 10 percent nitrogen content by weight, making it an excellent natural fertilizer for established plants with a mature root system.

Consumer acceptance of corn gluten has gained popularity as a natural alternative to synthetic pre-emergence herbicides. However, two important factors are necessary to ensure maximum effectiveness.

**Timing of the application** of corn gluten is critical. It should be disbursed four to six weeks prior to weed seed germination. Since pre-emergence products like this target annual weeds (which reproduce

❀ Most synthetic pre-emergence herbicides, such as Diuron, Oryzalin, and Dichlobenil, are widespread water contaminants. All are toxic to fish and aquatic plants.[1]

❀ While corn gluten inhibits the germination of about 50 to 60 percent of weed seeds, by the third year of application its results will match the performance of synthetic pre-emergence herbicides every year.[2]

❀ Corn gluten is an excellent source of nutrients for plants, containing about 10 percent nitrogen that will release slowly over a 3- to 4-month period.[3]

from seed), they should be applied in the late summer or early fall for cool-season annual weeds and again in late winter to early spring for warm-season annual weeds. First year reduction of targeted weed populations results in about a 50 to 60 percent success rate. Two to three years of repeated applications are necessary to match the effectiveness of synthetic counterparts.

Although perennial weeds also reproduce from seed, they can form new plants from the existing crown, rhizomes, and stolens as well. Therefore chemical pre-emergence weed controls are not effective against growth suppression other than from seed.

The **proper application rate**, in addition to the timing of the application, is the other critical issue involving corn gluten. As with any natural product, application of the appropriate amount is required for effective control. For corn gluten, that rate is twenty pounds per 1,000 square feet. Studies showed that higher rates of up to eighty pounds per 1,000 can be applied without damage to existing plants.

Moisture is needed to activate corn gluten, but extended moisture after application can reduce its effectiveness, just as with its synthetic counterparts.

Although corn gluten is somewhat more expensive to use as a weed-and-feed alternative to synthetic products, for eco-friendly gardeners and landscapers, it's a small price to pay for a more environmentally friendly options.

## THE IMPACT OF GARDENING GREEN

• By using corn gluten instead of traditional pre-emergence herbicides to prevent crabgrass and other annual weeds from germinating in your lawn, you can replace the need to use synthetic pre-emergence products and reduce your need to use synthetic chemical nitrogen fertilizer.

# If you need to use a chemical, follow the label.

*The label is the law.*

You may never fully appreciate the potency of chemical pesticides and their impact on man and the environment until you read Rachel Carson's classic book entitled *Silent Spring*. That's how it was for me. It is widely recognized as *the* book that first launched the environmental movement.

In it, she writes about how municipalities and federal agencies attempted to control specific pests, such as the Japanese Beetles. Time and again, she cites examples of how certain nonselective pesticides were used in mixtures from less than one part per million (PPM) to three or four PPM. It seems like an amount of chemical so small, how could it possibly work? Unfortunately, its effectiveness, even at such seemingly minute rates, was often catastrophic.

Unfortunately, we cannot change the past, but we can reduce the chances of repeating such mistakes. Many changes have taken place since then, such as the worldwide agricultural ban of DDT—a nonselective, widely used pesticide that is so lethal, it nearly wiped out the bald eagle population from the face of the earth.

Yes, we have learned a lot since Carson's written plea. Many chemicals have been taken off the market, standardized information is now a part of every chemical label sold in the United States and many other countries, and more information is available to handle and use chemicals properly. But in spite of multiple changes in the name of consumer and environmental protection, pesticides are still very powerful and very dangerous when improperly used.

Pesticides by definition are chemical agents that control pests. They are designed to kill an offending organism. In the garden, such products include insecticides, herbicides, and fungicides. Caution and restraint should always dictate how and when they're used.

The first step to proper use of pest control is to determine whether a problem truly exists. Identifying the specific problem is necessary before measures can be directed to solving it. In many instances, chemical pesticides are not the only way to control pests. Pest issues can frequently be controlled completely with non-chemical methods. Use these methods first.

DID YOU KNOW THAT...

❀ Suburban lawns and gardens receive more pesticides per acre (3.2 to 9.8 pounds) than agriculture (2.7 pounds per acre on average)—largely due to over-application and misapplication.[1]

❀ Surveys show higher concentrations of some pesticides, particularly insecticides and some herbicides, in urban streams than in agricultural streams.[2]

Once you have determined that the problem requires chemical control, use the least toxic option available. Product labels are required and are designed to provide critical information about how to safely handle and use the pesticide product. Once again, the label is the law.

Before using any chemical pesticide, *read the label completely*. Specific information about the following is included:

**Brand name**: the name used in advertisements and promotion.

**Formulation**: tells whether it's liquid, wettable powder, dust, etc.

**Name and address of manufacturer**: gives information on contacting the company which made the product

**List of active ingredients**: tells the percentage of active ingredient, common name, and chemical name

**Type of pesticide**: labels it as herbicide, insecticide, fungicide, etc.

**Signal words**: indicates the potential hazard of the product to humans. There are three signal words: danger, warning, caution.

---

### SIGNAL WORDS

| | | |
|---|---|---|
| **Danger** | Highly toxic | A taste to 1 teaspoon |
| **Warning** | Moderately toxic | 1 to 3 teaspoons |
| **Caution** | Fairly low toxicity | 1 ounce to over 1 pint |

---

**Precautionary statement**: describes how the product is hazardous to humans and animals and tells you measures you can take to reduce exposure

**Statement of practical treatment**: describes emergency first-aid measures

**Directions for use**: includes information on legal use for specific crops and pests. Also lists proper application rates as well as mixing instructions, necessary equipment, and the proper timing for application

**Storage and disposal precautions**: gives important information on how to properly store and dispose of pesticide

**Safety precautions**: lists protective clothing that is necessary to handle the product. This often includes rubber gloves, rubber boots, safety goggles, face shield, a respirator, and a waterproof hat. It may tell you to avoid any skin contact and wash protective clothing separately. This section also includes other important safety precautions.

**Misuse statement**: shares an important reminder that it is illegal to use the product in a manner inconsistent with its labeling

Many labels contain a phone number to call for questions or in case of an emergency. In case of an accident, it is important to have important phone numbers such as Poison Control and your local doctor on hand when using pesticides. Have the product with you when you call; the label contains important information that is needed in the event of an emergency. The national number for Poison Control is 1-800-222-1222.

The above information is only a partial listing of essential items included on pesticide labeling. All these statements are essential information for proper use and handling. It is tempting to skip over the fine print, but don't. If it weren't important, it wouldn't be there. Improper use poses significant safety risks both for the user and the environment.

> ## THE IMPACT OF GARDENING GREEN
>
> • By following the label carefully when applying garden chemicals (including fertilizers, pesticides, fungicides, and herbicides) you will significantly reduce their runoff, drift, misapplication, and over-application—all primary causes of garden-chemical pollution of the water supply.

The more I read about the historical and current implications of pesticide misuse, even when applied at the proper rates, the more I am determined to find alternative measures to chemical controls whenever possible.

# Good timing is everything.

*Use pest controls at the right time in a pest's life cycle and
they can be just as lethal as the most potent options.*

Timing is everything. How many times have you heard that? But
did you ever think it would apply to controlling pests in your lawn and
garden? In the eco-friendly landscape, it's the only proper way.

Harsh, non-selective pesticides are often formulated with a combination of chemicals engineered to "take out" offending pests at any stage
of their life cycle. Unfortunately those controls are completely contrary
to our attempts to be selective in our sustainable environments. In our
efforts for a better way, we must be a bit more diligent when it comes to
controlling pests in our landscapes.

If you're reading this book, you are looking for ways to be more
eco-friendly. Kudos to you for that. So when it comes to pest control,
you want something that works but imparts the least amount of impact
on non-targeted pests. And that's the way it should be. The first thing
I need to ask you to do is be more patient before intervening with
chemical controls. If you haven't been out there spraying lately, beneficial insects should arrive shortly to help manage the problem. However,
patience varies from one person to the next. If and when you feel the
need to jump in, being equipped with the most appropriate solution is
the next best thing.

When it comes to pest control in the eco-friendly garden, appropriate choices always means favoring the most selective method that will
have the least impact on non-targeted pests first. Knocking Japanese
Beetles into a cup of soapy water is an example of this: selective, effective, and benign to all but the beetles. A stiff blast of water to dislodge
aphids from their hiding spot or current meal is another example.

Other times, methods are not quite so simple. The good news is that timing your assault to an insect's life cycle can afford you the option of choosing a more benign yet effective solution. Before going into some specific examples, let's briefly cover an insect's life cycle stages.

Every insect starts out as an egg. Then depending on its type, it matures through various stages into an adult. Some insects change form completely. For example, during the larval stage the Mexican Bean Beetle transforms from the egg to a growing nymph. It then forms the pupae, where it will emerge as an adult in about ten days. Along the way, the beetle's body has transformed from a soft-bodied spiny-looking creature to a hard-shelled orange beetle that resembles a ladybug.

Knowing a pest's life stages is important in order to treat it in the most benign way possible. While it is young, the soft body nymph of the bean beetle is susceptible to the dehydrating effects of insecticidal soap. But as the nymph develops into an adult, the soap will have no effect on it. On the positive side, insecticidal soap won't harm most beneficial insects, either, making it an acceptable eco-friendly solution.

Another example of "perfect timing" involves the control of the Japanese Beetle. Throughout its life cycle from egg to adult, the beetle passes through a larval stage in late summer. It is during this earliest stage of its life as a grub that it is easiest to control. As larva, it is vulnerable to the biological control of a bacterium known commonly as Milky Spore. This control method is highly specific, affecting only the Japanese Beetle larvae and harmless to other insects, pets, and the environment.

Once a beetle's larvae are infected, the spores kill the grub and multiply by the billions to populate the surrounding soil and infect additional grubs. But for the unexposed grubs that survive to the adult stage, Milky Spore has no affect. At this point, non-selective, synthetic chemical controls are one of the few options. Certainly the most benign option is preferred for the eco-friendly conscience, and for this option, knowing the time of year that grubs are active and vulnerable is essential.

Controlling scale presents a unique challenge in which proper timing is critical. Scale insects attach themselves firmly to plant stems and foliage and secrete a protective, waxy, armor-like coating as they mature. Beneath this layer of protection, they can suck the juice from plants undisturbed, immune from almost all control measures.

It pays to be attentive to scale infestations in your garden because optimum control relies on monitoring them for their only vulnerable life stage, known as the "crawler phase." This phase takes place immediately after their eggs hatch while immature insects search for a feeding site. At this early stage of their life cycle, these juvenile crawlers have not yet developed the waxy protection and are very susceptible to horticultural oil or insecticidal soap.

Timing insecticide applications to coincide with the most susceptible life stage helps control pests and breaks their cycle of infestations. It's also the best way to choose a control option that minimizes the impact to other insects and the environment.

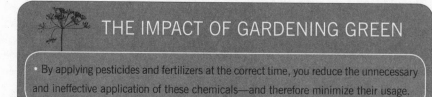

## THE IMPACT OF GARDENING GREEN

• By applying pesticides and fertilizers at the correct time, you reduce the unnecessary and ineffective application of these chemicals—and therefore minimize their usage.

# Don't spray on windy days.

*Too often, drift plays a role in chemical pesticides harming unintended targets.*

Every time we spray any pesticide (which includes insecticides, herbicides, fungicides, etc.), a chemical is being forced out of a small tip under high pressure. Inevitably, some amount of that solution disperses as vapor or drift. Higher pressure equates to more vapor.

Chemical drift has the ability to travel long distances. On a windy day, the chemicals suspended in the fine mist can travel untold distances and remain suspended until they come in contact with something or eventually fall to the ground. A number of factors influence drift, including weather conditions, topography, the area being sprayed, the equipment being used, and even decisions by the applicator.

Over the years, I've had several opportunities to spend time in a few university plant pathology labs, which frequently receive samples of damaged plant tissue and are asked to diagnose the problem. The paperwork accompanying the inbound sample from the homeowner or extension agent almost always assumes some sort of plant disease. And by looking at the tissue, you'd think that, too. But more often than not, the problem is something completely unrelated to disease.

> **DID YOU KNOW THAT...**
>
> ❀ One Cornell entomologist found that close to 99 percent of all sprayed chemicals land in the surrounding environment, leaving only 1 percent to hit the target pest.[1]

Chemical drift from herbicides is frequently the diagnosis for plants that show all the common symptoms of disease. Brown or yellow foliage, wilting, discoloration on the stem . . . the signs are varied but the

❀ More than 90 percent of pesticides are sprays or dusts that are prone to drift.[2]

❀ Spraying pesticides on a windy day can not only damage valuable ornamental plants on your property and your neighbor's, it can also lead to sickness in humans and pets and, if it reaches the storm sewer system, can eventually contaminate the water supply.

❀ In a 2003 study of indoor toxins in homes, researchers found varying and alarming levels of some of the most commonly used pesticides in dust concentrations in sampled homes. Most concerning is that 63 percent of the homes tested contained the commonly used herbicide 2,4-D, showing that pesticides can be tracked indoors or drift in through poorly sealed or open windows and doors.[3]

result is often the same. The follow-up questions are often even more surprising. When you suggest to the homeowner that herbicide drift is the diagnosis, a perplexed expression usually follows. "How could that be?" they ask. "I haven't sprayed anything all year!" Ah, but *you* didn't have to. "Does your neighbor spray?" the technician asks. Then the light bulb goes off.

Even calm days are not always a buffer against drift. My own story will explain why. Early one morning, on a very calm day years ago, I sprayed a non-selective herbicide to kill the many weeds that had taken over my lawn. I attached my hose to the ready-to-use spray bottle of broadleaf weed killer and went to work. I was careful to allow only the solution to come in contact with the target area.

The next day I was surprised to see my prized oakleaf hydrangeas, located far away from my area of spray, wilted and looking very sickly. In twenty-four hours, the plants had gone from thriving, beautiful specimens to sticks with limp, wilted leaves. They were victims of herbicide drift. The drift was the result of the solution being forced out of the nozzle under high pressure. Some of the chemical was dispersed as vapor and drifted a great distance, even on a calm day.

Fortunately the outcome of my experience was confined only to plant damage as far as I know. Even so, a few of my favorite shrubs never fully recovered. An insecticide could have been another story. With a creek and a lake on my property, several pets, and two children in the yard, its impact could have been much worse. However, the evidence of damage to my hydrangeas was a powerful reminder to me of the potential and very real consequences of "a little drift."

## THE IMPACT OF GARDENING GREEN

• Applying pesticides and other chemical sprays only at times in which the air is perfectly still will minimize not only the damaging drift of potentially dangerous chemicals into the yards of your immediate neighbors—it will also help prevent those chemicals from moving into the larger environment of the air and the water supply.

# Get a soil test before you add fertilizers and other amendments.

*Knowing important details about the soil materially affects your choice of amendments.*

I haven't met anyone yet who can simply look at his or her soil and know its complete chemical makeup. Sure, there are telltale signs and observations in the plant growth (or lack of) and color that can give an indication to possible nutrient deficiency, or even whether water is draining or not. Still, those clues are just usually not enough to make an informed decision about which nutrients and what amounts you should add to your garden or landscape. More often than not, we opt to toss out and onto our soil whatever fertilizer is left over from the last time. Although you may be pleased with the results from this random approach to a fertilizer program, it is rarely of benefit to your soil. It is more likely a detriment.

> DID YOU KNOW THAT...
>
> ❧ The forms of nitrogen in synthetic fertilizers are highly water-soluble and prone to leaching from the soil into groundwater and the water supply. Nitrogen from leaching and runoff finds its way into lakes, streams, and rivers, causing algal bloom and reduction of oxygen in the water, which is destructive to aquatic plants and animals. Nitrates and nitrites in the water supply can be difficult to remove and are toxic to humans.[1]

You'll never know for sure what the true chemical makeup of your lawn is until you have your soil levels analyzed for the all important primary nutrients (nitrogen, phosphorus, and potassium) as well as the secondary nutrients calcium, magnesium, and sulfur. And you can't leave out the nine other trace elements either.

Unfortunately, standard soil tests commonly obtained from county extension services and private labs—although excellent in quality and a good value at around ten to fifteen dollars—only provide minimal information to form a basis for fertilizer and liming recommendations. To further complicate matters, these tests routinely only offer synthetic fertilizer suggestions. Translating this information into useful organic fertilizer options is not an easy task for most gardeners.

There are resources, however, that can provide additional information geared toward the organic or eco-friendly gardener or even the weekend warrior who is serious about soil science. In addition to basic testing, private soil labs offer other valuable soil information such as respiration, infiltration, bulk density, aggregate stability, organic

DID YOU KNOW THAT...

❀ Only about 50 percent of applied synthetic nitrogen is used by plants; the rest is lost to the atmosphere, to runoff, or through leaching. It is important to apply only the nitrogen your plants can use, and in a form that doesn't quickly move through the soil—such as slow-release fertilizers.[2]

❀ Most urban and suburban soils already contain sufficient phosphorus—in one study 80 percent of soils from home gardens and landscapes had enough phosphorus already.[3]

matter, trace elements, and more for additional fees. An Internet search using key words like "soil labs" or "soil testing" will provide a great deal of information.

Another valuable information source for selecting a private lab suited to your needs is the National Sustainable Agriculture Information Service (http://attra.ncat.org/attra-pub/soil-lab.html).

## How to take a soil test

When you finally decide it's time to have your soil analyzed, contact the company or service that will be doing the testing, such as your county extension service or a private lab. They will be able to provide you with instructions and collection bags for obtaining your samples.

The basic technique for collecting a representative soil sample is to gather soil from random parts of the *total area* you want tested. This area may be a small raised vegetable bed, a large plot used for cut flowers, or an entire lawn.

Use a scoop, trowel, shovel, or spoon, but whatever you choose to collect your samples, make sure it is clean so that no foreign matter is being introduced into the sample. Place each scoop into a large bucket or bowl. Once you've collected a dozen or so samples, mix them together. Generally about two cups of the representative sample is needed by the lab to conduct its testing.

Deliver or mail the sample to the testing source. Make sure to include your contact information, along with what you plan to grow in the area from which you took the samples. For example, will you be growing vegetables, turf, flowers, or blueberries? These facts allow the scientists to determine which nutrients and what quantities are necessary to provide the optimum benefit.

Within a couple of weeks, a detailed report will be mailed or emailed to you that outlines the basic information you'll need to bring the soil into the ideal range. It will include instructions on what and how much to add in order to adjust the pH and nutrients to proper levels.

Keep in mind that basic tests from an extension service or private lab usually will not provide organic fertilizer and nutrient equivalents.

## THE IMPACT OF GARDENING GREEN

• By getting a good soil test before you apply fertilizers, you can help prevent unnecessary application of chemical nutrients—as well as over-application, which causes nitrate and phosphorus pollution of surface water and the water supply.

# Apply fertilizers responsibly and follow the label.

*Any chemical when applied improperly poses significant risks.*

Whenever you see a fertilizer product, it always has three numbers prominently listed on the package, usually in front. These numbers, referred to as the *primary nutrients,* are nitrogen, phosphorus, and potassium (N,P,K), and they tell a great deal about what the fertilizer will do.

Primary nutrients are always listed in the order of N, P, K and are expressed as the percentage of each component within that package by weight. For example, the common all-purpose fertilizer referred to as *10-10-10* represents a balanced blend of equal portions of nitrogen, phosphorus, and potassium. If you purchased a fifty-pound bag, five pounds (or 10 percent) would be nitrogen, five pounds would be phosphorus, and five pounds would be potassium. The remaining 70 percent is simply filler, or inert ingredients.

> **DID YOU KNOW THAT. . .**
>
> ❀ Applying fertilizer at the rate listed on the package provides the very best results. When you apply too little, you may be disappointed with the results, causing you to apply even more a second time. Or, you apply too much, potentially burning your lawn or plants and making excess fertilizer available to run off your property to pollute water systems.

On occasion, some fertilizers also include secondary or micronutrients. If present, they will be noted in the listing of ingredients, below the N, P, K reference. They will also be expressed as a percentage by weight of the total volume in the package. In addition to ingredients, other important information about application rates and safety information is listed.

Too often, consumers take for granted the potency of synthetic chemical products, including fertilizer. In our age of excess, it is natural to assume if some is good, more is better. But information like application rates on a chemical package is very specific for a reason. Appropriate distribution rates have been carefully tested for maximum efficacy while providing a reasonable level of safety to people, pets, and the environment.

Over-application of fertilizer products can have several consequences. One of the biggest concerns is the impact on soil health.

Manufactured fertilizers contain a great deal of salt, drawing moisture out of the earth as well as harming subterranean creatures responsible for creating healthy, living soil. Take table salt, for example. Remember how thirsty you get after eating pizza (lots of salt in there) —or better yet, the time you poured salt onto a slug?

Eco-savvy gardeners always concentrate on improving and feeding the soil—never the plants. They know that you can't feed living soil with synthetic fertilizers. In fact, quite the opposite is true. It's not that the fertilizer nutrients are harmful per se, but that the salts used to bind the fertilizers to the nutrients can build up in the soil to the point of adverse consequences to the earthworms and other billions of beneficial microbes thriving in healthy soil.

Even at the beginning of the soil food chain, once the smallest organisms are eliminated, everything else in the chain is eventually affected. Ultimately that soil becomes somewhat chemically dependant because there are no longer sufficient living organisms there to process the nutrients.

So every time you pour on liquid fertilizer to excess or toss out handfuls of granular fertilizer, be aware of what is happening. The salts are left behind in the soil when the nutrients are released. What's not taken up by the plants ultimately finds its way into the water table or into creeks, lakes, or other waterways. Such nutrient runoff and leaching are responsible for many environmental problems.

This leads me back to an expression in gardening I am very fond of, and one I live by: "Feed the soil, not the plants." When you focus on creating nutrient-rich soil, the soil then has sustainability to feed the plants as needed. For now, it's still a concept that is foreign to many of us. But I know the news spreads rapidly as we become more aware.

 THE IMPACT OF GARDENING GREEN

• By following the label carefully when applying chemical fertilizers, you avoid the misapplication and over-application of synthetic fertilizers that lead to water pollution. You also reduce the impact of excess salt buildup in the soil, which has an adverse affect on soil microbes and earthworms.

# Keep fertilizers and other chemicals off pavement.

*The issue is more in* how *they are used rather than that* they are used at all.

Here I want to pause to clarify an important point: Lawn and garden chemicals are not bad just because they exist, although I know I'll get some argument on that one. In fact, there are times that chemicals (organic or synthetic) provide the solution of last resort in an Integrated Pest Management (IPM) discipline.

> ### DID YOU KNOW THAT...
>
> ❀ Misapplication—not the type or amount of fertilizer used—is the most frequent cause of surface and ground-water contamination by fertilizers. Keep fertilizer and other chemicals away from streets, drives, sidewalks, and other hardscape areas because it is not only wasteful, causing you unnecessary expense—but also the chemicals are certain to get washed into the storm sewer system and end up in lakes, rivers, and streams.

In Rachel Carson's book, *Silent Spring*, she writes of horrific instances when chemicals such as DDT were used to deal with a particular pest problem. The results of widespread or off-target applications and misuse were often disastrous, killing and harming many non-targeted insects, birds, mammals, and sometimes, even humans. And even in the case of the extremely potent and nonselective DDT, while at times I question why it ever existed, I also know it has saved countless lives by wiping out insect populations that spread fatal diseases.

My point is that many people reading this book will never give up using chemicals completely in their gardens and landscapes. We are a society that is far too busy and has become all too conditioned to wanting and expecting results fast and easy. Frankly, many synthetic fertilizers and chemicals are formulated to give people just what they're looking for.

For these consumers, the biggest environmental problems involving the use of these products is more in how they are used (and abused) rather than that they are used at all. An easy first step to dramatically improve careless misuse is simply to start applying chemicals using the proper equipment, at the rates specified on packaging, and at the proper time. That, combined with keeping chemical products on target, off impervious surfaces, and disposing of them properly, would have a significant impact on building a more sustainable environment.

There are a number of specific measures that can be taken to make this conversion even easier. Here are a few:

### Equipment

Lawn and garden chemicals are applied either in liquid or granular form. Abuses arise when excess chemical is allowed to reach non-targeted areas. With granular applications, using a broadcast spreader around waterways, driveways, streets, and sidewalks will cast product into watersheds and onto impervious surfaces such as concrete or asphalt, where it will become part of the runoff.

*Drop spreaders* are a far more appropriate solution when working around these areas. Product is dropped straight down to the intended targeted area. Although this spreader takes longer to deliver the same amount of product as a broadcast spreader, it is the best choice around sensitive areas.

*Broadcast spreaders* are more appropriate where there is no risk of granular chemicals reaching waterways or impervious surfaces as it is broadcast from the hopper. These spreaders apply product much more quickly. But with speed comes the risk of misdirected applications of chemicals. Never use a broadcast spreader when a chemical has the potential of reaching beyond its target.

A compromise spreader is available to deliver the best of both worlds for those who only desire to have one device. The Scotts® Company offers a hybrid called the *Deluxe™ EdgeGuard® Spreader*. It has all the virtues of a broadcast spreader. But when you approach a waterway or impervious surface, one simple flip of a lever activates a shield on the right side that blocks the product from being broadcast in that direction.

*Hose-end sprayers* are another way that liquid products can be delivered quickly and efficiently. The biggest issues in misuse with these products stems from leaks and high pressure. Leaks allow product to flow out and away from an intended target area, oftentimes onto the applicator, impervious surfaces, or waterways nearby.

Remember, regardless of which type spreader you use, high pressure results in vapor drift and product reaching beyond its intended area. The best solution to both problems is to ensure that equipment is securely fastened and pressure is reduced so as not to create excessive drift or force.

### Cleanup to prevent contamination

Even when we are being careful, spills can take place. Nevertheless, some can be prevented.

Never fill spreader hoppers or spray applicators on impervious surfaces where the risks of runoff are obvious. Instead select an area within your target when filling an applicator.

Never overfill your equipment. Too much weight in the hopper can render it top-heavy and at risk for overturning. Similarly, never overfill liquid applicators. In addition to overflow and runoff, invariably you will run out of space before you run out of chemical. It is always better to mix more later if needed than to mix too much and be faced with the excess.

When mixing lawn and garden chemicals with a garden hose, a drop in water pressure can cause the entire contents to *back-siphon* directly into the water supply. To prevent this, always keep the end of the water supply hose above the water line in the fill tank. When drawing water directly from a well that will be used for mixing with chemicals, always use an anti-siphoning device. They are relatively inexpensive and readily available from product suppliers.

In the event of spills, prompt and complete cleanup is essential. Dry, granular products should be swept or vacuumed up and reused if possible. If unusable, dispose according to package instructions.

Liquid spills onto impervious surfaces should be cleaned up using absorbent materials. Non-chlorinated kitty litter is an inexpensive choice that works. Once the spilled materials have been absorbed, use a brush and scoop to place them in an appropriate container for proper disposal.

The most proactive steps we can take in our eco-friendly landscapes are always to use chemical products sparingly, apply them as directed and with the right equipment, and properly dispose of or store the excess. Those measures alone will bring about dramatic improvement in how we collectively will make a difference.

## THE IMPACT OF GARDENING GREEN

• By keeping fertilizer (and other garden chemicals) off of the pavement—both by not dropping it there in the first place and by sweeping it off into the lawn and garden beds when you accidentally do—you help to keep fertilizer runoff from entering storm drains, and from there into lakes and streams and other water systems.

# Store chemicals safely.

*Improperly stored chemicals can have lethal consequences.*

Perhaps you know of a case firsthand. A child is poisoned because she drank from a container she thought contained juice, soda, or milk. Instead, it was a container being used improperly to hold a pesticide. The results were fatal. What a sad story.

Of course these are extreme cases, but unfortunately they happen all too often. I've personally known of several such tragedies. What makes stories like this even harder is that they were easily preventable. In no case should any chemical be stored, even for a moment, in a container other than the one it originally came in.

> **DID YOU KNOW THAT...**
>
> ❀ A nationwide survey by the EPA revealed that almost ½ of surveyed households with children under the age of 5 had at least one pesticide stored within the child(ren)'s reach.[1]

There are a number of precautions we can take to ensure accidents with pesticides don't happen under our watch[2]:

• Follow all storage instructions listed on packaging and labels.

• Always store pesticides in their original containers. In addition to the proper identification of the contents, important safety information specific to that product is listed on the container. Such information includes what to do if accidental poisoning takes place, emergency contact numbers, and necessary first aid steps.

• Keep pesticides stored out of the reach of children and pets. When possible, store them in a locked but ventilated cabinet. Even if you don't have children, you never know when a curious person may happen upon these dangerous chemicals. Be safe and take the path of caution.

• Pesticides should never be stored in the same location as food, medical supplies, or animal feed.

• Never transfer pesticides to soft drink bottles or other containers, including milk jugs, juice or water bottles, or coffee cups. It is easy for children and even adults to confuse them for something to drink or eat.

• Use child-resistant packaging correctly. Be sure to close containers tightly and properly after use. Just because a product says "resistant" does not make it child-proof. These products should receive the same care and caution as any other when storing.

• Don't stockpile chemicals. Only buy what you will use that session or season. The less pesticide remaining after it is needed, the lower the risk of accidents.

• Pesticides should be stored away from places where flooding is possible or where spills or leaks could run into drains, surface water, or watersheds.

• Flammable liquid pesticides should be stored away from the living area and away from any risk of sparks, such as near gas grills, furnaces, and power lawn equipment.

THE IMPACT OF GARDENING GREEN

• By storing garden chemicals safely, you protect children and pets from accidental poisoning, you protect the environment from accidental chemical spills, and you protect your chemicals from losing their effectiveness.

• Never store pesticides in the application equipment. To avoid the problem of having excess product, only mix what is needed for that application. If excess mixture remains after application, apply where appropriate to other parts of your property.

• When in doubt as to the identity of a product or container, do not use. Be sure to dispose of it properly.

*If man cheats the earth,*
*the earth will cheat man.*

CHINESE PROVERB

# Dispose of chemicals safely.

*Improperly disposed chemicals can make their way into storm drains which feed into streams, rivers, ponds, and lakes.*

Over the years, I've managed to do a pretty good job eliminating chemicals from my garden shed. Yet in spite of my best efforts, they keep showing up. I've accumulated pesticide containers from a prior gardening life, inherited my dad's collection when they moved from a home to an apartment (so that I could dispose of them properly), and even uncovered a stockpile after moving into our current home.

It's scary to think how many people out there are like me . . . or worse. I really have worked hard to properly dispose of the chemicals that I will never use again. But it's amazing how quickly these remainders add up. Collectively I can only imagine how many leftover containers are sitting around the sheds, garages, and basements of the world!

> ### DID YOU KNOW THAT . . .
>
> ❀ The average home can accumulate as much as 100 pounds of household hazardous waste (HHW) per year.[1]
>
> ❀ Americans generate 1.6 million tons of HHW per year.[2]
>
> ❀ One gallon of used motor oil can pollute up to 2 million gallons of water.[3]

In our very busy lives, it would be easy to pour the excess liquids out into the street or down a drain. But we know better than that, don't we? Pesticides poured into the street often travel directly into storm drains, which feed into streams, rivers, ponds, and lakes. When pesticides reach waterways, they can harm fish, plants, and other living things.

Chemicals should never be poured down the sink, tub, toilet, or into the sewer or street drain. Pesticides can interfere with the operation of wastewater treatment systems, and many municipal systems are not even equipped to remove all pesticide residues.

So what can we do to dispose of chemicals properly and safely? The following are some suggestions:

The Environmental Protection Agency and other sources advise that the best way to dispose of small amounts of excess pesticides is to apply them (according to the directions on the label) or give them to your neighbor so they can use them to treat a similar pest control problem. Although this is certainly a valid way to consume the product, I find it hard to suggest using *more* pesticide chemicals in your landscape simply to use it up.

As an alternative, most local municipalities have a department that deals with waste management and can advise you on how to dispose of excess chemicals—other than by using them. Some even have a household hazardous waste collection program. Once or twice a year, many cities or counties provide a place for you to take such chemicals where they can be properly and professionally disposed of.

You can find more information on these programs by contacting your local government agency. You may find the appropriate department listed under *solid waste, public works, garbage, trash,* or *refuse collection.* In the United States, there is a telephone number that you can call to find information and sites for recycling and disposing of hazardous household waste. The number is 1-800-CLEANUP. An automated recording will guide you through the process, and the number is accessible 24/7.

According to the EPA, empty containers can be disposed of with your other solid waste after proper rinsing. A triple rinse is suggested before disposing, but do not triple rinse pesticide containers in a kitchen sink! First, fill the container one-fourth full with water, close the lid tightly, and shake vigorously. The rinse water should be applied to an area needing treatment. Never pour the contents down the sink. Repeat the process two more times.

Whenever you are going to dispose of chemicals of any kind, be sure to read the product label for disposal information. Be aware, however, that state and/or local laws may be more restrictive than the Federal requirements listed on the label. You should check with your local authorities before disposing according to information listed on the product label. Some municipalities do not allow even empty pesticide containers to be disposed of with solid waste. Instead, they are seen as household hazardous waste and treated accordingly as mentioned above.

Before I wrap up this subject, let me share a saying we use around my house to reduce the clutter: "When in doubt, throw it out." Although that applies to much of the junk we accumulate in life, it does *not* apply to pesticides, at least not in the same sense. Disposal of pesticides should never be acted upon without taking the proper precautions. Our health and environment depend on it.[5]

## THE IMPACT OF GARDENING GREEN

• Disposing of garden chemicals safely by taking them to a hazardous chemical waste site rather than dumping them down a drain, into a storm sewer drain, or on the ground protects our water supply from a host of dangerous chemicals that are difficult to remove from water.

# Use bagged soil and mulch that is certified.

*That organic garden of yours just might be topped off with a nice thick layer of arsenic or chromated copper arsenate (CCA).*

What's in *your* mulch? That's right, mulch. More and more people are making an effort to be more eco-friendly, from the cars we buy to the food we eat and the products we use in our gardens and landscapes. But have you ever thought about mulch?

Believe it or not, that organic garden of yours just might be topped off with a nice thick layer of arsenic, chromated copper arsenate (CCA for short), or one of many not-so-organic chemicals. The potential health risks are sobering. So is the thought of knowing I may be using contaminated mulch in my garden where my children and pets play, where I grow organic food, and where nature abounds.

Fortunately, consumers who are concerned about what might be in their mulch, especially when it comes to *hazardous materials* such as the chemicals used for treating wood, now have a valuable resource. In 2004, the Mulch and Soil industry adopted standards prohibiting the use of CCA-treated wood in all consumer mulch and soil products.

One of the greatest benefits to consumers arising from these standards was a product certification program developed by the Mulch & Soil Council (MSC). The program's purpose was to help consumers identify mulches and soils that comply with industry standards and contain no CCA-treated wood.

The Council supports and encourages wood recycling as an environmentally friendly practice when and if it is done correctly. However, removal of all CCA-treated wood and other potential contaminants must be a required part of responsible wood recycling.

Certified mulches and soils can be found at major retailers and garden centers across the country. They are easily identified by the MSC Certification logo on the package and are listed on the Mulch & Soil Council Web site (www.mulchandsoilcouncil. org). Their Web site provides more information and important related links.

I wish this were true of bulk soil and mulches sold on the market today, but knowing that I have a choice when it comes to buying and using mulch that is certified to be free of potentially harmful contaminants is reassuring, and the best choice for my eco-friendly garden. I can't imagine buying mulch any other way.

> **DID YOU KNOW THAT. . .**
>
> ❀ The EPA instructs consumers that they "should never use CCA-treated wood (wood preserved with chromated copper arsenate) as compost or mulch." Mulch made from CCA-treated wood is contaminated with arsenic, which can leach into the soil.[1]
>
> ❀ Bagged mulch that is certified by the Mulch & Soil Council is free of contamination by wood preserved with chromated copper arsenate (CCA).
>
> ❀ Bulk mulch is not certified by the Mulch & Soil Council. To be sure that mulch is free of CCA contamination, it needs to be bagged and marked with the logo of the Mulch & Soil Council.

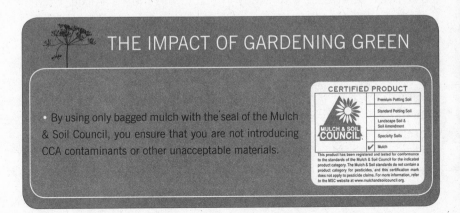

## THE IMPACT OF GARDENING GREEN

• By using only bagged mulch with the seal of the Mulch & Soil Council, you ensure that you are not introducing CCA contaminants or other unacceptable materials.

CERTIFIED PRODUCT

| | |
|---|---|
| | Premium Potting Soil |
| | Standard Potting Soil |
| | Landscape Soil & Soil Amendment |
| | Specialty Soils |
| ✔ | Mulch |

MULCH & SOIL COUNCIL

This product has been registered and tested for conformance to the standards of the Mulch & Soil Council for the indicated product category. The Mulch & Soil standards do not contain a product category for pesticides, and this certification mark does not apply to pesticide claims. For more information, refer to the MSC website at www.mulchandsoilcouncil.org.

# Use alternatives to CCA-treated wood.

*Today there are many options that have none of those risks.*

Pressure-treated (CCA) lumber has enough toxic chemicals to qualify as a hazardous waste. It's hard to believe: one twelve-foot-long two-by-six piece of CCA lumber contains enough arsenic (one ounce) to kill over two hundred people. Ironically (or not), industry lobbyists in Washington, D.C. secured an exemption from hazardous wastes disposal laws.

No doubt, you've heard the rumblings about using pressure-treated wood, not only in garden beds but for playsets, decking, picnic tables, and more. The concerns are valid and have led to safer alternatives. From changes in the chemicals used to treat wood to more rot-resistant, natural offerings and even post-consumer recycled products, today's eco-friendly gardeners have plenty of choices.

All the hype came about when lumber was impregnated with chromated copper arsenate. You know it as "CCA." It was supposed to be the answer for anyone needing an inexpensive choice for long-lasting, rot-resistant lumber. It was readily available and touted as safe. Even though the wood was treated with chemicals that were all toxic (chromium, copper, and arsenic), *somehow* they remained locked in the wood. An answered prayer indeed for gardeners!

Time has a way of revealing many truths. In this case it was determined that CCA-treated wood carried a number of risks. Of main concern to gardeners was the risk that the toxic chemicals, primarily the arsenic, would leach into garden beds that were being used to grow edibles. As it turns out, some of the chemicals *did* leach from the wood. It was found that most leaching occurs during the first season and then subsides to a slow release.

Numerous studies have shown that although chemicals do leach from the wood, they do not travel very far. Most notable and significant concentrations are within immediate proximity to the wood itself, from zero to two inches (zero to five centimeters). Migration was minimal although measurable, as little as six inches (fifteen centimeters) away. Samples taken twenty-four inches (sixty-one centimeters) away showed no effects of migration.

> DID YOU KNOW THAT...
>
> ❀ The annual market for pressure-treated lumber is extremely large (currently estimated at $10 billion in the U.S., $4 billion of that for decks) and will continue to grow.[1]
>
> ❀ Even faster growing (increasing at the rate of about 40 percent per year) is the market for plastic lumber. There is even plastic lumber available made from recycled plastics such as milk jugs.[2]

In beds containing some amount of inorganic arsenic, the concern is whether it is absorbed into the plants, especially if they are edible crops. Studies show that, in general, plants tend to hold the arsenic in their fibrous roots. Although there are exceptions, the risk of uptake into the plant tops and fruit was very small. Exceptions included carrots, radishes, and spinach, which tend to store arsenic in their edible parts.

The more likely risk in the presence of arsenic-treated wood is for people and animals that may come in physical contact with it. As arsenic leaches from wood, it can easily be transferred to children or pets when the wood is touched. In addition, one must never burn wood containing arsenic due to the risk of breathing in the smoke. Repeated exposure to arsenic can increase the odds for lung, liver, skin, and other cancers.

Because these are such real possibilities of danger and due to the public outcry, CCA-treated wood was taken off the market in 2004.

Another treated wood, which was considered safer and less controversial, was already on the market by then. It is know as "ACQ"®, which stands for alkaline copper quaternary. Since arsenic was considered the biggest risk, it was removed entirely. None of the chemicals in ACQ is considered hazardous by the EPA.

The most popular alternatives to treated wood include the following products:

*Manufactured lumber products* are from wood fiber and post consumer plastics such as milk jugs, plastic grocery bags, and recycled tire rubber. These choices are long-lasting (up to fifty years) and take advantage of sustainable and recycled products.

THE IMPACT OF
GARDENING GREEN

• By using safe alternative to CCA-treated wood, you reduce to zero the risk of the introduction of arsenic, chromium, and copper into your soil.

*Weather-resistant hardwoods* include redwood, cedar, cypress, black locust, red mulberry, Osage orange, Pacific yew, catalpa, juniper, oak, mesquite, and others. Before selecting one of these options, give careful consideration to the environmental impact of its use. Select wood only from sustainable sources, not from clear-cut, old growth forests. Depletion can cause serious environmental damage, habitat loss, and watershed issues.

Of course there are many other options. And the great debate on the use of treated wood in the garden goes on. As for me, I choose to use alternate sources for my garden beds. Erring on the side of safety makes sense always, especially in the eco-friendly garden.

# Beware of the unintended effect of deicers in winter.

*Deicers are loaded with chemicals that can seep into groundwater and storm drains.*

Sometimes it's not an easy choice between our safety and the safety of our plants and soil. If I lived alone, a tie would go to the plants! But since I'm not the only one living here, I must be prudent to protect my family and guests from winter perils, namely an icy, slick sidewalk or driveway.

If you live in an area with this problem, you know deicers are a common preference. But too often we don't use deicers properly. Their job is to *loosen* ice for removal, not remove ice completely.

So why a discussion about deicers in a gardening book? Because *improper or overuse of deicers is detrimental to plant life and the environment.* Most deicers are chemicals containing high concentrations of salt. As a result, deicers do more than melt ice. Excess salts build up in the soil, just as with the overuse of chemical fertilizers, impeding the uptake of moisture and nutrients. Other deicers can cause leaching of heavy metals which can eventually make their way to water supplies.

Even the fertilizers used in an attempt to be more environmentally responsible are high in salts, nitrogen, phosphorus, and other harmful chemicals that can impact the soil and surrounding ecosystems. Symptoms of salt damage are stunted growth, wilting, desiccation, and burned leaf tips or margins. It can also cause permanent root damage. Flooding areas exposed to excess salts as soon as possible in the spring may help to alleviate the problem.

REDUCING GARDEN CHEMICALS

The following list includes some of the most common ingredients used to battle ice and snow each winter:

*Sodium chloride*, commonly known as rock salt, may be the product we are most familiar with. The most popular deicer since the 1940s, an estimated ten to fourteen million tons will be used yearly on roads in the United States and Canada.[3]

*Calcium chloride* is produced in flakes, pellets, and as a liquid. It is sometimes sprayed over rock salt to lower its melting temperature. Although this increases the efficiency of snow and ice removal, it also increases plant and soil exposure to salt damage. Even though calcium chloride is considered to be practically non-toxic to aquatic life, it does increase algae growth, which poses a problem for our waterways.

*Potassium chloride* occurs naturally in the mineral form of Sylvite and can also be extracted from saltwater. Ok, that's a clue . . . more salt. It is also used as a fertilizer (muriate of Potash) and as a salt substitute.

These chloride salts, although common choices, present their own set of problems. As a group, they are corrosive to metal and concrete, damaging to plant material, irritating to skin, and potentially lethal to pets. Please be sure to read the label before purchasing.

*Urea,* which is a source of nitrogen fertilizer, has less burn potential than potassium chloride but can cause excessive plant and algae

---

**DID YOU KNOW THAT...**

❀ The most commonly used salt for de-icing roads is sodium chloride. Calcium chloride and calcium magnesium acetate are less damaging to the environment but are more expensive.[1]

❀ Salts affect plant growth in several ways: by accumulating specific ions in toxic concentrations within plant tissues, by increasing osmotic pressure differences and causing desiccation (drying), by altering mineral nutrition balances, and by altering soil structure.[2]

160

growth, choking out other vegetation and aquatic life. For this reason, it is probably the worst choice. Urea that is not absorbed into the soil breaks down into ammonia, which is eventually released into the atmosphere.

Some people will even broadcast common garden fertilizer, thinking they are providing a more benign solution. They are not! Salt is salt (at least from the standpoint of what it does to your soil and plants), and synthetic fertilizer has a lot of it. Excessive runoff of any of these materials is capable of damaging our lakes and streams.

## Eco-friendly alternatives

Considering that pets are a part of the equation too, the choice to opt for salt-free alternatives provides for their safety as well. Salt buildup from deicers accumulates on an animal's paws and coats, causing mild to fatal illnesses as they lick themselves clean.

Covering key areas with plastic before a storm and removing it before it has a chance to freeze in place is a good preventative measure against ice. Spreading sand or gravel over slick spots will not melt the ice or snow, but offers some traction. If you must use a product containing chloride salts, use it sparingly.

An alternative salt-free deicer, guaranteed not to be harmful to humans, pets, or the environment, is trademarked as Safe Paw™.

### THE IMPACT OF GARDENING GREEN

• Avoiding the use of sodium chloride as a deicer will reduce damage to your plants and to plants near your property. Not only is sodium chloride harmful to vegetation, but because deicers are used specifically on impervious surfaces, the excess salts find their way into storm drains and, ultimately into rivers, lakes, and streams.

# Avoid fuel spills when filling gasoline-powered equipment.

*Because gasoline is such a fundamental part of our lives, many homeowners never stop to think about its proper handling and potential consequences.*

It happens all too often. We're gassing up the lawnmower, blower, or tiller, and in our effort to fill it to the brim, we spill a little over the top. After a small "Oops," we think "Oh well, that was just a little. It couldn't possibly do any harm." But little bits add up.

DID YOU KNOW THAT...

❀ One-third of all emissions from small gasoline engines are either from gasoline spillage by the operator or evaporation from the gasoline container or equipment.[1]

❀ One gallon of gasoline can contaminate a million gallons of groundwater.[2]

❀ A typical gas can emits about *8 pounds* of hydrocarbons through spills and evaporation each year. There are about 78 million gas cans in the United States. In total, they emit about *621 million pounds*, or *310,000 tons*, of hydrocarbons each year.[3]

Consider this: in 1999 Americans spilled more than nine million gallons of fuel, enough to fill an oil supertanker. Gasoline is such a fundamental part of our lives that many homeowners never stop to think about its proper handling and potential consequences. But it is a sobering thought to know that even the effects of a small gasoline spill can contaminate soils and wells a quarter of a mile away.[4]

Besides the obvious danger of explosion, how many of us store the gas can without a cap? This habit alone introduces 50 percent more hydrocarbons into the air than a new car. As we all know, gas emission plays a major role in ground-level ozone's increasing contribution to greenhouse gases and pollution.

Just a few minimal precautions when handling gasoline can contribute greatly to cleaner air and safer groundwater[5]:

• Use proper containers such as those approved by a nationally recognized testing lab like Underwriters Laboratories (UL).
• Use the container's spout or a funnel when fueling.
• Keep the container tightly sealed and out of direct sunlight.
• Never store gasoline in the basement or a car trunk.
• Fuel equipment on a hard surface to minimize contamination of soil.
• If there is a spill, use kitty litter, sawdust, or absorbent cloths, and dispose of them properly.
• Never pour gasoline down the drain, into surface water, on the ground, in the trash, or in a storm water gutter.
• Dispose of old or unwanted gas at your municipality's hazardous waste collection site.

We may not completely eliminate gas engines from our landscape, but in the meantime, consider opting for electric or rechargeable versions. I have done so myself, and I must say, I'm pleased with the results I'm getting while doing my part to protect and preserve our planet. It all adds up!

## THE IMPACT OF GARDENING GREEN

• If you use a secure gas can with a tightly-fitting lid, store it in a cool place out of sunlight, and carefully avoid all spills and leaks when filling the tanks of your garden equipment, you can personally avoid emitting an average of 8 pounds of hydrocarbons into the air and water every year.

• If everyone took this kind of care with handling gasoline, it could reduce the amount of hydrocarbons emitted into the air by 310,000 tons per year.

# CHAPTER FOUR

# LANDSCAPING TO CONTROL RUNOFF

Water pollution—what do you think of when you hear that term? Factories, pumping contaminated wastewater directly into rivers, perhaps? Maybe you envision a massive tanker, leaking millions of gallons of oil into the ocean. I know I do. But let me ask you this: when you wash your car in the driveway or see rainwater flowing across your yard as it leaves your property, do you associate *that* as part of the problem of water pollution?

The fact is, we're all part of the problem. Indeed, industrial sources have had a massive impact on our environment globally and in our own communities. And because of that, they're often highly regulated. Certainly it doesn't completely solve the problem, but imagine the devastation if they weren't. But there's another group that collectively has the potential to contribute just as much to this crisis. It's you and me and everyone we know. In neighborhoods, subdivisions, homesteads, and farms around the world, trillions of gallons of stormwater flow from our roofs; across our farms, landscapes, and driveways; onto our streets, and ultimately into the same waterways as our industrial neighbors' oil spills and leaks.

As that water migrates across our home landscapes, it is collecting and transporting a host of pollutants. Unfortunately, there is no system in place to process this massive volume of wastewater where it can be captured, purified, and made available again as water we can use in our homes and on our landscapes. Instead, this tainted water flows to the nearest watershed. Creeks, streams, rivers, tributaries, ponds, lakes, and even the ocean are all recipients.

Of course, the first and most obvious change we can make to lessen this environmental impact at home is to *reduce the pollutants going into runoff* in the first place. It sounds too simple, doesn't it? The truth is, as you learn to reduce your reliance on certain chemicals and find alternate yet effective, eco-friendly ways to tackle some common challenges outside your house, you *will* make a difference.

DID YOU KNOW THAT. . .

❀ Runoff from urban areas is the largest source of water quality impairments to surveyed estuaries (areas near the coast where seawater mixes with fresh water). The most common pollutants in this runoff water are sediment and nutrients (fertilizers).[1]

❀ About 60 percent of soil that is washed away ends up in rivers, streams, and lakes, making waterways more prone to flooding and to contamination from soil's fertilizers and pesticides.[2]

Radical transformation is not a requirement to effect change in your own personal corner of the world, nor do I even recommend it. Drastic alterations in how we live and function rarely stick. Rather, as you become aware of the many factors contributing to the problems, you can more easily develop solutions. It may be as simple as timing fertilizer or pesticide applications to avoid a forecasted rain. Maybe you wash your car on the grass instead of the driveway. There are plenty of ideas, and I'll provide ample specifics to get you going.

*Landscaping* to slow the flow, increase infiltration, and reduce the runoff is another satisfying way to mitigate erosion and runoff, and one where you can enjoy immediate gratification for your efforts. Again, the alterations to your landscape need not be extreme to reap the benefits.

Simply adding mulch to bare soil or using the right kind of mulch can have a bearing on erosion runoff. Another easy solution is creating a way to capture surface water long enough so that it is able to seep into the ground first. Swales and rain gardens are both excellent conservation methods, and by adding plants that are adapted to wet conditions, a highly functional feature becomes a beautiful four-season garden as well.

Although stormwater is unavoidable, you can significantly reduce its effects by modifying the way water flows through your property. As clean as the rain appears that falls from the sky, by the time it gets into waterways, it has carried with it particulate pollutants and gases along with nutrients picked up from the surface, like nitrogen and phosphorus—all harmful to aquatic life. Antifreeze, salts from deicing chemicals, oil from leaking cars, zinc from metal gutters, and carelessly applied pesticides are just some of the toxic chemicals along for the ride.

The fragile eco-systems in and around our water systems continue to be threatened by the pressures placed upon them from our unwitting contributions. The harmful effects that we don't see downstream still affect us upstream, no matter where runoff originates. Remember, the balance of nature connects us all, and we are collectively all responsible for taking a more proactive role to protect and preserve it. Simple actions we take at home can result in significant results across our planet when we each do our part.

# Protect topsoil on construction sites.

*Without topsoil little plant life is possible.*

By definition, topsoil is the uppermost layer of soil, usually the top two to six inches. Topsoil is where the highest concentration of nutrients, organic matter, and beneficial microbes are found. So it's no surprise that most of the earth's biological activity takes place there, where plants concentrate their roots and draw most of their nutrients.

Why then are we so careless about allowing this precious resource to literally wash away? The term is *erosion,* and it's what happens every time it rains or water splashes onto exposed soil. To bare soil, a raindrop is like a miniature water bomb, hitting the ground at an explosive rate of twenty miles per hour! When the drops hit the exposed soil, water can splash the soil up to six feet away, and soil particles and heavy metals can migrate off the property, ultimately carrying harmful sediments into water systems.

DID YOU KNOW THAT...

❀ One rainstorm can wash away 1 millimeter (.04 inches) of dirt. It doesn't sound like much, but that's the equivalent of 5.2 tons of topsoil on one acre of land.[1]

❀ When stormwater runs off a construction site, it carries sediment and other pollutants. The EPA estimates that between 20 and 150 tons of soil per acre is lost every year to stormwater runoff from construction sites. Other estimates of soil loss due to erosion on construction sites run as high as 500 tons of soil per acre.[2]

As conditions dry and winds pick up, they too contribute to the erosion problem. After water, wind is the second most damaging influence, dislodging soil particles and transporting them far away.

## THE IMPACT OF GARDENING GREEN

• If the site for your new home is ½ acre, by protecting the topsoil on it during construction you prevent the erosion and loss of from 10 to 75 tons of topsoil. That's 3 to 25 dump truck loads of topsoil that would otherwise end up in waterways (depending on where you live). And that's 3 to 25 dump truck loads of topsoil you would need to purchase as a replacement for a healthy landscape and garden.

• If all U.S. home construction sites protected topsoil from erosion, it would keep around 80 million tons of soil from eroding into the nation's waterways.

Some soil erosion is natural. It's the *accelerated erosion* that is the biggest problem. This type of erosion occurs at the hand of man during construction, timber harvesting, and poor tilling practices. The costs are high, financially and environmentally. Erosion creates sterile soils, fills the air with dust, blocks road ditches and drainage ways, carries pollutants, and destroys fish habitats.

Since construction plays such a major role in the amount of erosion that takes place each year, it helps to know what we can do to prevent or minimize its impact and keep as much topsoil on our property as possible. As offered by the Tualatin, Oregon, Soil and Water Conservation District, here are some simple yet significant actions you can take when it's time to protect your topsoil[3]:

• Schedule construction activities for the driest times of the year. Dry conditions reduce the chance of water runoff and soil compaction.

• Before ever beginning the grading and construction phase, identify and install erosion controls where eroded soil could leave the site.

• Leave plant buffers as wide as possible to help keep erosion in check. Buffers slow and trap sediment erosion. You can also plant cover crops. Grasses work well. Even weeds serve a purpose. The bottom line is to keep or plant as much vegetation as possible. Leaves soften the impact of rain, and roots anchor the soil.

• Silt fences, which should be positioned on the down-slope perimeter of the site, will catch and prevent much of the sediments from running off your property. Most construction sites require silt fences.

• Remove the topsoil (the top six to eight inches) and store it away from the construction area. Be sure to cover it to protect it from the eroding effects of wind and rain. Planting grass over the pile and adding a silt fence around it provides additional protection.

• Restrict traffic to a gravel driveway and parking area. This prevents soil from sticking to equipment and leaving the property or washing into the street.

• Protect storm drains near the site with gravel-filled geotextile bags or socks. Straw bales also work. The objective is to trap sediment while allowing water to pass through.

• Inspect erosion control measures frequently and especially after storms or high winds. Make any necessary adjustments immediately.

• Install downspout extenders that carry water beyond exposed soil.

• Return topsoil to disturbed areas as soon as possible after construction is completed. Replant with vegetation immediately.

For more information, contact your local Soil and Water Conservation District, or the USDA Natural Resources Conservation Service (NRCS).

# Add organic matter to the soil for percolation and retention.

*The proper cultivation of our soil includes regularly adding organic matter.*

Soil. It takes approximately five hundred years for one inch to be deposited, yet there are twenty-five billion tons of it being lost each year. Just imagine the ultimate effect of such erosion. You can't find a more dramatic yet historical illustration of eroding soil than the series of dust storms during the 1930s that sent massive amounts of American and Canadian prairie land topsoil blowing into the Atlantic Ocean.

Severe drought conditions coupled with years of extensive farming and poor soil management practices turned the top layer of earth literally into dust. Excessive use of the land without crop rotation, overgrazing, the removal of grass during plowing, and the elimination of organic matter all contributed to severe erosion.

What can we learn from this tragedy? The lessons are many, but we gardeners must remember that the proper cultivation of our soil is vital for a healthy, productive garden that retains soil and protects our ecosystem.

Most garden soil starts out either too heavy or too sandy. Heavy soil rarely drains well enough, while sandy soil never retains water long enough. A gardener just can't seem to get a break! But he or she can improve the conditions of that soil so that it provides just the right amount of percolation. The added reward for these efforts is soil that fosters more life and is less susceptible to soil erosion.

When organic material is added to loose soil, aggregates are formed that help particles join together. In addition, various size particles work together to help slow down the effects of gravity on drainage, and some aggregates even bind moisture to their surface. Those same binding properties prevent the situation that happened with the Dust Bowl. Aggregates stick together, retain moisture, and become heavier and less mobile (relatively speaking) than simple dried out particles of silt, clay, or sand.

DID YOU KNOW THAT...

❀ Once incorporated into the soil, compost can increase water infiltration up to 125 percent.[1]

❀ A mere five percent increase in organic matter quadruples the capacity of soil to hold water.[2]

In the same manner, aggregates help to break up the tight-fitting bonds of heavy soil. Space is created between the particles, and water is allowed to migrate down more freely. From an erosion standpoint, soil that is allowed to drain offers less opportunity for surface water to run off, taking with it valuable topsoil. Any time water can flow down through the soil, rather than across its surface, runoff is avoided.

Adding organic matter will help to improve the condition of any soil and minimize the chance of runoff. You've worked too hard to have great soil. You might as well keep it. It's good for your garden, and it's good for the planet.

## THE IMPACT OF GARDENING GREEN

• Adding organic matter to your soil can reduce soil lost to erosion by up to 85 percent. This is especially important to reduce the runoff of phosphorus into waterways, as phosphorus is relatively insoluble and is carried chiefly in eroding sediment. Adding organic matter can also reduce water requirements because organic matter increases the water-holding capacity of soil.

# Don't till—let earthworms do the job.

*Earthworms are important in a garden for several reasons.*

If having loose soil that incorporates lots of organic material is so good, then what's so bad about tilling? It's a fair question, but consider this: you're killing the good guys. Allow me to explain.

It's one thing to have soil rich in oxygen. It's another to have so much oxygen that the precious organic material in it is rapidly decomposing. Tilling is the number one way extra oxygen enters the soil, and it's the fastest way to hasten the decomposition of organic matter. Secondly, earthworms and tillers don't mix. Well . . . they do, it's just not pretty. And earthworms are far better in the long run at doing what our mechanical tillers are not able to do.

In areas where tilling is frequent, worm populations can be reduced by as much as 90 percent. Tilled soil can dry out rapidly, bury the plant residue that worms feed on, and crush the vertical worm burrows. Finally, any time soil is tilled and left bare, erosion is possible. Even barely noticeable, small amounts of erosion are harmful over time. A better alternative to creating healthy, friable soil is to nurture it. If you provide the most inviting habitat for earthworms, they'll do the work for you.

Earthworm burrows are so important in an eco-friendly garden because they enhance water infiltration and natural soil aeration. In fact, according to the National Sustainable Agriculture Information Center, earthworm tunneling can increase the rate of water entry into the ground four to ten times more than soil that lacks worm tunnels.

Worms' vertical burrows also pipe air deeper into the soil, cycling microbial nutrients farther as well. The burrows are lined with these nutrient-rich compounds and will remain for years if left undisturbed. Furthermore, the tunnels allow plant roots to penetrate more deeply into subsoil levels where moisture is more likely to be present during times of drought.

Earthworms aren't the only beneficial soil-dwellers. From arthropods (there are many, including beetles and spiders) to microscopic fungal hyphae, the soil food web is an amazing community of symbiotic relationships. As one or more of these organisms are damaged, the adverse affects can snowball. So just relax: keep the tiller in the shed and let the good guys do the work.

> **DID YOU KNOW THAT...**
>
> ❀ Newly tilled soil is the most susceptible to soil erosion. Rainfall on a tilled plot of land will result in 285 percent more soil erosion than on a comparable plot that hasn't been tilled.[1]
>
> ❀ Each year, 15 tons of dry soil per acre travel through earthworms. Earthworms eat soil to get the organic materials in it. The rest passes through them.
>
> ❀ Worm castings are richer than the surrounding soil. Besides being high in organic matter, they contain nutrients changed into forms that are more available to plants. For example, one study found that a sample of soil with 4 percent organic matter from worm castings contained 246 pounds of nitrogen per 1000 square feet, while the surrounding soil contained 161 pounds of nitrogen per 1000 square feet.[2]

Even the hardest soils can eventually become rich, deep plantable beds without tilling, through a process known as *lasagna gardening*. The term, coined by Patricia Lanza in her book by the same title, is for gardeners who dream of creating rich, healthy soil while saving work, time, money, and energy!

Lasagna gardening comes from the way the organic ingredients in the garden are layered to create the bed. It's truly an eco-friendly approach to gardening because the ingredients are all natural so there's no digging, sod removal, or tilling; no power tools, heavy equipment or special additives; and earthworms do all the work. As long as you know where you want to put your garden and what you want to grow, you can get started.

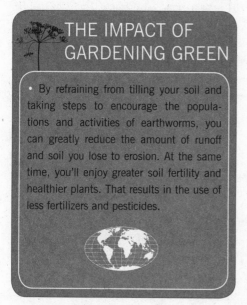

## THE IMPACT OF GARDENING GREEN

• By refraining from tilling your soil and taking steps to encourage the populations and activities of earthworms, you can greatly reduce the amount of runoff and soil you lose to erosion. At the same time, you'll enjoy greater soil fertility and healthier plants. That results in the use of less fertilizers and pesticides.

The key ingredients in any lasagna garden are organic materials; essentially any and everything you would put in a compost pile can go into making your lasagna garden.

Making a simple lasagna garden works like this: Determine your bed size or dimensions and apply the first layer. Use something heavy to smother the existing grass or weeds. I think stacks of wet newspapers work well for this (and it is also a gratifying way to recycle). Cardboard boxes are another option. Next you should add a two- to three-inch layer of peat moss, then a four- to eight-inch layer of compost or mulch. Repeat this process, starting with the peat moss, until you have built up the bed to at least eighteen inches.

Finish off with a spray of water to give your bed the damp-sponge feel and cover with black plastic for about six weeks. Although you *could* plant into the garden the day you make it, allowing the elements time to decompose and the layers time to blend together is well worth the wait.

This is just a brief sample of what is covered in much greater detail in Patricia's book. Creating a deep, rich garden bed with earthworms as your workhorses doesn't get much easier!

# Mulch to reduce runoff.

*The benefits of mulch are many, but this may be
the most important one for the planet.*

There's much more to know about mulch. I've written about it
often, but usually in the context of how it keeps weeds at bay, moderates soil temperatures, reduces plant disease, and holds in precious
moisture. But guess what? It does something even more important
for our planet than any of those: it helps keep soil sediment in place
rather than running off our property and polluting surface water.

If that doesn't sound like a big deal, consider this: sediment is the
number one pollutant in surface water. The average home construction site can lose from twenty to five hundred tons of soil per acre
each year to erosion. Most of that ends up in our waterways, replete
with fertilizers and pesticides.[1]

Not only are we polluting our planet, we're letting the most valuable part of our soil wash away in the process. Every cubic inch of
topsoil contains over a billion microorganisms, mostly bacteria and
fungi. Washing them away may sound like a good thing to you, but
it's those creatures that are responsible for life in the soil, leading to a
more nutrient-rich environment for plants and trees to thrive.

Providing a protective cover over bare soil will do more than any
other single action to keep soil erosion in check. Certainly a living
plant cover is the most effective because the leaves cushion the impact
of wind and rain while the roots anchor the soil. The next best option
is mulch.

## Choosing your mulch

Although when it comes to reducing the effects of runoff and erosion, any mulch is better than no mulch, but some are better than
others. The irregular shapes of some mulch allow them to bind or

lock together, reducing the potential for washing or blowing away. Read on for some of the popular choices.

**Shredded wood** mulch, especially from hardwoods, tends to stay in place better than other options when exposed to wind or water.

**Wood chips** are also a good choice when selecting a mulch to stay put, although heavier hardwood mulch is more likely to stay than softwood such as pine, given the same conditions.

**Bark chips** are more migratory than shredded wood but still hold in place better than some options. However, pine bark does tend to float and is not the best choice. Hardwood bark is the better option.

> DID YOU KNOW THAT...
>
> ❦ About 60 percent of soil that is washed away ends up in rivers, streams, and lakes, making waterways more prone to flooding and to contamination from fertilizers and pesticides.[2]
>
> ❦ A thick layer of mulch will reduce runoff and soil erosion by as much as 70 to 80 percent.[3]

**Processed hulls** of cocoa, buckwheat, peanut, and cottonseed are aesthetically pleasing, but they are very prone to washing and blowing away.

**Pine straw** is flexible and does a nice job of matting and weaving, keeping it in place in moderate wind and rain. It can also last for a year or more in the landscape.

**Wheat straw,** on the other hand, will do a nice job buffering rainfall, but the straw is light. It blows away easily and breaks down quickly. Therefore, it's not the best straw choice.

**Leaves** are plentiful and a good choice for mulch that decomposes quickly to improve the soil. However, as you know, leaves will not stay around long in even a moderate wind, so they're not the best choice when you're counting on mulch to stay put. For that, you really need **stone** or **gravel**. It's not right for every location, but you can bank on it to be there for many storms to come.

## THE IMPACT OF GARDENING GREEN

- By mulching all landscape beds on your property, you can reduce the runoff and accompanying loss of soil to erosion by as much as 80 percent.

*A garden is a thing of beauty and a job forever.*

RICHARD BRIERS

# Plant perennials to control erosion beautifully.

*If a lawn isn't the answer for you, turn to perennials.*

Erosion and perennials, they don't seem to belong in the same phrase. But I can't think of a more beautiful way to control such a serious problem than with perennials. Many perennials have colorful flowers and interesting foliage texture. They come in all sizes, shapes, and forms, and there are certainly numerous varieties suitable for your growing conditions.

> DID YOU KNOW THAT . . .
>
> ❀ Depending upon the plants selected and the density of the plantings, perennials and groundcovers can be almost as effective at preventing runoff and erosion as turfgrass. Densely planted groundcovers can cut runoff by as much as 83 percent.[1]

By definition, perennials return year after year. Some are evergreen, unfazed by months of inhospitable weather. With others, only the tops die back, leaving their roots intact to sprout new foliage in the spring. It's those omnipresent, living roots that are one of the main benefits of planting perennials for erosion control.

Living roots entwine in the soil, working to bind soil particles together. As roots reach farther into the earth, they open the soil and create new opportunities for water infiltration—and less chance for runoff.

Besides the obvious aesthetic benefit of growing perennials for erosion control, their variety of shapes, forms, and heights above-ground work in concert to cushion the force of falling raindrops' velocity. Adding mulch at their base provides yet another stabilizing factor.

Perennials can provide just the solution to controlling runoff and erosion on a slope, a most challenging problem. Low-growing, spreading groundcovers are a common option. Although English ivy is one perennial often planted because of its tenacious habit and ability to withstand deep shade, this highly invasive plant is more than opportunistic and should not be used. Depending on where you live, suitable native options may include creeping phlox, Meehan's mint, Plantain-leaved sedge, or marginal woodfern. Check with experts in your area for other options as well.

As you seek perennial choices for your landscape, look for plants that are native to your region, have fibrous root systems as opposed to tubers or bulbs, have the ability to grow quickly, and are relatively drought tolerant. Plants at the top of the slope will be drier than those at the bottom, where water has a tendency to collect. Select plants that can take periodic drought and occasional wet feet if you plan to use only one variety for your planting. If utilizing non-natives, keep in mind that since cold air settles, a marginally hardy plant may not survive the lower areas of a steep slope.

## THE IMPACT OF GARDENING GREEN

• Planting perennial groundcovers helps to slow water runoff, decrease erosion (especially on a slope), and allow greater water infiltration. That eases the amount of harmful sediments and pollutants going into our water systems.

# Plant trees and shrubs to control erosion

*Trees and shrubs actually have the ability to store water.*

Just as utilizing perennials, turf, or mulch helps slow down erosion and runoff, using a combination of trees and shrubs can have the same effect on an even grander scale.

> **DID YOU KNOW THAT. . .**
>
> ❀ Trees protect water and soils resources by reducing the amount of runoff and pollutants entering creeks, ponds, rivers, and storm drains.[1]
>
> ❀ Leaves, branches and trunks intercept and store rainfall, reducing runoff volume, while root growth and decomposition increase the capacity and rate of soil infiltration.[2]
>
> ❀ Tree canopies reduce soil erosion by diminishing the impact of raindrops on barren surfaces.[3]
>
> ❀ One large deciduous tree in coastal Southern California reduces stormwater runoff by over 4,000 gallons per year.[4]

Obviously it's easy to envision how a tree canopy slows down the velocity of rain drops, and how its root system aids in soil infiltration and soaks up water. But consider this: trees and shrubs also mitigate stormwater runoff by actually *storing* rainfall *on* their leaves, *in* their branches, and *on* their trunk. Water droplets are either held temporarily, falling to the ground later, or eventually evaporate into the air, reducing runoff volume. This ability to intercept such large volumes of rainfall is especially valuable in slowing the effects of erosion.

Of course, not every tree or shrub captures and stores water at the same rate; some are better at it than others. For instance, in areas that get more rain in the winter, evergreens would be a better choice. In fact, some conifers are capable of intercepting a larger volume of rainfall than a deciduous tree of similar size. Conversely, deciduous species may work best where summers experience more precipitation.

On slopes, trees should be mixed with shrubs and perennials as well as mulch. All should have a significant root zone capable of supporting the above-ground growth. Don't use shallow-rooted varieties with large canopies either, as they will be more susceptible to uprooting during significant winds or unusual downpours. For the best results, use species that are native or adapted to the conditions in your area.

## HELPFUL TREES AND SHRUBS

*Some of the best trees and shrubs for preventing runoff and soil erosion include:*

**Sweetgum** (*Liquidambar styraciflua*)
**Sweetbay magnolia** (*Magnolia virginiana*)
**Bald cypress** (*Taxodium distichum*)
**Heritage birch** (*Betula nigra*)
**Black gum** (*Nyssa sylvatica*)
**Serviceberry** (*Amelanchier* spp.)
**Larch** (*Larix decidua*)
**Quaking aspen** (*Populus tremuloides*)
**Summersweet** (*Clethra alnifolia*)
**Redtwig dogwood** (*Cornus sericea*)
**Winterberry holly** (*Ilex verticillata*)
**Inkberry holly** (*Ilex glabra*)
**Virginia sweetspire** (*Itea virginica*)
**Spicebush** (*Lindera benzoin*)
**Highbush blueberry** (*Vaccinium corymbosum*)
**New Zealand tree** (*Leptospermum scoparium*)
**Pittosporum** (*Pittosporum* spp.)
**Mirror plant** (*Coprosma grandifolia*)
**Pampas grass** (*Cortaderia selloana*)
**New Zealand flax** (*Phormium tenuosum*)

## THE IMPACT OF GARDENING GREEN

• Each tree on your property can prevent as much as 4,000 gallons of runoff every year. While it may seem a long-range plan, planting trees is an important part of developing a landscape with minimal runoff and soil erosion.

# Use porous paving.

*It may be hard to imagine, but some pavements can slow water runoff.*

One of the sounds I love most in the garden is footsteps on a pea gravel walkway. There is something very gardenesque about it to me. Maybe because it seems so natural, and it is. Loose stone, either crushed or in small pebble form, is one of the better ways homeowners can control runoff and erosion in their own yards. It's not terribly complicated; simply pour several inches onto a pathway and enjoy. That's what I call a simple, significant step!

---

**DID YOU KNOW THAT...**

❀ In most urban areas, 2/3 of the impervious surfaces are pavement, the other 1/3 are roofs. These are the surfaces where water runs off to be collected by stormwater systems. That means that pavements are producing 2/3 of the runoff.[1]

❀ Properly designed and installed porous paving *can completely eliminate* rainwater runoff. For example, a porous driveway consisting of concrete blocks filled with gravel that comprises 12 percent of the surface area has an infiltration rate of more than 100 inches per hour.[2]

---

Another simple technique is to use stone pavers set into a gravel base without permanently cementing them in. This also slows runoff, which increases the ability of water to be absorbed into the soil.

Over the years, more sophisticated systems have been developed. Most are suitable for driveways and sidewalks on individual lots, but many have a more far-reaching application for restricting water flow and urban runoff in our over-paved cities. The benefit of these systems is that many are plantable, providing not only purification of the water but increased $CO_2$ absorption and cooling effects as well.

Sadly, these anti-runoff surfaces are little understood and rarely used. Porous asphalt and pervious concrete allow water and air to pass

THE **green** GARDENER'S GUIDE

rapidly through to a highly permeable layer of gravel and stone. An underlayer of filter fabric helps to screen out small particles. When installed properly, this design slows runoff, increases infiltration, allows roots to breathe, helps replenish groundwater, and mitigates the total volume of stormwater excess.

You've heard the expression, "Necessity is the mother of invention." In the need to find new and improved ways to control erosion and runoff, other systems like Grasspave™ and Grasscrete™ have been designed. While installation is more involved, these systems allow for plantable surfaces over load-bearing ring and grid designs. The result is a more sophisticated filtering system using vegetation to further mitigate water flow and enhance purification. As a matter of fact, this turf-based model has been installed at the Orange Bowl in Miami, Florida. Considering how close any place in Florida is to a potential watershed, it's a great place to have them in use.

One of my next outdoor projects is to take out the asphalt-paved driveway at my house and replace it with pea gravel. Besides the pleasant sound it makes under foot (and tire), it's one more way I can do my part to reduce surface runoff. The collective actions of homeowners, businesses, and even sporting venues to use porous material will have a great impact on reducing runoff, one of our greatest global environmental problems.

 THE IMPACT OF GARDENING GREEN

- By replacing the impervious paving of your driveway, parking area, walks, patios, and other hard surfaces with porous paving such as pea gravel or Grasscrete, you can reduce the runoff of your paved areas virtually to zero.

www.greengardenersguide.com 183

# Grade for on-site drainage.

*Keep water on your property and reap the benefits locally and globally.*

How many times have we passed a construction site and wondered why on earth it needs to be reduced to a barren tabletop for a few houses or buildings? What's wrong with working around the existing trees and grading? Does that thought even cross builders' minds? Having never worked as a developer, I'm sure I'll get a list a mile long of the reasons why it's done this way. But with my limited knowledge on the subject, I'm betting it mostly comes down to two factors: it's easier and costs less.

Unfortunately, the vast majority of contemporary developments still rely on traditional stormwater management practices. The initial phases of the project involve clearing and grading the site while removing all existing vegetation. This makes it very hard if not impossible to keep stormwater on the property. During development, grading and conveyance pipes are arranged to move water off the property. In the end, very little pervious surface remains. Statistically, it's less than 40 percent on average. This despite the one thing about water that will forever be true—it always wants to go somewhere!

An essential part of stormwater management, whether it's new construction or an existing renovation, is keeping water from leaving the property, or at least slowing it down as much as possible. And yet many of today's home landscapes are sloped to encourage water runoff onto adjacent property or the street rather than retaining it on-site.

When water is kept from leaving the property, it is better able to soak into the ground, where it is purified naturally, to recharge drinking water, streams, and wetlands. There is also less pollution damage to nearby streams, watersheds, and wildlife habitats.

In an eco-friendly landscape, runoff should be managed and directed to bioretention areas. These can be as simple as locations around the landscape that allow for greater infiltration, native landscape plantings, areas of improved soil, or even rain gardens.

In response to the need for more natural, environmentally sensitive methods to land development and stormwater management, an approach known as Low Impact Development (LID) evolved. The methods used in LID significantly reduce the harm caused to our environment by traditional development practices. At the heart of LID is its central focus on stormwater management. Rather than attempting to alter topographic conditions, which leads to increased stormwater runoff, site plans are adapted to natural constraints, managing and keeping the water at the source whenever possible.

Through on-site assessments, areas are identified that are most appropriate for surface water flows and drainage patterns. Any necessary grading is managed to minimize off-site runoff, instead directing water to on-site areas with improved soil characteristics and natural buffers. LID focuses on utilizing a combination of water management traits: high infiltration capacity, evaporation, and transpiration.

DID YOU KNOW THAT...

An effective drainage system that keeps storm and irrigation water on-site without runoff will: (a) reduce or eliminate peak flows of water to lessen flooding, (b) pre-filter any pollutants from entering streams and rivers, (c) allow gardeners to utilize the water for plant needs, lessening the need for irrigation, and (d) in the case of combined sewer systems, lessen the chance of sewer overflow and resultant pollution in rivers and lakes.

During heavy rain, a combined sewer system can be overloaded and dump a mix of polluted runoff, pathogens, toxins, and other contaminants directly into nearby lakes or streams. The U.S. EPA reports that the nation's combined sewer systems dump about 1.2 trillion gallons of raw sanitary wastewater, untreated industrial wastes, and stormwater runoff into receiving waters each year.

In LID's approach, vegetative buffers play an important role in controlling site runoff by providing infiltration, slowing and dispersing water flows, and trapping sediments and pollutants. Whenever possible, large continuous open spaces, vegetative buffers, and sensitive areas should be protected and preserved in their natural condition. Some areas may need to be enhanced with additional plantings of water-tolerant native selections.

In the next few tips, I'll give you some more down-to-earth ideas on ways water runoff can be moderated and managed effectively in your own little corner of the world. Remember, little things add up.

 THE IMPACT OF GARDENING GREEN

• By managing your property to keep storm and irrigation runoff on-site for percolation into the soil, you can prevent thousands of gallons of runoff from entering the storm sewer system every year. It wouldn't take many of us doing that to keep literally billions of gallons of sewage out of our storm sewer systems and our surface water every year.

# Install a drainage system.

*Directing water to a safe place on your property has multiple benefits.*

As precious as water is, it also carries a great amount of pollution as surface runoff in the form of fertilizers, pesticides, and heavy metals. Drainage systems that capture runoff and carry it to another area in the yard allow water to percolate back into the soil, recharging groundwater supplies rather than burdening our aquifers with the accumulated silt and sediment from millions of square feet of impervious surfaces.

Once installed, a French drain is an effortless way to redirect runoff from downspouts or slopes. Simply put, a French drain is a trench filled with coarse gravel and topped with three to four inches of coarse sand that catches water, allowing it to seep back into the earth. Although the drain can be any size, it is typically five to six inches wide and eight to twelve inches deep. A French drain doesn't require steep grading, just enough to allow the water to flow. It can be disguised with grass or perennials planted into the sand.

> **DID YOU KNOW THAT...**
>
> ❀ A standard 4-inch diameter, corrugated plastic pipe is large enough to convey a 30-gallon per minute flow, the equivalent of 3 or 4 garden hoses on residential taps running at full capacity.
>
> ❀ The runoff from 1,000 square feet of roof area during a 3-inch per hour rainstorm (a very intense storm) would equal about 30 gallons per minute for that 1-hour period. Therefore, if you had all of the downspouts from this roof section plumbed into a 4-inch diameter corrugated plastic pipe, the pipe would be adequately sized to carry that runoff to an on-site collection spot away from the house.

Some people construct French drains out of perforated plastic drain pipe—you know, the black kind sold at home improvement stores. In this case, the pipe needs to be covered with a fabric sock that serves as a filter. The drain must be surrounded by at least one inch of coarse gravel on each side before being topped off with course sand.

Utilizing a French drain in your own yard can ease the burden of excessive water being deposited in one area of your property. In the bigger picture, it can also have a positive impact on your municipality's stormwater management, especially when many people in the community utilize this simple but significant solution.

## THE IMPACT OF GARDENING GREEN

• Installing drain lines is an important way to manage the flow of water on your property, to ensure that drainage reaches the appropriate collection points for infiltration and percolation into the water table.

# Use terracing and walls to slow the flow of water.

*One of the most effective actions you can take to mitigate the problem of an eroding slope is to interrupt the rate of water descent.*

I get a lot of questions from gardeners of every level. One of the most common is how to plant a garden on a slope. I'm always happy to answer this frequent inquiry because it gives me the opportunity to talk about the more important issue first. Knowing how to plant on a slope is important, but of even greater significance is knowing *why* to plant on a slope.

Soil erosion and surface runoff occur as water moves across the ground. The more exposed the soil and the faster the rate of flow, the greater the damage and the bigger the problem. The fact that I'm being asked this question tells me it's not too late for those asking (I think). But it is imperative to make sure a slope is covered or planted so that erosion is minimized.

> **DID YOU KNOW THAT...**
>
> ❀ Terraces and walls prevent erosion by shortening the long slope into a series of shorter, more level steps. This allows heavy rains to soak into the soil rather than run off and cause erosion.

## Terraces

One of the simplest and most significant actions you can take to mitigate the problem of an eroding slope is to break up the rate of water descent by constructing *terraces*. In addition to providing a way to garden on difficult terrain, terraces give you the opportunity to create a series of mini-gardens. Erosion is prevented by shortening a potentially long slope into a series of more level steps. This allows heavy rains to soak in rather than run off, taking soil with it.

Think of terraces like steps in an embankment. Soil is cut out of the hill to create the level tread or landing area. As with garden steps, the level area is not exactly level. Sloped terraces should be graded by about 2 percent perpendicular to the incline in order to gently direct drainage towards one side or the other.

Proper spacing between terraces on a slope depends on the slope itself. But in all cases, the shorter the slope length, the less chance there is for runoff. Terracing is most effective when the slope is divided into discrete segments.

For extra water management, you can capture and redirect excessive runoff by installing perforated drainage pipe just below the surface. Run the pipe across the direction of the slope. Position the drainage pipe in a gravel bed, with the perforated side down. Again, position the drain pipe at a 2 percent slope in the gravel bed.[1]

When constructing terraces, it is important to retain the exposed side. A number of building materials can be used. Some of the most common include landscape timbers, railroad ties, interlocking landscaping blocks, stones, bricks, and treated and weather-resistant wood. Whatever you use, be sure the material is firmly anchored against the soil. If you are stacking material, angle it back slightly towards the terraced level with each course. The force of water is powerful. It is always flowing downhill, and the pressure can easily push out against the wall, especially in freezing and thawing conditions.

## THE IMPACT OF GARDENING GREEN

- Terracing walls are important ways to slow and direct the flow of water to allow it to percolate into the soil, reducing erosion and avoiding runoff.

The height of a terraced wall depends on the steepness of the slope. Because of the force of a wall under pressure, it is advisable to seek the help of a professional for heights greater than twenty-four inches (sixty-one centimeters). Also check local building codes for constructing walls and terraces.

## Retaining walls

*Retaining walls* are another way to slow runoff and erosion, but their primary function is to support and retain an embankment. Unlike a terrace that is designed to have a level surface area (hence the name), the area behind a retaining wall can be either level or sloped.

Materials used for constructing retaining walls are generally more decorative. In addition to the resources listed above, native stone or stack stone is often used. Whatever material you choose, remember that the weight must be strong enough to hold back the pressure of a great amount of soil, yet porous enough to allow for adequate drainage. Pipes for drainage are often installed every twenty-four inches (sixty-one centimeters), and six inches (fifteen centimeters) from the ground.

Retaining walls can be stacked either without the use of mortar or with a bonding agent such as cement, concrete, or mortar. Dry walls should be sloped back against the soil to give it greater strength. The general rule is to slope the wall back four to six inches per foot of rise. Another guideline is that the width of its base should be about one-third of its height.

Do you remember the often-asked question that began this section? Well, now that you know why it's so important to retain that sloped area of your yard for runoff and erosion control, I suppose I can go ahead and tell you how to plant that garden on the slope. It's easy. Simply make sure the soil behind the terraced support or retaining wall is well amended and plant away. The hardest part is getting the soil level!

# Use swales to slow or capture drainage.

*Swales are designed to redirect and moderate water flow while at the same time removing toxic pollutants from stormwater runoff.*

The use of swales to slow and direct stormwater runoff is nothing new. Swales consist of very shallow, wide, linear depressions typically planted with turf, but they may also utilize compost or stone. Their success is mainly determined by their length, and they are primarily used when developing large tracts of land. Basically, swales are like mini-water treatment plants, improving water quality before it reaches the storm drain.

Although it is typically used in commercial and larger developments, some very clever people are bringing the swale concept home . . . literally. They're utilizing swales on a smaller scale in their own backyards with the primary purpose of keeping water on their property and not sending it off-site or down the street, at least not initially.

DID YOU KNOW THAT. . .

❀ Swales are depressions used to hold or divert water for percolation into the soil.

❀ A swale that is 20 feet by 15 feet, with an average depth of 8 inches, is large enough to hold about 1,500 gallons of water from a single rain event.

Similar to rain gardens, swales are designed for the purpose of redirecting and moderating water flow, while at the same time removing toxic pollutants. Swales need a very wide basin with minimal slope. This gives water the maximum amount of time to be absorbed back into the ground, allowing for the natural process of purification.

Creative, *water-retentive* homeowners are utilizing swales as part of their landscape design to handle the inevitable occasional overflow of rain barrels or cisterns, as well as natural rainfall. A swale can be attractively planted with any suitable vegetation, but natives are more adapted to the local climate and rainfall patterns. And many natives also offer the added benefit of being lower maintenance and more pest- and disease-resistant.

Swales offer yet another way to capture and ease the flow of water from properties of all sizes. When planted with native vegetation, swales are swell (sorry, I couldn't resist) and another simple and significant step to a more eco-friendly garden.

## THE IMPACT OF GARDENING GREEN

- Swales are one more tool for managing the flow of water and keeping it on-site without runoff. They are a part of the whole picture of on-site drainage retention.

# Plant a rain garden.

*Underneath a glamorous cover of lush vegetation, lies a workhorse.*

So, culverts, landscape grading, swales, and French drains just aren't striking your fancy as chic ways to reduce runoff and pre-filter pollutants from entering streams and rivers around your house? Then maybe I can interest you in something a little more your style. How does a *rain garden* sound to you?

Indeed, rain gardens certainly can be beautiful. And they do have a nice ring to them. In reality, though, storm gardens might be a more appropriate name, and here's why: underneath a glamorous cover of lush vegetation lies a workhorse waiting to take on the next wave of stormwater coming its way.

After a squall, stormwater runoff rushes towards the closest drain, stream, or river. Unfortunately, the stormwater reaching these areas is full of contaminants, including gasoline and oil deposits, animal wastes, and pesticides and fertilizers, namely nitrogen and phosphorus. A rash of problems is created in its wake.

Rain gardens are man-made shallow areas that collect and hold water temporarily. Nature allows some stormwater runoff to settle into shallow depressions and wetlands before seeping in to recharge groundwater and aquifers. In the land of McMansions, where impervious surfaces are as common as the lawns around them, surface water rarely makes it to such natural areas. Rain gardens help to minimize this impact.

> ## GOOD PLANTS FOR RAIN GARDENS
>
> **Sedges** (*Carex* spp.)
> **Swamp milkweed** (*Asclepias incarnata*)
> **Jack-in-the-pulpit** (*Arisaema triphyllum*)
> **Joe-pye weed** (*Eupatorium maculatum*)
> **Boltonia** (*Boltonia asteroides*)
> **Hardy hibiscus** (*Hibiscus moscheutos*)
> **Serviceberry** (*Amelanchier* spp.)
> **Black chokeberry** (*Aronia melanocarpa*)
> **Pagoda dogwood** (*Cornus alternifolia*)
> **Red-osier dogwood** (*Cornus sericea*)
> **American hazel** (*Corylus Americana*)
> **Elderberry** (*Sambucus* spp.)
> **Winterberry** (*Ilex verticillata*)
> **Highbush cranberry** (*Viburnum trilobum*)

## Creating your rain garden

Your rain garden can be as small or as big as you'd like. A typical rain garden is not elaborate, but whatever the size, the gardens are set far enough away from the house so collected water doesn't affect the foundation. A low or wet spot where water naturally drains is a good place to put your garden. Close to the street is ideal so as to minimize the amount of water reaching roadway storm drains.

There's no rule for what shape your rain garden needs to be, either. What is important, though, is depth and drainage. A shallow depression with a center depth of twelve to eighteen inches, feathering out to the edge, is ideal. If the native soil is dense and holds water too long or drains poorly, it is advisable to replace this soil with a sandier texture, usually to a depth of a foot to allow for better percolation.

Just as there are no hard and fast rules for the shape of a rain garden, there are no rules for the type of plants that go in them either. However, you should consider the extreme conditions a rain garden can face. Deeply rooted native plants are a good choice, as well as varieties that can take drought and extreme moisture conditions for extended periods. Deep roots help retain soil and create pathways for better percolation. Consider selecting plants for four seasons of interest and use a diverse mix, especially when you want to attract beneficials to your garden.

You can facilitate the flow of water into your garden by digging a shallow trench or burying a plastic drainage pipe, connected from a downspout. But no matter how it gets there, collected water is what a rain garden is all about. The premise is for the garden simply to retain the water only long enough to allow it to seep into the soil.

While the intercepted water is collected in the rain garden depression, so much good is being done to prevent contamination problems downhill. As the water calms, plants in the rain garden absorb nitrogen, phosphorus, and other chemicals; pollutants such as gas and oil are converted to organic compounds; and sand and silt settle—all as water slowly seeps and filters toward the groundwater below.

In spite of all the advantages provided by rain gardens, there are still those who are concerned that rain gardens may detract from the aesthetics of the property. That never has to be the case. There are many native plants that are not only well suited for these gardens but also they are visually pleasing as well. Even so, plants in a rain garden environment may very well thrive, and occasional taming may be required to keep it looking its best.

Another concern that arises on occasion is the misconception that having a rain garden will provide a breeding ground for mosquitoes. On the contrary, mosquitoes need several days of standing water to reproduce. Rain gardens are designed to dry up well before that. Even better, rain gardens *do* attract dragonflies, one of a mosquito's worst nightmares!

Although there are a number of effective ways to deal with stormwater in our yards, rain gardens are indeed a beautiful solution to the challenges of on-site water management issues. They're also a smart way to create a more biodiverse environment for native plants and to attract wildlife, minus the mosquitoes!

## THE IMPACT OF GARDENING GREEN

• Rain gardens can play a significant role in reducing or eliminating runoff from your home landscape. They are beautiful and add value to your home.

# Create a seasonal water feature.

*A dry stream bed can be a beautiful and significant way to manage water flowing across your property.*

Many parts of the country experience periodic heavy rains that can overwhelm stormwater management systems, while the region's drought-prone areas need to retain as much precipitation as possible. Dry stream beds can be the answer to both challenges.

A dry stream bed, in very simple terms, is a shallow trench filled with stones in which water follows the chosen course. An underlayer of landscape fabric works to provide additional soil stabilization while allowing water to seep slowly back into the ground, and it blocks weeds from emerging between the stones. If your purpose is to direct water more quickly to a localized area such as a catch basin, you might want to use plastic or a rubber pond liner material. You can even set the stones in concrete.

DID YOU KNOW THAT...

❧ In arid climates, dry creek beds are interesting natural features rich in attractive plant life that serve the important ecological function of handling the "boom and bust" rainfall of occasional cloudbursts followed by long periods of drought. They are an excellent arid-climate alternative to rain gardens.

The most likely place for a dry stream bed is where water naturally drains across your property. The stones placed in the bed serve to break up the rate and reduce the flow, helping to filter water back into the soil. In dryer times, the rocks and stones can also serve as mulch to trap moisture and provide a microclimate that sustains a number of living organisms and aids in water infiltration.

A dry stream bed doesn't need predefined dimensions. Visualize natural streams and how they flow. Areas where water flows more rapidly are usually narrower, deeper, and steeper while slower water is found in wider, shallower areas. Of course, a meandering stream is more interesting than a straight one and also does a better job of slowing down the flow.

When stocking your dry stream bed, use a variety of stone sizes, from boulders to pea gravel large enough not to get washed away in a heavy downpour. Boulders are typically placed toward the outer edges of the bed and occasionally positioned as "islands," while in the middle, smaller stones gradually lead to larger ones. The stream bed will appear more natural if you use rounded stones rather than sharp ones.

To complete the look, landscape with plants you would find growing naturally in your area. If the stream bed traverses a hillside, plants will be especially effective for additional erosion control.

When artfully created, a dry stream bed adds much more than just erosion control. It enhances the beauty of the landscape, which can increase the value of your home as well. It's easier to construct than you think and is a significant step to managing water flow across your property.

## THE IMPACT OF GARDENING GREEN

- Similar to rain gardens, dry creek beds provide an attractive way to reduce the runoff of rainwater from your property.

# CHAPTER FIVE

# TURNING WASTE INTO GARDENING GOLD

As a gardener, having a pick-up truck offers many advantages. As I think back on my pre-truck days, the sedans I owned must have been quite confused. Although they were made for hauling people, I used them more to haul my latest gardening stuff. It was quite a sight; I'd fill the car so full there was barely enough room left for me to drive my latest score home.

My plan eventually worked. My wife got so tired of competing with the plants and future yard art for a place in the car that I finally got the green light to buy my first truck. It wasn't a moment too soon. On the way home I passed a yard where they had just put out a dozen sacks of fresh grass clippings. Since I hate to see perfectly good grass go to waste and was anxious to try out the new hauling features, I pulled over next to the sacks and jumped out. Much to my wife's surprise (and embarrassment), I started loading this stranger's clippings into the bed of my truck.

And that's pretty much how my life has been ever since. As much as I want everyone to keep their clippings, leaf debris, and other organic matter at home to use as compost and reduce landfill space, I'm always happy to take a few extra bags off someone's hands (or curb), and I do so quite often. My truck gets more miles bringing home composting ingredients and making runs to the recycling center than anything else.

At home, my family and I compost or recycle just about everything we can, from inside and outside the house. It's hard to believe just how much waste is generated each day not only at our house but in homes around the world. In the United States, it's about 4.5 pounds per day per person. Canada and the Netherlands are not far behind at about 3.75 and 3 pounds per person.

The U.S. holds the distinction as the world leader in municipal solid waste, but on a brighter note, we're also the leader in recycling, finding ways to keep about 25 percent of that waste out of the landfill.

As gardeners, we have such a wonderful opportunity to do something good for ourselves and our gardens, while at the same time doing our part to relieve the pressure of overburdened landfill space and reduce emissions from carbon dioxide and methane gas. So much of what ends up as municipal solid waste and discarded junk is just what we need and can use in our eco-friendly gardens and landscapes.

> **DID YOU KNOW THAT...**
>
> ❀ The average American generates 1,500 pounds of trash per year—about 4.5 pounds per day, a total of 246 million tons per year—more than the citizens of any other country.[1]
>
> ❀ The U.S. also leads the industrialized world in recycling—about 1.5 pounds per day. Composting recovered about 21 million tons of waste in 2005, and other recycling (excluding composting) recovered another 58 million tons.[2]
>
> ❀ Compostable organic materials continue to be the largest components of our waste stream. Paper and paperboard products account for 34 percent, and yard trimmings and food scraps account for about 25 percent.[3]

## Landfill limits

Picture any landfill. Have you ever seen one that didn't look like a small mountain? Now imagine that landfill at only one-third its original size. The two-thirds that you just vaporized in your mind is the portion of that mountain that could have been composted or recycled. It's true, plain old paper accounts for over 40 percent of landfill mass on average, while an additional 25 percent is made up of yard trimmings and food scraps. All of that could have been compost!

❀ Solid waste landfills are the single largest man-made source of methane gas in the United States.[4]

❀ The processs of collecting, transporting, and consolidating trash uses up a great deal of energy, especially considering all of the associated air pollutants and greenhouse gas emissions.[5]

❀ Landfills use up large areas of land. In some highly built-out urban areas there is little room remaining available for landfills.[6]

❀ About 86 percent of U.S. landfills are currently leaking toxic materials into lakes, streams, and aquifers. Once groundwater is contaminated, it is extremely expensive and difficult, sometimes impossible, to clean it up.[7]

Just in case you think there's no difference in depositing paper, yard trimmings, and food scraps into the landfill versus recycling or composting them, think again. For organic material to break down, it must have carbon, nitrogen, moisture, and oxygen. The better the ratio among those ingredients, the faster the process of decomposition occurs. At home, we can control those variables rather easily. With the right combination, we can have finished compost as quickly as several weeks to several months.

In a landfill environment, the ideal combination for decomposition rarely if ever exists. Instead, the compaction that occurs from the addition of more and more material and the weight of heavy equipment at the surface deprives potentially decomposing matter of sufficient oxygen and prevents moisture from reaching the material as well. In fact, the breakdown process happens so slowly that one researcher was able to excavate newspapers from the 1960s that were still intact and readable!

This massive amount of organic material creates an even greater problem in a landfill. As organic matter attempts to decompose, in the absence of sufficient oxygen, *methane* is created. A powerful greenhouse gas, methane is twenty-three times more effective at trapping heat in the atmosphere than carbon dioxide. It's no surprise that solid waste landfills are the single largest man-made source of methane gas in the United States.[8]

In addition to organic matter taking up unnecessary space, many items that may never break down, like heavy plastics from garden containers, metal, stone, and concrete, find their way into landfills. Many of these products can be repurposed in some form or another. In fact, the garden has many uses for these very materials.

In the following pages we'll explore some simple yet significant ways you can reduce, reuse, and recycle items from inside and outside your house. In addition to the benefit of knowing you're doing something valuable to protect and preserve our planet, you'll be beautifying your garden and landscape at the same time.

(And don't worry—you don't have to own a truck to do it!)

# Compost your garden waste.

*For every item that you can throw in the compost pile,*
*that's one less for the landfill.*

Fortunately, there is measurable progress in reducing the amount of yard waste we are keeping out of our landfills, and there are a number of reasons why. First, many municipalities no longer allow yard debris to be included with other household waste. Instead, trimmings are set aside in biodegradable paper bags and collected separately. They're then taken to a municipal composting site where they are deposited for the slow decomposition process.

DID YOU KNOW THAT...

❧ Yard trimmings (grass clippings, leaves, tree and shrub branches, etc.) account for 13.1 percent by weight of the total solid waste generated in the U.S. That amounts to about 32 million tons every year.[1]

❧ The methane produced by yard waste dumped in landfills is 23 times more damaging in causing global warming than carbon dioxide is.

Elsewhere, many cities and counties across the country offer curbside pickup of items too bulky for paper sacks. Tree limbs, shrubs, and other such items are the usual components of this part of the recycling campaign. Even fall leaves are sucked up and hauled off to a composting facility by some solid waste departments.

For me, surrendering my yard trimmings to a third party is only a measure of last resort. After all, I want as much compostable material as I can get. The thought of handing it over, even the big stuff, seems ludicrous. I admit, it is sometimes tempting to leave cumbersome branches and bags of leaves on the curb rather than haul them to the backyard compost pile, but like most things in life—no pain, no gain.

When you're outside working in the yard, it's always surprising how much yard debris accumulates so quickly. Can it all go into the compost pile? Yes, it probably could, but should it? Well, that's another story.

## What goes in the compost pile

**Outside**, anything that was growing is fair game . . . almost. A few exceptions are mentioned below. First, however, great additions to a compost pile from outside the house include grass clippings, hay, straw, pine needles, leaves, wood chips, bark, and other yard trimmings.

You may have heard that for compost to break down quickly, there needs to be the right ratio between carbon (the brown stuff) and nitrogen (the green stuff). Although that is true, compost happens in nature with no help from us, although it may take longer.

Rather than get bogged down in trying to provide the perfect ratio, just be sure always to have some of both working all the time. The rate of composting can be accelerated by simply keeping the pile moist (like a damp sponge) and turning it often to provide oxygen to the center of the pile.

Now, the outdoors has a few limitations on what *not* to put in a compost pile. First, avoid adding weeds that have gone to seed. Weed seeds often survive the decomposition process, only to be spread next season under the cloak of perfect compost.

**Diseased plant material** also poses risks to your compost. The pathogens may survive the composting process and reinfect other plants later as they are distributed about your garden. Play it safe and remove this material from your property completely. Although burning would destroy the pathogens and infected plant material, it's not an option in the eco-friendly garden.

**Fireplace ashes** present yet another problem. Ashes are highly alkaline. More harm could be done by raising the soil pH of acid-loving plants than the small benefit from potassium inherent with ash. I leave them out of my compost.

Personally, I don't add twigs or branches to my pile that are thicker than a pencil. It's not that they won't become compost; it's just that I'm too impatient. Instead, I toss all my thicker branches into a pile of their own. As they slowly break down, the added benefit is that they provide cover and protection for birds and many of the smaller wildlife that live in the area. I also keep thorny branches and twigs such as roses and briars out of my compost. They go into that separate pile and provide additional protection for the smaller animals.

So although there are some *don'ts* when it comes to what to put into your compost, the exceptions are very few. Just remember this: for every item that you can throw in the compost pile, that's one less for the landfill. If that's not motivating enough, know that what you are putting in your compost pile will provide the very best soil amendment you can give to your garden, and no store-bought product can match it!

## THE IMPACT OF GARDENING GREEN

• By composting your yard waste instead of sending it to the landfill, you will help decrease the need for landfill space, reduce the production of methane in your landfill, and enjoy a better soil amendment than you could buy in any store.

# Compost grass clippings as a valuable resource.

*Grass clippings contain nitrogen, a key nutrient for lush growth and deep green color.*

I have issues. I'm not sure mine are all that serious in the big picture. But on a Saturday morning, they're huge! As I prepare to mow my lawn, I have some pretty tough decisions to make. For example, do I mulch my grass this time, or do I bag the clippings and place them in the compost pile. Oh, the pressure!

You'll be happy to know that I've come to terms with problems like these. Actually, I can't go wrong either way. Why can't the rest of my life be like that? The fact is, whether I bag and compost, or grasscycle, the nutrients from the clippings are being put to work. It's simply a matter of where I choose to employ them. Since I have strong feelings about this, as I'm sure you can tell by now, I'll break this tip into two parts. Grasscycling with a mulching mower will be discussed separately. But for now, let's get started with composting grass clippings.

## Composting your clippings

Can you imagine how many bags of grass clippings are collected on any spring or summer day? The EPA tells us yard clippings make up over 20 percent of the entire waste stream entering public landfills. If it were up to me, I'd take them all at my house. Grass clippings are loaded with nitrogen, a key nutrient to lush growth and deep green color. They're also a necessary part of helping other organic material break down quickly.

Nitrogen provides the food source for microorganisms to decompose carbon, that brown waste in our compost such as twigs and leaves. You only need about 20 percent as much nitrogen as carbon, but it is essential that you have both for efficient decomposition. In fact, a compost pile without green waste will seem to just sit there. It will eventually break down, but it takes *much* longer. Add some grass clippings to the mix and watch that pile start to cook! That heat is from the microbes hard at work again, nourished and fortified from the addition of their essential food source.

Now, even though I've said I'd take all the grass clippings I could get, that's not exactly true. In my eco-friendly garden, I don't want to add clippings that have been doused with herbicides and pesticides. Some of those chemicals don't break down in the heat of composting, and I'm not interested in adding tainted compost to my otherwise chemical-free garden.

The same goes for grass containing a lot of weeds. It's not the weeds I'm worried about as much as the seeds they make. Weed seeds have the ability to survive some pretty harsh conditions, including a hot compost pile. The seeds could remain viable, only to germinate later in other parts of the garden where you apply the finished compost. If I keep my grass cut often enough, weeds are rarely a problem since frequent mowing cuts off emerging seed heads.

DID YOU KNOW THAT . . .

❀ During the growing (and mowing) season, grass clippings cause the amount of yard waste entering landfills to rise by 50 percent. During the growing season, grass clippings compose 20 percent of the waste entering landfills.[1]

❀ The average home that grasscycles or composts grass clippings typically diverts more than 1 ton of grass clippings each year from disposal in landfills.[2]

❀ Grass clippings are a rich source of nitrogen, phosphorus, and potassium.[3]

Finally, too much of a good thing can be, well . . . too much. If you've ever placed a large amount of grass clippings in a pile, added water, and come back later, you may have noticed a strong and not so pleasant aroma much like the smell of ammonia. It's simply a matter of chemistry—too much moisture and not enough oxygen to process the decomposition of the nitrogen-rich grass clippings. But it's an easy fix. Just spread the pile out to allow more oxygen in, add some carbon-based brown ingredients, and then mix it all together. The problem should resolve itself within a day or two.

So now, do you see why I consider my grass clippings to be such a precious natural resource in my yard and garden? As it turns out, deciding between grasscycling and composting from one week to the next isn't so bad. But sending them off to the landfill? Now that's a problem!

## THE IMPACT OF GARDENING GREEN

• Recycling your grass clippings into compost provides the important nitrogen necessary to break down the other waste. The addition of organic nitrogen sources, such as grass clippings in compost, helps round out the finished product into a full spectrum of plant nutrients to reduce or even eliminate synthetic fertilizers—all while avoiding the ecological cost of transportation and storage elsewhere.

# Compost kitchen waste, paper, and other items to reduce landfill costs.

*One of the easiest ways to add to your compost is to toss in those food scraps from salads, vegetables, and fruits.*

I certainly try to do my part to reduce the pressure on our community landfill. In fact, I've indoctrinated my family into this composting-recycling obsessive world in which I live. But I may have gone a little too far with it. Now I have them afraid to throw *anything* away. I must admit, my fervor has resulted in a plethora of recyclables at my house. And I am happy to say that anything that *can* be composted *is* composted.

As part of our system, we now have a dedicated cabinet in the kitchen that houses two bins. One is for the daily compost and the other for recyclables. I thought it would be a tough sell to get my wife to go along with the ongoing storage of food waste inside the house. As it turns out, the biggest challenge is my remembering to take it out at the end of each day. After all, that was our deal.

The total acceptance by my family of "The System" has resulted in my having to fish out some pretty crazy items that just don't work in the compost bin. That's all right though. I'd rather fish them out than have them thrown out—there's no chance to compost then. So just what can and *can't* go into the compost bin?

From inside the house, just about anything that once came from a living source can be composted. From the *kitchen*, add all fruit and vegetable scraps, coffee grounds and filters, paper towels and the roll, napkins, oatmeal, banana peels, eggshells, and tea bags. You'll find more items.

From *around the house*, add vacuum cleaner bags and contents, dryer lint, cardboard rolls, clean paper (shredded is best), newspaper, cotton and wool rags, hair and fur, and houseplants.

As with everything in life, there are exceptions to the rule, including household compost. First, don't add meat products, bones, fats, grease, oils, or dairy products to compost. They create odors that can attract pests such as rodents and flies. And don't compost pet or human wastes. These can contain parasites, bacteria, germs, pathogens, and viruses that are harmful to humans.

## The thrill of shredding

Inside my house, the shredder is the equivalent to the compost bin outdoors, based on how much it is working. I shred everything! In fact, I derive great pleasure from it. If you think there's something wrong with that, just know that my kids fight over who gets to shred the next stack.

Think about all you can shred: bills, junk mail, school papers, printed emails and articles, oh the list goes on, and so does the pleasure. And while we're having some good clean family fun (except for all the paper dust), I am creating a wonderful carbon-rich addition to the compost pile.

> **DID YOU KNOW THAT...**
>
> ❀ Compostable food scraps amount to about 11.7 percent by weight of the waste stream entering landfills, which amounts to a total of about 29 million tons every year. Another 17 million tons of food scraps that go through garbage disposals go to wastewater treatment plants.[1]
>
> ❀ Disposing of kitchen scraps in landfills uses up energy, contributes to global warming through the production of methane, and takes up valuable landfill space.

Shredders are readily available today from many sources—drug stores, office supply stores, and the big warehouse clubs all sell them. I purchased a high quality, home/office version for about $150. It can take about fifteen sheets at a time, cuts paper into confetti, and handles a large volume, all without removing a single staple or paper-clip. It can even cut through CDs, DVDs, and credit cards. However, knowing that everything I shred is destined for the compost pile, I don't include these.

> **DID YOU KNOW THAT...**
>
> ❀ Disposing of kitchen waste through the wastewater treatment system uses water, is expensive, and can lead to water quality problems when the effluent is released.
>
> ❀ On average, about 40 percent of a landfill's contents is plain old paper. Paper and paperboard products constitute about 34 percent of the total waste stream, by weight.[2]
>
> ❀ Paper is many times more resistant to deterioration when compacted in a landfill than when it is in open contact with the atmosphere (such as a compost pile).[3]

I've had the small trashcan-size shredder in the past and to me, they're more trouble than they're worth. The small cans fill up too quickly for all the trash I have. On my current model, I even enjoy hauling out the container of confetti paper to dump into the compost pile. It's actually quite attractive. In short order, all the different colors from the paper confetti are soon reduced to the same unrecognizable common denominator of finished compost.

As long as there is junk mail, school work, and bills, there will be an endless source of compostable material from inside the house . . . meaning there will *always* be an endless source! Besides the true pleasure I get in reducing junk mail to confetti, I must say, I am amazed at how quickly that paper adds up. I'm sorry to say that, for much of my life, I was contributing so much unnecessary waste to the landfill.

Now, with the affordability of quality shredders for the home, I encourage you to get one and start using it right away. I promise, you'll enjoy it too, and the compost you'll make is the icing on the cake. Above all though, it really is a simple and significant way to keep a great deal of solid waste from inside your home *out* of the landfill.

I must admit, now that the family is on board, our household composting machine is running smoothly. It took a little work at first, but now it's a healthy habit that I doubt we'll ever break, nor should we. Besides the good we're doing for the environment and our garden, my children are learning important lessons on stewardship. And when they get to eat fresh vegetables from the garden, nourished by the compost they helped make, green gardening is an easy sell.

 THE IMPACT OF GARDENING GREEN

• By composting your kitchen scraps and your paper waste in addition to all of your yard debris, you can reduce the amount of waste you send to your landfill by at least 50 percent.

# Mulch or compost your leaves—don't send them to the landfill.

*Leaves contain more than half the nutrients they took in during the season.*

When the mornings are cool and crisp, the leaves are starting to change colors, and college football is in full swing, that's clearly my favorite time of year. But these thrilling signs of autumn aren't what make it so for me.

> **DID YOU KNOW THAT...**
>
> ❀ Leaves comprise about 25 percent of the total amount of yard trimmings that enter the waste stream, about 8 million tons per year.[1]
>
> ❀ Up to 4,000 pounds of leaves per acre can be shredded and mulched over a lawn with no negative effects on turf quality, color, thatch accumulation, weed populations, or disease.[2]

As lovely as hardwood trees appear with their leaves in glorious shades of red, yellow, orange, and rust, my favorite part of the season is *after* they have fallen. The now brown leaves begin to blanket my lawn and beds, and I know that it is compost time!

No, I haven't lost my mind. I don't relish the work of clearing off those leaves any more than you do. But, I do have a deep appreciation for what they will mean to my garden and landscape in just a few months.

I suppose it goes back to that old saying: "Beauty is in the eye of the beholder." Where most people see leaf debris, along with hours of raking, bagging, and hauling, I see garden beds blanketed in rich organic compost. These leaves contain 50 to 80 percent of the nutrients that their trees extracted from the earth this past season. I will use them to replenish the soil and nourish all that grows within it.

Earthworms will feast on this debris, burrow deeper into the soil, and then deposit the matter as castings, adding even more valuable nutrients, oxygen, and drainage in the process. Beneficial fungi and bacteria will assist in the decomposition process, consuming this raw leaf material and returning it in a nutrient-rich form that can be utilized by plant and tree roots more efficiently and effectively than anything man has ever created.

Mere months after these shredded leaves are applied around my garden, they'll transform into matter that promotes the life of soil-dwelling organisms, which in turn will fortify my plants and trees to be more pest- and disease-resistant . . . ah, I can see springtime already.

But let me interrupt this vision to ask you a question: Have you ever stopped to consider that no matter what condition soil is in, leaf compost will help make loose soil retain moisture and compacted soil drain better?

Rather than being viewed as unnecessary trash, these leaves, grass clippings, and other garden trimmings should be going into our own gardens to enrich the soil while reducing the need for supplemental fertilizers and other harmful chemicals.

Yes, I'll look forward to gathering up and shredding not only the leaves falling from my trees, but from my neighbor's (and the stranger's down the road) as well. I also have the landscaping crews ready to bring me the leaves they've collected from their jobs.

What leaves I don't spread into the beds, I'll store somewhere else in my yard. I'll worry about them later. You're welcome to bring me all you have. It's my organic fertilizer, multi-vitamin, and soil conditioner all-in-one, both plentiful and free. It doesn't get any better.

## THE IMPACT OF GARDENING GREEN

- Shred your leaves for the compost pile or mulch instead of setting them out for collection, and you can reduce the amount of waste you send to the landfill in the fall by as much as 50 percent.

*One touch of nature makes the whole world kin.*

WILLIAM SHAKESPEARE

# Use a mulching mower and grasscycle

*Grasscycling does not cause thatch, and it reduces nitrogen fertilizer needs.*

With the arrival of spring, cutting the grass becomes another weekly ritual to promote the health and beauty of a great-looking lawn and landscape. But many homeowners don't realize it's not necessary to bag those grass clippings. In fact, leaving them on your lawn offers several advantages.

Grasscycling is the natural recycling of grass clippings by leaving them on your lawn when mowing, rather than bagging and removing them. It's such a simple way to mow that I don't know why more people don't do it.

Actually I do. My mother was one of those people. After she retired, I would go over and cut her grass, but I wouldn't bag the clippings. Instead, my mulching mower did a fine job of cutting those blades into pieces so small, it was impossible to find them. But mom was always concerned that by not bagging the clippings, thatch would build up, weed seeds would be scattered everywhere, and it just wouldn't look as good. To this, I'd say (as politely as possible), "Wrong, wrong, and wrong!" Read on for the facts.

**Grasscycling does not promote thatch.** According to university studies and abundant research, it is a common misconception that grass clippings are a major cause of thatch buildup in lawns. Thatch buildup is caused by grass stems, shoots, and roots, not grass clippings. Clippings, which consist of about 75 percent water, decompose quickly while adding nutrients to the soil.

**Grasscycling contributes valuable nutrients.** Studies indicate that as grass clippings decompose on your lawn, they contribute enough organic matter and nitrogen to reduce lawn fertilization needs by about 25 percent per year.

DID YOU KNOW THAT...

❀ Each home that grasscycles typically keeps more than 1 ton of grass clippings out of the waste stream annually.[1]

❀ Modern mulching lawn mowers make grasscycling easy—and certainly easier than bagging lawn clippings and sending them to the landfill. You can reduce your mowing time by 30 to 40 percent by not having to bag clippings. In one study of 147 homeowners in Fort Worth, Texas, grass recyclers spent an average of 7 hours less during the grass cutting season on yard work.[2]

❀ Leaving your grass clippings on your lawn does NOT contribute to thatch. Grass clippings quickly decompose and act as a natural mulch, helping to shade grass roots and conserve important soil moisture.[3]

**Grasscycling does not promote weed growth.** One of the keys to proper grasscycling is to remove only one-third of the grass blade each time you mow, always keeping in mind the recommended height for your type of grass. This may necessitate that you cut your grass a bit more frequently, especially during peak growing times. Consistent, regular mowing reduces the chances of weeds going to seed and dispersing throughout your yard.

It's also important to use a sharp blade. Sharp blades make clean cuts, thus reducing the chance for lawn diseases and pests. A healthy lawn is a lush lawn and one that does not create a favorable environment for weeds to grow and flourish.

**Grasscyclng leaves no visible residue.** The key to having a freshly cut lawn free of unsightly clippings is to make note of the comments above. Again, always use a sharp mower blade to ensure a clean cut. Avoid cutting off more than a third of the grass blade any time you mow. This not only reduces the size of the clippings, it is also less stressful on the grass. Finally, don't mow when the grass is wet. Clumps will ultimately develop, no matter how hard you try to avoid it.

If you follow these guidelines, you can zip through your mowing sessions faster than ever, add valuable organic nutrients into your lawn, keep excess waste out of the landfill, and still achieve, tidy results.

Even after my mother won the coveted "neighborhood lawn of the month" award, I'm not sure I ever sold her on the virtues of grasscycling. Mom finally moved to an apartment before we ever resolved that debate. I think she did that rather than concede and allow me to go "bagless" in her yard whenever I wanted. She's as stubborn as she is sweet.

## THE IMPACT OF GARDENING GREEN

• Use a mulching mower and let your clippings decompose into the lawn, and you'll send a ton less waste to the landfill every year—as well as the need to apply 25 percent less fertilizer to your lawn. You'll spend less time doing yard work, too!

# Use a chipper to break down tree branches.

*To get great compost faster, you want your yard debris to be as small as possible from the start.*

Do you ever find it annoying that while harvesting apparently finished compost you are constantly having to remove sticks from the pile? It's simply the "law of the compost pile"—smaller particles decompose faster than larger ones. So, to achieve great compost faster, you want your yard debris to be as small as possible. The solution for large stems, vines, and branches is a chipper/shredder.

> **DID YOU KNOW THAT...**
>
> ❀ Tree and shrub prunings contribute about 25 percent of the waste stream from yard and garden waste. That amounts to about 8 million tons per year.[1]

When choosing your chipper/shredder, electric models would be my more eco-friendly choice. Besides not spewing pollutants into the air, they are quieter than most gas-powered models. And, if you are not chipping debris that is larger than about two and a half inches in diameter, electric models work fine.

If you decide you'd rather not compost the chips, they make great mulch and will decompose naturally in your garden bed. By knowing the exact ingredients of your own mulch, you can certify it yourself!

## THE IMPACT OF GARDENING GREEN

• By using a chipper-shredder to compost your tree and shrub prunings, you will save about the same amount of space in the landfill as when you compost your grass clippings—about 1 ton per year.

# Recycle those plastic pots.

*Of most of the plastic recycled today, very little is garden garbage.*

When we think about the act of gardening, we often assume we are doing wonderful things for the environment. But many of us don't realize the amount of trash we generate at the same time we are creating that beautiful garden.

Take plastic pots, for instance. They come in all sizes from little cell packs to very large containers. Once we've planted the beauties that came in them, where does the pot go? Hmmmm . . . lots of time it's into the trash, or at best it's into the curbside recycle bin or municipal recycling center.

DID YOU KNOW THAT . . .

❀ Only a very small percentage of agricultural and gardening plastics are recycled. Many recycling programs don't take the Number 4, 5, and 6 plastics used in most pots, or they discard them because they have soil clinging to them.[1]

❀ Nursery pots, flats, and cell packs alone use up to 320 million pounds of plastic a year. Since little of this is recycled, it ends up in landfills.[2]

❀ In 2006, an Oregon company called Agri-Plas, Inc., accepted and recycled approximately 15,600,000 pounds of plastic that included nursery pots, trays, plug trays, as well as bulk bags and pesticide containers. It used this plastic to make more nursery pots, plastic lumber, and railroad ties.[3]

According to the EPA, of the nearly 27 million tons of plastic generated in the United States in 2003, only 3.9 million tons of it was recycled. But as Beth Botts, a writer for the *Chicago Tribune* points out in her article "Beauty and the Plastic Beast," most of that was soda, water, and milk bottles; very little was garden garbage.

Looking deeper into the issue, we find that one main problem is the variety of plastics that are used in making garden containers in the first place. Even if everybody sent their containers to the recycling center, most are not accepted and end up in the landfill instead.

## Solving the plastic problem

So what's an eco-friendly society to do? Solutions range from asking manufacturers to standardize the type of plastic they use for garden containers and for growers to use them, to creating biodegradable pots and asking municipalities to segregate plastic pots for recycling. While these and more ideas are being researched, progress isn't going to happen overnight.

Still, there are some things we as individuals can do to help. Ask your local garden center if you can return empty containers. We can also request programs that offer garden container recycling for all types of plastic pots, including recycling numbers 2, 4, 5, and 6. Or we can seek out garden centers or botanic gardens that make this service available. Maybe you can begin a program in your community.

In 2007, the Missouri Botanical Garden successfully recycled over one hundred thousand pounds of horticultural plastic originally destined for the landfills. The Garden's successful Plastic Pot Recycling program in St. Louis is the most extensive public garden recycling program in the U.S, collecting over three hundred tons of waste in the past ten years. Think what would happen if every city in the United States followed suit.

## THE IMPACT OF GARDENING GREEN

• Use the Missouri Botanical Garden program as a model and organize your local arboretum to sponsor an annual pot-collection day for your community. By collecting and sending your local community's pots to Agri-Plas in Oregon for recycling, you can keep thousands of tons of plastic out of the landfill every year.

# Think outside the pot by reducing the use of other garden-related plastics.

*Once you're in the mindset, you'll discover numerous other ways to reduce, reuse, or recycle many of the gardening by-products we use every day.*

If you really stop to think about it, there is a lot more we can do right at home to reduce the plastic pot proliferation paralyzing our landfills. (Excuse the tongue twister—but it was fun!) But seriously, consider that every pot you can reuse is one you have kept out of the garbage. Here are some ideas for reusing those pots:

• First, you can grow your own plants from cuttings or seeds. That's another pot you don't have to throw away. Either use a container from an earlier purchase or repurpose food containers. (A simple solution of 10 percent bleach will sterilize it, and be sure to provide a hole in the bottom for drainage.)

• You can also donate your unused plastic pots to schools for school gardens and to botanical gardens for their own propagation usage. Contact garden clubs and your local County Extension Office Master Gardener Program to see if you can donate pots for plant sales.

> **DID YOU KNOW THAT...**
>
> ❀ The agriculture industry is responsible for generating at least as much plastic as the total amount of curbside recyclables collected across the United States. Yet a very small percentage of those plastics are recycled.[1]
>
> ❀ Recycling 1 ton of plastic saves the equivalent of 1,500 gallons of gasoline.[2]

• Another option is never to bring the plastic home in the first place: a cardboard box makes for easy, tidy transport from the garden center to your home and leaves the plastic tray in the hands of the retailer to reuse.

• When considering your planting scheme, use perennials extensively in your landscape, saving small islands for annual color. This will save you not only time and effort, but you will also have fewer containers to deal with.

• When you are comfortable with the retail source, purchase mulch, compost, topsoil—anything that comes in a bag—in bulk. Just be sure you know the products don't contain pressure-treated wood, painted wood, or other unhealthy particles. If you use fertilizers or chemicals, buy the concentrated form and mix it at home. It reduces the resources needed for disposal, and you'll probably save money as well!

• If you order plants from a mail-order nursery, you can even ask if they use plastic or foam peanuts in their packaging. If they do, look around. There are plenty of businesses out there that are more eco-conscious.

• Finally, encourage the places where you do business to do their part in helping to keep plastic pots out of the landfill. Urge them to find other resources such as biodegradable pots and to persuade their industry leaders to adopt standardization methods for producing plastic pots. As I keep saying, every little bit helps!

## THE IMPACT OF GARDENING GREEN

• Taking multiple steps to reduce your consumption of plastic with your gardening can help save tons of plastic from going into the landfill every year.

# Buy plants in pots made from biodegradable material.

*Eco-friendly garden containers are nothing new.*
*But what is new is what they're being made from.*

It is mind-boggling to consider that every product we consume, from the foods we eat to the items we use every day, took energy to make, package, ship, store, and sell to us. A big part of that energy is the fossil fuels consumed in this process. We might be astonished to know actually just how much energy is used for that toothbrush or paper clip. The question of how we as individuals can take a bite out of that consumption can seem overwhelming at times.

As gardeners, we have a number of opportunities to conserve energy from products. One of the more interesting choices is the use of biodegradable plant containers. True, it may be only a small factor in the big picture, but it is one way for us to reduce the pressure on landfill space and fossil fuel consumption.

> ### DID YOU KNOW THAT...
>
> ❀ Ball Seed Company, a large wholesale distributor of plants and seeds for growers, recently introduced its "Circle of Life" pots made out of rice hulls. The pots look like brown plastic with a rough texture—but unlike plastic pots, they will break down in a landfill in 8 months.[1]
>
> ❀ CowPots™, which the manufacturer calls "the pots you plant," are a biodegradable planting pot made from composted cow manure.[2]

Eco-friendly garden containers are not new. Terra cotta pots have been around forever, but in our lifetime, plastic pots are the ubiquitous choice by the nursery industry. In terms of water retention, weight, durability, and cost, they have no equal, which is unfortunate.

The true cost to our environment from making all these plastic pots may be higher than anyone imagined, as the amount of fossil fuels used in the manufacture of all types of plastic is significant. Fortunately, options to plastic containers are becoming more popular as we find creative ways to manufacture them at a cost effective rate.

## Options besides plastic

For seedlings and smaller plants such as annuals and perennials, pots made from pressed paper pulp, peat moss, and even composted cow manure are an eco-friendly option to plastic. They can be planted directly in the ground, making it easier on us and easing the risk of transplant shock to the seedlings.

But these containment methods have not been completely embraced by the nursery industry yet. For retail sales of plant material, these pots' propensity to decompose while in inventory makes for a messy problem. But this decomposition is exactly why we should use them in our gardens as an alternative to plastic for cuttings and seedlings. Composted cow manure pots have the added advantage of fertilizing plants as they break down.

Biodegradable pots have been available for a while but are recently gaining attention as gardeners attempt to "go green" in their landscape. Coir, a product made from coconut hulls, has been used extensively as liners for open-weaved hanging baskets and window boxes. Now this natural material is being translated into compostable garden pots.

Although many biodegradable materials have been available for a while, what is new is how decorative these containers have become, making them not only functional homes for plants but artful accessories for our homes as well. Take bamboo, for example—a renewable resource with a multitude of applications. We can now add to its extensive list of uses fashionable, decorative containers with an eighteen to twenty-four-month shelf life. They're stylish and colorful, and when you're through with them, you can toss them into the compost pile where they'll break down in about six months.

Similarly, a material made from a combination of grain husks (rice shells) and coconut shells offers other decorative options. Its products last from three to five years, as long as the pot is not broken. Once broken, they will compost in nine to nineteen months.

Even old wine barrels that have outlived their original purpose can be pressed into service as planters. The wood will eventually break down over time, making them an eco-friendly alternative to plastic.

Finally, one of my favorite recyclable pots is a good old-fashioned toilet paper or paper towel tube. They make a great way to start seeds indoors. Just fill it with your favorite potting soil, place a seed or two inside, and plant it directly into the ground once the seedlings are ready for the great outdoors. If seedlings are susceptible to cut worms, leaving the top of the tube out of the ground a bit acts as a protective collar. How's that for recycling?

## THE IMPACT OF GARDENING GREEN

• Assert your convictions to nurseries and garden centers to supply plants from growers that use biodegradable pots and cell-packs. The sooner we can help this nation save millions of tons of plastics from going into the landfill every year, the better.

# Recycle old bricks and broken concrete, windows, etc.

*When you design or accessorize your garden using recycled products, you're only limited by your imagination—and ambition.*

I've already given you some ideas for composting and recycling inside your home; now take a little trip with me outside my house. I have a nice stream running through the back of my yard; it's quite wide and feeds a pond down the street. This lazy stream becomes a raging river during heavy rains, eroding its banks in its race to the pond downstream. I even built a bridge to traverse it, creating a park-like setting beyond.

DID YOU KNOW THAT. . .

✤ Construction and demolition debris account for as much as 22 percent of the waste stream entering landfills.[1]

But the banks of the stream have always bothered me. I knew they were exposed to the eroding effects of stormwater runoff, and I envisioned the banks washing away, slowly but surely. One day one of my neighbors destroyed their old driveway to make way for a new one. It occurred to me that I could use those broken pieces of concrete to line the banks, the same way rip-rap is used on lakes for erosion control.

Now this was no easy task, and yet it wasn't as hard as I thought, either. Hauling and placing large pieces of concrete all along the banks of the stream is just a grown-up version of what I did as a child all the time. Although this one driveway didn't provide all that I needed, I persevered and found other sources until the job was eventually completed.

Looking back, it is gratifying to know that I kept that concrete out of the landfill and protected the banks of the stream and the pond below.

The vegetation I planted within its pockets complemented it quite well. In fact, the combination looks so natural that most people don't even realize it is simply stacked concrete! Now I have a beautiful water feature to enjoy. You, too, can just as easily create walls, paths, or raised beds by collecting and reusing broken concrete or old bricks.

Being the passionate gardener that I am, I'm forever trying to extend the gardening season on one end or the other. Cold frames are one of the best ways to accomplish that. I fashioned a cold frame next to my house out of used windows. I was quite proud of myself, considering I'm not a carpenter. I am also able to say that these windows didn't find their way to the landfill but served a useful purpose instead.

My next project involves the 1,406 bricks I recently removed from an old walkway. Yes, I did actually count them! It was hard work moving them load by load to the back corner of my yard where they sit in neatly stacked rows, patiently waiting for their next assignment. I'm sure there's another pathway in their future soon. In the meantime, I challenge you to find ways to use, or re-use, items outside of your house. Consider what you are about to throw away, where it will end up, and whether you might be able to repurpose it in some other way. Who knows just how creative and eco-friendly you can be? You're only limited by your imagination—and ambition!

## THE IMPACT OF GARDENING GREEN

- While no one expects you to use 22 percent of the nation's waste stream as hardscape in your back yard, every little bit helps. Recycle the concrete from your old driveway into attractive retaining walls, or use those old bricks to create an inviting curved pathway, and you'll do your part in keeping rubble out of the landfill.

# Create garden art out of found objects.

*Some of the most ingenious pieces of garden art come from rescues and found objects in places ranging from the obvious to the obscure.*

Now I don't consider myself artistic by any means. I may be clever, but I can't take every remnant of an architectural item and create art out of it. That doesn't mean I'm not fascinated by the ability of others to recycle found objects into interesting pieces of garden art. I even have a book on it. It is appropriately called "Garden Junk", by Mary Randolph Carter, and provides me with inspiration if not actual application.

> **DID YOU KNOW THAT...**
>
> ❀ Cracked Pots in Portland, Oregon, is the brainstorm of garden designer Tess Beistel and artist Mary Lou Ablen. It supplies novel materials salvaged from landfills and junkyards (Portland sends more than 1,500 tons of discarded items to landfills daily) to artists throughout the area. In one of its yearly sales of art made from castoffs, Cracked Pots raised more than $90,000.[1]

One of my favorite garden junkies is Felder Rushing, author and former Mississippi extension agent. If anyone epitomizes the ability to be creative with cast-offs, he does! Nothing is sacred. From old tires used as planters to "bottle trees" fashioned by using dowels inserted into old tree trunks. Even lumber posts can serve as makeshift trunks to display a collection of colorful bottles supported by dowels that become the branches. (I'm too right-brained to think of that!)

Even if clever construction is not your forté, collections can be. Consider the lowly wheelbarrow, a piece of garden history that can be utilized visually as well. I remember neatly arranged, colorful, old wheelbarrows in a Seattle community garden, lined up against the fence. Although still put to use, they struck me as architectural, more art than utilitarian. I have the pictures to prove it.

Perhaps you've even noticed a rusty old bicycle, propped against a garden fence. The wicker basket strapped to the handle bar explodes with color from seasonal annuals. What a sight!

I'm not saying we must all run out to the salvage yards, scooping up bits and pieces to save them from the landfill. Oh heck, yes I am! Some of the most creative uses of garden art were rescues from such places.

There is an all too forgotten saying: "Use it up, wear it out, make it do, or do without." That may be a mouthful, but it's true. I prefer a simpler version that says the same thing; "One man's trash is another man's treasure." We are a society of planned obsolescence. Why not put some of those obsolete *treasures* to use in your garden?

 THE IMPACT OF GARDENING GREEN

- With a little creativity, by recycling what used to be junk into attractive and unique garden features you can help save just a little more space in the landfill.

# CHAPTER SIX

# CONSUMING LESS ENERGY

I have enjoyed gardening so much as a hobby and passion in my life, and I've been fortunate enough to earn my living at it as well. Some might think that when you're immersed in something so much, you may start to take some things for granted that less seasoned gardeners still find fascinating. I'm happy to say that has never happened with me. I'm every bit as excited to spend time in a garden today as I was when I was first bitten by the gardening bug—many years ago.

Part of the reason for my never-ending obsession with gardening is that the more I know, the more I realize I don't know . . . and that creates passion and a thirst to immerse myself in it even more. As a lifetime student of gardening, nature, and the environment, I find myself wanting to protect it and nurture it, to keep it pure and untarnished. Without even realizing it, I've been enlisted as one of her most devoted guardians.

Yes, I do this for myself so that I will have a place to go like the haven I discovered when I first fell in love with gardening and the outdoors. And I have children. I protect her for them so they won't have to only imagine the wonders I've known. I protect her for all the others, the ones who may never have the chance without help from people like me to look after her. This is why I've become so aware of the changes happening all around us, every day of our lives.

The natural resources that many of us still take for granted are diminishing, and it's happing at a faster rate than ever before. I know this is the case around our land, and so much of what has been damaged may never recover. And although I know our earth is resilient, I feel the burden not only to stop the decline but also to help lead in her recovery.

But how does one person go about such an ambitious mission? Thankfully, there isn't just one person—not just you and not just me—although it may seem like it sometimes. There are many, many others who share the same desire and vision. But until most, if not all, of us grasp the depth of the consequences and height of the opportunity, we will have our work cut out for us.

Another challenge we face as individuals trying to make a difference on this planet is wondering if our efforts really make a difference. In this book, I refer to the expression, "It's the little things that add up." I think about this truth often as I face off against a plethora of obstacles. Indeed, there are numerous simple actions we can take (and *not* take as well) if we're going to impact our planet in a positive way.

Life seems to be all about the dos and don'ts, doesn't it? As a parent, I am reminded of this every day. It seems I'm always telling my girls what they *can't* do, and their question back is always, "Well then, what *can* we do?" There's a lesson here as we look for ways to be more eco-friendly in our gardens and beyond. Although we hear about all the steps we should take, there are also many things we shouldn't be doing as we find ways to protect and preserve our planet. After all, seemingly small bad habits and actions are how we got into this

> DID YOU KNOW THAT. . .
>
> ❀ Fifty-seven percent of the energy used in the average U.S. home is for heating and cooling. Plants, particularly as they provide shade, protection from the wind, and the cooling effect of evapotranspiration, can play a significant role in the amount needed to heat and cool our homes for comfort.[1]
>
> ❀ The energy used in the average U.S. residence results in the emission of 26,000 pounds of carbon dioxide per year. Of those 26,000 pounds, 14,800 are from heating and cooling.[2]

❀ Gasoline-powered lawn equipment is responsible for about 10 percent of all mobile-source hydrocarbon emissions in the U.S. and is the single largest contributor to non-road emissions.[3]

❀ The amount of natural gas required to make approximately 200 bags of lawn fertilizer would heat the average U.S. home for a year. Each 40-pound bag of fertilizer contains the equivalent of approximately 2.5 gallons of gasoline.[4]

predicament in the first place. *Little things add up.*

On a positive note, there are so many wonderful and effective actions we can take as gardeners to actually reduce energy consumption, conserve water, and purify the air we breathe. And that's one reason I love gardening. In addition to the beauty it provides and the healing it brings to our minds, the very act of gardening can benefit our world in simple yet significant ways. Enjoy the information ahead as we focus in this chapter on ways to reduce nonrenewable energy consumption and protect our air quality.

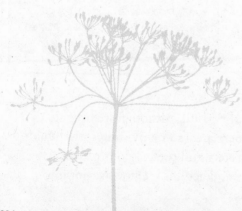

# Plant trees, tall shrubs, and vines to reduce your home's cooling needs.

*The shade cast by plants can play a vital role
in energy savings for cooling our homes.*

How many of us can remember a time when homes were only heated in the winter and not air-conditioned in the summer? Back then, we weren't used to having the perfect climate inside, and as kids, I don't think we really knew what we were missing.

That was a long time ago. Today, the majority of us live in a year-round, climate-controlled environment. In fact, 78 percent of single-family homes in America have some form of air conditioning. That's a lot of energy demand, especially as our climate heats up. Going forward, think about how much energy is needed to keep that perfect climate going year-round in your house.

Just as we humans benefit from the cooling effects of shade outside, our home's

> DID YOU KNOW THAT...
>
> ❀ Nearly all air conditioning is accomplished with electricity. The average amount of electricity consumed for cooling per home is about 11,000 kilowatt hours per year; nationwide, that accounts for about 9 percent of our total residential energy consumption.[1]
>
> ❀ Well-positioned, appropriately chosen trees around your house can reduce indoor temperatures by up to 20 degrees and save between 10 to 40 percent in energy use for cooling each year, compared to a wide open landscape.[2]

interior climate benefits as well. It's easy to forget that what's going on outside can profoundly affect how our homes operate and feel inside.

Planning ahead for plants that keep your home cooler naturally can affect how much energy we consume.

On the west or south side of your house, planting a combination of deciduous trees and very tall shrubs will block those summer rays. The trees will eventually drop their leaves, allowing the warm winter sun into your home. Consider planting large deciduous vines trained on a trellis, arbor, or pergola running in front of or over south- or west-facing windows, doors, and porches. They too will cast welcome shade in the summer and allow sunlight in the winter.

 THE IMPACT OF GARDENING GREEN

• By growing well-positioned trees around your home, you can reduce your energy use for cooling by 10 to 40 percent.

• With the average household using about 11,000 kilowatt hours a year for air conditioning, if just 100,000 households in the U.S. improved their shade plantings and saved a conservative amount of 10 percent of the energy they use for cooling, that would result in a national savings of 110 million kilowatt hours every year.

• If every homeowner planted shade trees around his or her house, the energy used for cooling our homes could be slashed by 20 to 40 percent nationwide.

# Plant an evergreen hedge or windbreak to reduce your home's heating needs.

*One of your tree's specialties is taking a bite out of your heating bill.*

Protecting your home from cold winter winds is a job for evergreen trees and shrubs. They are the ideal windbreak plant. Even in the coldest weather, their leaves or needles will diffuse winds. On the north side of your home, especially in the colder climates of the northern half of the U.S., plantings to slow those howling winter winds can help prevent wind from working its way into your home's nooks and crevices.

As a rule of thumb, plant the windbreak as far away from your home as the plant's mature height. For instance if you're planting a hedge of yews that will top out at eight feet, plant them so their outermost branches will be at least eight feet from the north wall of your home. Similarly, if you're planting a hedge of cedars that will top out at forty feet, plant them so that even when they have a mature spread of perhaps fifteen feet, the perimeter of the trees is still forty feet from your home.

> **DID YOU KNOW THAT...**
>
> ❀ According to one government study, smartly planted windbreaks can reduce heating bills by as much as 15 percent.[1]
>
> ❀ Windbreaks not only reduce your heating bill and result in a subsequent reduction of power plant emissions, they also create wildlife habitat, clean the air, and have a cooling effect on your yard, neighborhood, and community in the summer time.[2]
>
> ❀ Nearly 48 percent of the energy we use in our homes is for space-heating.[3]

This assures that you won't plant your windbreak so far away from the house that it's useless, or plant it so close that it overwhelms your home; endangers the foundation, sidewalk, and driveway; or blocks healthy natural light during winter. The ideal windbreak stretches somewhat longer than the width of your home so that the house also has some protection from northeast and northwest winds.

The east side of your home is not as critical for protection since winter winds usually intrude from the north and west. In fact, in the northern third of the country where nights can be cool during the summer, the summer morning sun is often welcome. Plant evergreen trees and shrubs on this side of the house with caution, or use them in combination with deciduous varieties.

## THE IMPACT OF GARDENING GREEN

- Plant a windbreak to reduce your home's heating energy usage by as much as 15 percent.

- With a typical home responsible for the emission of around 12,500 pounds of carbon dioxide a year, if 100,000 homes in the northern regions of the U.S. planted trees as a windbreak and reduced their energy use by 15 percent, 1.25 million pounds less of carbon dioxide would be emitted into the atmosphere every year.

# Plant trees to purify the air.

*Trees are a feast for the eyes and a breath of fresh air . . . literally!*

All too often I think we take the *functionality* of trees for granted. I know I do. When I look at trees, I am in awe of their beauty. I marvel at their shape, sculptural features, or the color and texture of their leaves. I'm taken aback at the symphony of hues that color the landscape in the fall. With so much to admire visually, I often fail to appreciate trees for their greatest gift, one more important than even their aesthetic qualities.

Trees have been called the lungs of the planet, and for good reason. They play a vital role in helping to control air pollution by taking in carbon dioxide, storing the carbon, and then releasing oxygen during photosynthesis. Of all the vegetation on our planet, trees are the real workhorses in this department.

According to the Maryland Department of Natural Resources, over a year's time, trees absorb enough carbon dioxide on each acre to equal the amount you produce when you drive your car twenty-six thousand miles. That's an impressive amount of work for a plant revered for its pleasure and beauty.

> **DID YOU KNOW THAT...**
>
> ❀ Over time, planting just one tree can have a big effect. An 80-foot beech tree has been shown to remove daily carbon dioxide amounts equivalent to that produced by two single-family dwellings.[1]
>
> ❀ Tree foliage also removes nitrogen oxides, airborne ammonia, sulfur dioxide, and ozone from the air—all pollutants that contribute to smog and greenhouse gases. According to the Center for Urban Forest Research, an average tree absorbs 10 pounds of such pollutants from the air each year, including 4 pounds of ozone and 3 pounds of particulates.[2]

In addition to trees' overall benefits, tree leaves remove harmful chemicals such as nitrogen oxides, airborne ammonia, some sulfur

## THE IMPACT OF GARDENING GREEN

• If 100,000 homeowners planted a tree, they would collectively remove one million pounds of pollutants from the air each year.

dioxide, and ozone—harmful gases that contribute to smog and "greenhouse effect" problems. At the same time, trees are cooling the air by releasing water vapor through their leaves in a process known as *transpiration.*

Trees also serve as collection sites for massive amounts of dust and harmful man-made particulates that can be eventually washed to the ground by rainwater, then filtered and purified through the earth.

The benefits of trees are compounded when you consider that they not only store such huge amounts of carbon but also reduce carbon emissions by decreasing energy use. And if that weren't enough, shade trees are primarily responsible for reducing the intense "heat island effect" created in urban areas by high concentrations of impervious surfaces such as buildings, roadways, and sidewalks.

You don't have to have a large yard to make a difference; all plants clean the air. Even shrubs and houseplants are helpful to some extent. Give the gift of a tree to a friend or family member or even to yourself, because young trees are more efficient at cleaning the air than some very old ones. Donate one to a school on Arbor Day or Earth Day or any day! I can't think of a better gift to give that looks so good, lasts so long, and does so much. Now if they could only invent kid's toys this way . . .

# Install and plant a green roof to reduce cooling needs.

*Green roofs slow runoff, reduce temperatures inside and out, and purify the air.*

One of the biggest global opportunities we have to positively impact our carbon footprint is to plant green roofs. They cool the air in and above our homes and offices, absorb carbon dioxide, return oxygen, reduce runoff, filter pollutants, and provide habitats for birds and other wildlife—and even provide a respite for our mind and body. So much space, so much opportunity.

The concept of green roofs is far from new. Probably the most famous "green roof" is the Hanging Gardens of Babylon dating from 500 BC. Green roofs have been used extensively across Europe for energy savings and aesthetics and are only relatively new to the United States. You may be surprised to know that Rockefeller Center in New York has a green roof that was planted in the 1930s.

Even though green roofs have been around for a while, constructing one is not a simple matter of dumping some soil on your roof and planting it with grass or flowers. A considerable amount of engineering goes into such a project and is better left to professionals. Besides calculating the weight limit of the roof structure, waterproofing is the most important factor to consider. Green roofs can contribute a minimum of twelve to more than one hundred fifty pounds of extra weight per square foot. And even the greenest of roofs won't do you much good if it collapses on you or leaks water every time it rains!

## Understanding green roofs

Simply put, a green roof is made up of a waterproof layer covered with layers of a variety of growing mediums. To drastically reduce runoff, these mediums are specifically engineered to be light, yet

✿ Studies have shown that green roofs can reduce the cooling load in a building—and the energy costs for cooling—by 25 percent. It is not unusual for a green roof to reduce the cooling load of the upper floor directly under the roof by as much as 60 percent.[1]

✿ According to the U.S. Environmental Protection Agency, green roofs also reduce sewage system loads by absorbing large amounts of rainwater and preventing runoff; by absorbing air pollution, collecting airborne particulates, and storing carbon; by serving as living environments that provide habitats for birds and other small animals; by offering an attractive alternative to traditional roofs; and by reducing noise transfer inside the home from the outdoors.[2]

stable enough, for plant roots to hold water long enough for adequate filtration, yet still drain properly.

*Intensive* green roofs take the concept even further. They contain a foot or more of planting medium that allows for a wider variety of plant material, including even some large trees. But they do require elaborate drainage systems and significant maintenance. *Extensive* green roofs are designed for more drought-tolerant, shallow-rooted plants that penetrate the surface from one to five inches deep. They are probably most appropriate on the flat roofs of office buildings, parking decks, and industrial parks, although the concept can be applied to slightly sloping roofs as well.

"Why a green roof?" you might ask. Where else can you get that much flat open space in the middle of a concrete jungle? Actually, there's much more to it than that. A multitude of benefits exists to planting a green roof, and most are related to reducing pollution. Green roofs can alleviate stormwater runoff by 60 to 80 percent. That's significant when you consider just how many office buildings and flat roofs there are in any given city. Just take note the next time you fly into your own hometown or visit another city.

Along with the reduction and filtration of water runoff, the plants on a green roof act as they do in nature: trapping particles, absorbing pollutants and carbon dioxide, giving off oxygen and transpiring water vapor. The payback is substantial in energy savings and in easing the heat island effect by reducing temperatures both inside the building and on the roof. The roof itself is protected from damaging UV light, extending its life two to three times (which is always a good thing—who wants to replace that planted roof any sooner than you have to?).

Speaking of benefits, green roofs insulate buildings from more than just high outside temperatures; they shield them from noise as well. Other pluses include providing habitats for birds and insects, providing space for recreation, and even allowing for food production. The psychological benefits of having a green roof are enormous, but difficult to calculate.

As for concerns, the most problematic issue about a green roof is that it's usually practical only with new construction, but not always. Also, it can be difficult to find a knowledgeable contractor to install a green roof. Search the Internet. Greenroofs.com is an excellent source of general information and provides a directory of green roof contractors.

## THE IMPACT OF GARDENING GREEN

- Install a green roof on your home and you can reduce your air-conditioning costs by 25 percent.[3]

- If 100,000 households nationwide (that's just one household in every city and town in the U.S.) installed a green roof, we would reduce electricity consumption in the U.S. by 275 million kilowatt hours every year.

# Plant a large perennial garden, prairie garden, or meadow garden.

*Perennials, grasses, and native plants offer more than an aesthetic appeal.*

Whenever you opt for plants rather than pavement, the net effect is to cool your immediate area and provide a visual treat for you and your neighbors as well.

Lawns are good. Trees are better. But I find something especially appealing about perennials, grasses, and native plants. They contribute shade, trap pollutants, and afford infiltration of rainwater like other plants. They are virtually carefree, providing a visual treat without being finicky, and their ease of culture may give the beginning gardener the confidence to try something different.

A perennial garden is a richly diverse habitat, perfect for butterflies, bees, and other beneficial wildlife to make use of. Better yet, once planted and established, a perennial garden returns year after year.

I also love the look and feel of a prairie or meadow planting—a large, sunny spot filled with those native and other plants that practically take care of themselves—oxeye daisies, purple coneflowers, black-eyed Susans, asters, native grasses, perennial sunflowers, beebalm, butterfly milkweed, or just about anything else that grows well (but not too well!) in your community.

Remember, some plants are considered invasive in some parts of the country but not others. Plan to do a little research before committing to plants that may be considered *overly enthusiastic* in your region. Your county extension service is a good place to start.

Native perennials and grasses require less of a space commitment, and you don't have to wait as long for them to reach maturity compared to trees. Another benefit is that they require less water, fertilizers, and care than lawns. For the time-challenged, most perennial, prairie, and meadow plantings need little more than an annual cutting back in late fall. Depending on your region, perennial gardens may only need an occasional watering once established, while meadow and prairie plantings can often go without supplemental watering after the first year.

Native plantings perform well without repeated applications of fertilizers and chemicals to control disease and insect problems. Properly planted, natives are content with an annual topdressing of compost. The bonus is two-fold: Not only are you limiting the release of chemicals into the soil, but in the process of composting, you are contributing far less to landfill volume.

## THE IMPACT OF GARDENING GREEN

• Replacing large areas of lawn with native herbaceous perennials can help reduce the consumption of fossil fuels used in maintaining that lawn. If you replaced half of the area currently occupied by a lawn with herbaceous perennials and shrubs, and reduced your gasoline consumption by half, the average household would save about 3 gallons of gas per year. If every household in the U.S. did this, it would save about 300 million gallons of gas per year and cut the total amount of non-road-source hydrocarbon emissions in the U.S. in half.

# Use eco-friendly paving for driveways and parking areas.

*Porous paving can have a cooling effect as well as controlling runoff.*

You've heard the expression, "cat on a hot tin roof," of course. I imagine that expression would be just as appropriate if you inserted "driveway" or "parking lot" for tin roof, judging from the heat I've seen and felt rising from those surfaces.

> **DID YOU KNOW THAT. . .**
>
> ❀ Eco-Pavers, a Japanese product that looks like regular pavers, is highly porous, so the pavers stay cooler and hold moisture; they are purported to stay 3.5° F to 5.5° F cooler than the air above them and about 18° F cooler than asphalt.[1]
>
> ❀ When planted with grass, an open-cell paver driveway or parking area laid with the pavers that allow soil to be packed into them can be as much as 70 percent turf.[2]

As I mentioned in Chapter 4, the use of porous paving reduces runoff and erosion but can also have a net cooling effect as well. We should all fight the paving of America! Individually, we can opt for using open-cell or porous material blocks instead of solid cement. These can be placed so that plant material can be used in the joints. Some designs allow grass to grow within them, and all minimize reflected heat, absorb water runoff, and help us all keep our cool.

Open-cell concrete block is available in an assortment of designs under a variety of names. Essentially, they're hollow concrete blocks or tubes, often with a decorative pattern, set so soil can be spread inside for growing grass or other traffic-tolerant plants.

Open-cell concrete is ideal for driveways, patios, parking areas, alleys, pathways, and just about any other place you might use concrete or traditional pavers. They're just as easy to install as cement, and if you're a real plantaholic, instead of using grass or allowing wild plants to reseed in them, you can plant them with compact, traffic-resistant, drought-tolerant groundcovers. In a cool, moist climate, you can plant them with mosses, if the foot traffic isn't too heavy.

Much research is being conducted on the use of reflective paving to greatly limit the amount of heat that is absorbed and later released into the atmosphere. "Plantable" pavers and so-called "cool" paving work together to reduce the overall heat island effect of many of our large cities. On a smaller scale, these types of surfaces can work to cool your own little corner of the world, too.

## THE IMPACT OF GARDENING GREEN

• Grass paving is a way to have the structural benefits of hard pavement for driveways and parking areas while still enjoying the cooling effects of a lawn. When it's time to replace your concrete or asphalt driveway and parking areas, replace them with open-cell concrete block paving, grow grass inside the cells, and you'll enjoy an area near your house that is 3.5° F to 5.5° F cooler in the summer than it was before.

# Use passive solar design in a greenhouse.

*Building a greenhouse with passive solar heating extends the season and the ways you can save energy, too.*

Greenhouse. The word itself is like music to my ears. I've always wanted a greenhouse, and in the future I will have one . . . just not today. Although I think I'd be happy with about any type of "glass" house, in my mind's eye my greenhouse is a passive solar design that doesn't rely on complicated electrical systems for heating and misting.

While all greenhouses collect and retain heat for periods of time, a passive solar greenhouse is as natural as they come. A free-standing design integrates the thermal mass of materials like concrete, stone, and water, used on the floor and/or the north wall so that heat is collected and stored during the day. With proper insulation of the thermal mass, this warmth is then slowly released at night or on cloudy days.

DID YOU KNOW THAT. . .

❋ A passive solar greenhouse supplies a large portion or all of its own heat. It's designed with materials that absorb heat and then store it. This "heat sink" can consist of barrels of water, rocks, concrete walls, or other thermal mass. At night, the stored heat emanates back through the greenhouse.

Of course I'm making this sound much simpler than it is. The reality is that multiple components factor into the construction of passive solar design. Designers must consider the area's latitude, the building's orientation, the angle of both the sun and the glazing (glass or plastic), in addition to providing adequate insulation and natural ventilation. When any of these mechanics are off balance, you risk freezing in the winter and frying in the summer. These issues are one reason that the construction of passive solar greenhouses is one project best left to professionals.

Passive solar greenhouses can become a large foundation for your home's heating and cooling. Lean-to designs can be attached to the main house, making it possible for enough solar heat to be captured during the day to actually contribute warmth to the home. This is also true of a well-designed passive solar atrium incorporated into a house.

The greenhouse I envision has a beautiful stone foundation about three feet high with a thick stone wall on the north side. Its longest side will face due south with no trees obstructing the sun's rays from the stone surfaces. I will use it to overwinter tender perennials, to start seeds, and even to produce a few edibles. Of course there will be a place to sit on sunny winter mornings to take in the arrival of a new day. I'll have an extra chair, so come by for a visit. I'll keep the coffee hot.

## THE IMPACT OF GARDENING GREEN

• A greenhouse in New York City could require 108,000 Btu on a typical winter day to keep it heated. A comparable greenhouse with passive solar design would not require any heat and perhaps could even contribute heat to an attached home.[1]

• If 100,000 people who currently heat their greenhouses for ninety days of the year with electricity had similarly sized passive solar greenhouses instead, they would annually save more than 113 billion pounds of carbon dioxide from being put into the air.[2]

# Buy locally grown and processed garden materials.

*Buying locally produced gardening and landscaping material reduces countless energy miles burned in the transport of those products from far away places.*

Many of us are already familiar with the term *food miles*. It refers to the distance that food had to travel to get to your kitchen table. Today's fruits and vegetables often travel thousands of miles before reaching the produce counters at our grocery stores. Although this global transporting isn't ideal, it is the reason why you can buy watermelon twelve months a year if you really want one. But I hope you are patient. Why? Because eating food that's local and in-season cuts down tremendously on the energy and fuel consumption needed to import out-of-season products. It also supports our local economies. Besides, local in-season food is fresher; it tastes better and is better for you.

> **DID YOU KNOW THAT...**
>
> ❀ Depending on how you calculate it, if you purchase 10, 3-cubic-foot bags of mulch that have been delivered from 200 miles away, the bags' delivery used up half a gallon of diesel fuel for their delivery. This doesn't even include the energy used to produce and package that mulch before it arrived.

The same reasoning behind the concept of food miles can apply to *everything* we buy. So why not consider saving *energy miles* too? Energy that would otherwise be consumed to package and transport materials such as mulch, stone, topsoil, vegetables, plants, and more can be saved by buying locally whenever possible. It is an especially smart idea to purchase local and regionally grown plants, as they are more adapted to your area and often perform better. It makes perfect sense.

The ultimate ideal of course is to recycle as many materials as you can that are already in your landscape—grass clippings and wood chips for mulch, compost for nutrient-rich topsoil, fieldstone collected with permission from a local farmer or landowner to be used for hardscapes . . . you get the idea. But if you cannot collect these materials yourself, do your community a favor and try to buy locally—in other words, something generated within fifty to one hundred miles or so from your home. Community-supported endeavors such as this are solid and significant ways to vote with your conscience and your pocketbook.

It's not hard these days to find sources. Check the Yellow Pages and the Internet for suppliers near you that carry the materials you're looking for. And if you can't find what you want, call a nearby landscaping company and ask them. They may have access to special stockpiles of materials they can sell from, or they may be willing to recommend a small, independent supplier that derives its stock from local sources.

## THE IMPACT OF GARDENING GREEN

• Purchase garden materials locally rather than making a purchase originating 200 or more miles away, and you'll save an average of nearly ½ gallon of diesel fuel per purchase.

• If just half of the 90 million gardeners in the U.S. made one local purchase a year, it would save 16.65 million gallons of diesel fuel, not to mention the pollution the diesel engines emit.

# Grow your own fruits, vegetables, herbs, and other edibles.

*Homegrown fruits and vegetables taste better than any store-bought product, plus it's healthier for you, your family, and your planet.*

And I thought *I* traveled a lot! Recently I was on an overseas trip and was bumped from First Class by a crate of tomatoes that had more frequent flyer miles than I did! But seriously folks, do we really need to eat watermelon in the winter? It just doesn't seem normal, and it's not. Buy strawberries out of season or pick up a rock-hard tomato in February, and you know they've traveled hundreds if not thousands of miles. That doesn't even take into consideration the fuel costs of heating the greenhouse and producing the fertilizer and chemicals to keep plants pumped up or even to create the packaging it arrives in.

DID YOU KNOW THAT...

❧ In a Midwestern state, such as Iowa, most fruits and vegetables have traveled an average of 1,500 miles (according to the Leopold Center for Sustainable Agriculture at Iowa State University).[1]

The whole "buy local" movement that I mentioned in the previous tip is a result of environmentally aware consumers taking note of the incredible environmental costs associated with shipping foods across vast distances.

For me, a much nicer solution is a vegetable garden at my fingertips in my own back yard. That way I'll have a much clearer picture of the fuel costs of growing my own. While I can't predict precisely the amount of fossil fuels I'll save by using fewer chemical products, I know I'm contributing something to cleaner air and a healthier body.

There is little that is more gratifying to me than harvesting the fruits of my own labor, with the added pleasure of eating in tune with the seasons: early spring's first radishes and greens; summer's bounty of tomatoes, peppers, and berries; and fall's harvest of pumpkins, squash, and cabbages. And here's a final thought to consider: there are no fuel costs or food miles associated with walking into your backyard to pick the perfect meal. (That is unless of course you have a really, really big backyard.)

## THE IMPACT OF GARDENING GREEN

• When you grow produce in your own backyard, not only do you save on the fuel costs for each meal, but you also become part of a collective trend that diminishes demand for produce transported long distances.

• When you choose to eat only fruits and vegetables in season, you directly support your local growers and help the environment. The resulting reduced demand for "out of season" produce will slash the number of food miles being consumed from all the imports that travel thousands of miles to get here.

# Reduce the use of fertilizers made from fossil fuels.

*Gardening as chemically free as possible has many benefits in my eco-friendly garden.*

I try to garden as chemically free as possible and encourage others to do so as well. But, I realize there will always be those who won't give up their traditional chemical fertilizers and pest controls.

Environmentalists' concerns have been primarily from the perspective of the amount of salts left behind in the soil and the effect of excess nitrogen entering our waterways. These ills can be mitigated by prompting the user to follow the package directions appropriately.

DID YOU KNOW THAT...

❀ An average lawn of 5,000 square feet with a typical application of 3 pounds of nitrogen per 1,000 square feet per year equates to the use of about 25 cubic feet of natural gas and 367,500 Btu of energy— the equivalent of 3 gallons of gasoline.[1]

❀ The amount of natural gas required to make approximately 200 bags of lawn fertilizer would heat your home for a year, according to the University of Vermont Extension Service.[2]

But there are mounting concerns about how much natural gas, a key ingredient in synthetic fertilizers, is gobbled up in their manufacturing process. Since it takes fossil fuels to manufacture synthetic fertilizers, limiting their use in the garden will reduce the expenditure of an environmentally limited resource.

The U.S. Department of Agriculture reports that it takes 1.65 cubic feet of natural gas, along with 24,500 Btu of energy, to produce just one pound of nitrogen fertilizer. And according to the EPA, seventy-eight million pounds of herbicides and pesticides are used by homeowners on just their lawns each year. American consumers have a tendency to think that if one tablespoon is good, two or even three is better. That can't be further from the truth, and the cumulative effect is very dangerous.

## Finding a fix for fossil fuels

So what can we do to combat the consumption of fossil fuels? There's no denying, compost is king when it comes to an easy, natural way for creating a nutrient-rich soil amendment for your lawn and garden. I do realize making the quantity needed to cover the average-sized residential landscape is a tall order, even for the most enthusiastic composting fans out there. But there are other sources for the consumer, and if you can't make enough yourself, you should be able to purchase the rest in bags or bulk.

Creating and promoting the existence of healthy living soil and then feeding it with natural, organic amendments and nutrients will keep your lawn and garden thriving, without the need for excess or supplemental chemicals. I can't think of any better way to rehabilitate our chemically dependent lawns and gardens!

For more about the many benefits of compost as a great soil amendment and an alternative to fertilizer, be sure to review the tips in Chapter 3. There are also other helpful ideas for alternative ways to provide nutrients to your lawn and garden while reducing the amount of manufactured chemicals you use.

## THE IMPACT OF GARDENING GREEN

• If each of the estimated 90 million gardeners in the U.S. reduced fertilizer use by just 1 pound of nitrogen a year, it would result in a savings of more than 138 million cubic feet of natural gas and more than 2 billion Btu of energy.

# Reduce the use of gasoline-powered engines.

*Cleaning up our landscapes is creating a much bigger problem abroad. And it's getting out of control.*

OK, I'll admit it . . . I'm a tool guy when it comes to gardening. I can relate to Tim Taylor and his quest for "more power." But, over the years my attitude has well . . . softened. As I sharpen my eco-friendly savvy, my desire to rev up the machines dulls. The more I realize how the use of gasoline-powered tools impacts the environment we all share, the less apt I am to pull out a flame thrower when a match will do.

The Environmental Protection Agency tells us that eight hundred million gallons of gasoline are being burned each weekend by fifty-four million Americans simply mowing their lawns.[4] And that figure doesn't even include gas-powered chipper-shredders, snow blowers, leaf vacuums and blowers, hedge trimmers, power washers and the like that keep our homes and gardens looking pristine.

DID YOU KNOW THAT. . .

❀ According to a Yale University study, the U.S. used more than 600 million gallons of gasoline every year in lawn mowing and trimming alone. (The EPA has estimated it at as much as 800 million gallons.)[1]

❀ Compared to a battery-powered and corded mower, a gasoline-powered mower emits far more contaminants: 1,500 times more carbon monoxide, 31 times more hydrocarbons and nitrogen dioxides, and 18 times more carbon dioxide.[2]

❀ The gasoline-powered small engines used for lawn maintenance in the U.S. (mostly mowers, string trimmers, and blowers) contribute about 10 percent of the total mobile-source hydrocarbon emissions each year. They are the largest single contributor to non-road emissions in the U.S.[3]

Gasoline-powered garden tools not only suck up fuel, they also emit air and noise pollution. We learn from the EPA that one gasoline-powered mower used for an hour pollutes as much as forty late model cars. And all those other gas-powered tools like leaf blowers and weed eaters pollute even more. Not to mention how much engine oil they consume in their crankcases, or fuel in their two-stroke engines.

Electric models tend to be a better choice, though even they take fossil fuels to manufacture and ship. And the spent battery of a cordless model can emit lead as it breaks down, a real hazard if it ends up in a landfill. That's why it is imperative to dispose of these items properly. Corded models are a bit more planet-friendly even though they require the use of electricity, pulling power off the grid. I haven't seen a solar model yet, but perhaps it's out there on the horizon!

Of course the most environmentally responsible tools also offer the greatest health benefits. They're the ones fueled by good, old-fashioned muscle and grit: "people power" for lack of a better term. A reel mower, a saw, grass shears, a rake—all these are highly cost effective and don't take a drop of gasoline to power. With the occasional glass of iced tea or lemonade, the fuel tank of the operator should run just fine.

## THE IMPACT OF GARDENING GREEN

- If just 1 out of every 4 gardeners switched to a reel mower and grass shears, that would save from 75 to 200 million gallons of gasoline each year. It could also reduce the total amount of mobile hydrocarbon emissions in the U.S. by 2.5 percent.

# Reduce the size of your lawn—and care for it more responsibly.

*To benefit from a lawn's redeeming qualities*
*perhaps a compromise is in order.*

Each year I find that my lawn gets smaller and smaller . . . by design. Although I have many friends who have sworn off their lawns for eternity, opting instead for a low maintenance groundcover alternative, I have not yet reached this level of extreme. In fact, I doubt I ever will. I still enjoy the look and feel of a well manicured lawn, even if it is a small one. On the other hand, I recognize the responsibility to maintain my lawn in an environmentally responsible manner and know it can be quite demanding if I let my guard down.

DID YOU KNOW THAT. . .

❀ Each weekend, about 54 million Americans mow their lawns, using an estimated 800 million gallons of gas per year and producing tons of air pollutants, according to EPA figures.[1]

❀ An average suburban lawn of 10,000 square feet with a typical application of 3 pounds of nitrogen per 1,000 square feet per year would use about 25 cubic feet of natural gas and 367,500 Btu of energy—the equivalent of 3 gallons of gasoline—every year.[2]

As the previous tips illustrate, a heavily maintained lawn is an environmental disaster in the making. While lawns are lovely to look at and have numerous benefits, the traditionally coddled lawn wastes natural resources and human energy. Lawns are the greatest consumers of water compared to other vegetation, and we tend to waste that water by applying much more than is needed. In our maintenance regimes, lawns consume a great deal of fossil fuel to run mowers, trimmers, and edgers, and natural gas is used in the process of creating the fertilizers, pesticides, and herbicides that carpet it. Whew!

But once again, a lawn, especially a thoughtfully maintained lawn, does have certain advantages. It is, after all, made up of plants that through the power of photosynthesis cool and purify the air. Its leaf blades trap dust and other particles that would otherwise become pollutants. Its cooling expanse helps moderate temperatures around our homes and buffers the flow of runoff into storm drains and watersheds.

In my ecological journey, I've reconciled my lust for lawn with my sense of responsibility to be a better environmental steward. My compromise gives me the best of both worlds—a smaller lawn that I can still enjoy and a more eco-friendly environment.

As I reduce the size of my lawn each year, I always think I'll miss the part I'm giving up. The truth is, by the time I go back and fill in that space with a variety of different plants, I can't wait until the next year, when I get to plant more new things. But those years are numbered. I only have so much space left to sacrifice.

## THE IMPACT OF GARDENING GREEN

If each household reduced its traditionally maintained lawn by ¼, the EPA estimates that our country would use 200 million fewer gallons of gasoline a year. It would reduce the nation's air pollution by more than 2.5 percent, and it would reduce the nation's use of fertilizer by nearly 2 billion pounds—the equivalent in fossil fuel consumption of 192 million gallons of gasoline.

# Keep engines properly maintained for maximum efficiency.

*An ounce of prevention . . . is worth far more than that in saved fuel and reduced emissions.*

Any handyperson knows to maintain his or her tools for maximum performance. To do so, start with a novel idea: Read the instruction manual. Following the manufacturer's guidelines for maintenance should provide maximum efficiency of the tool. It's amazing how hard that is for some of us to do. Even when the directions are still close at hand, we often ignore them, from the chemicals we use to the equipment we purchase. My set of instructions? Well, they've already been shredded and composted!

> **DID YOU KNOW THAT...**
>
> ❀ The EPA has stated that "small engines are big polluters. And power equipment users inadvertently contribute to the problem by carelessly handling fuel and by improperly maintaining their equipment."[1]

The environmentally conscientious gardener knows that maintenance is important. After all, good maintenance also means that you'll use less fuel, pollute less, and your tools will last longer, saving the energy that goes into purchasing new ones and the waste of tossing poorly maintained ones into the landfill.

## Maintaining engines

Each time you use lawn and garden equipment, try to remember these suggestions: remove debris from the air intake screen, muffler, oil filter, and other areas as needed. It's amazing how simply keeping a tool clean will help to make sure it runs well. If it's a four-cycle engine, check the oil level. If it's a two-cycle engine, be sure to use the correct fuel/oil mixture.

Otherwise, once or twice a year (in cold climates, right before you put the tool away for the winter) with a four-cycle engine, drain the old oil into a container through the drain plug or pour it out through the filler hole and refill with new oil. (Dispose of the oil properly; check with a local gas station or auto mechanic for regulations in your area.)

Also in cold climates, as the end of the season nears, add fuel sparingly. Tools should be stored without fuel, so if there is only a little bit in the tank at the end of the season, you may need to run the engine until it's empty. On the other hand, if you end up running an engine in your driveway for an hour or so, it's just a waste of fuel and unnecessary air pollution. Perhaps the best option is to remove the fuel and store it in an approved container with the rest of your gasoline. Be careful when refilling the engine; the EPA points out that even small gasoline spills evaporate and pollute the air.[2]

As needed, apply a small amount of lightweight oil, lithium grease, or silicone lubricant to all exposed control cable and pivot points, usually at the clutch and throttle controls. Then clean or replace any air filters as specified by the manufacturer.

If you aren't a knowledgeable mechanic (and I'm not), timely tune-ups at a small engine specialty shop will ensure your engine is running at maximum efficiency and prolong its useful life.[3]

## THE IMPACT OF GARDENING GREEN

• Maintaining a tool well hits several important environmental issues. You buy fewer tools, saving on fuels costs and pollution in manufacturing and transport. The machine operates with fewer emissions. And you're less likely to have to haul it away before its time, another drop in the huge ocean of waste we Americans produce each year.

# Replace your outdoor light bulbs with more energy-efficient types.

*Compact florescent light bulbs (CFLs) are one of the easiest options, and there are even more efficient, eco-friendly ones on the horizon.*

Compact florescent light bulbs (CFLs) are winning fans and influencing people all over the planet indoors because of their long life and impressive energy savings. So, it would seem that they would be a good choice outdoors as well, with the proper precautions and caveats.

Read the package first to ensure that the bulb is suitable for use outdoors. A CFL should be housed in a fixture that protects it from moisture which could shorten its life, and may need special adapters to operate at temperatures of 32°F (0°C) or below. On/off applications of features like motion detectors and timers also tend to shorten their life span.

> **DID YOU KNOW THAT...**
>
> ❁ Compact fluorescent bulbs last up to 10 times longer than traditional bulbs, produce 75 to 90 percent less heat, and use anywhere from 25 to 70 percent less electricity, according to various estimates.[1]

While CFLs are indeed capable of reducing energy consumption, it is important they are used and disposed of properly. (All fluorescent bulbs contain some amount of mercury, which is dangerous when released into the atmosphere.) Never just throw them in the trash where they will end up in a landfill. Sooner of later they'll break, releasing their mercury. According to the Web site http://earth911.org, even the small amount in one low-mercury CFL can contaminate one thousand gallons of water beyond safe drinking levels.

So rather than leaving them like ticking bombs in a landfill, dispose of them at a hazardous waste collection site— the same location where you deposit paint and household chemicals.

While florescent lights take five times more energy to make than incandescent bulbs, they last six to ten times longer. Although more expensive, the energy savings more than make up for it. And there are even more exciting developments emerging on the energy efficient, eco-friendly lighting scene.

The best of all worlds is on the horizon. Pricier than CFLs, *light emitting diodes* (LEDs for short) have the lowest environmental cost yet. Typically used individually in electronics or in Christmas lights, they can now be clustered for use in many of the same applications as incandescent bulbs, but with the staying power of up to 133 times longer than CFLs. Even better, they contain zero mercury.

For now, LEDs are not readily available and are still too pricey to be widely accepted by consumers. But as this exciting and environmentally responsible lighting option develops, prices will fall and availability will increase. Expect to see LEDs as a staple inside and outside the homes of people around the world relatively soon. That will make for a pretty bright future for our planet and a significant action to protecting and preserving it, too.

## THE IMPACT OF GARDENING GREEN

• If every U.S. household were to change just 1 light bulb to a compact fluorescent, it would be the equivalent of removing 800,000 cars off the road, with respect to greenhouse gas emissions, according to an EPA spokesperson. That's enough energy to light 3 million homes and accounts for 600 million dollars in energy costs.[2]

# Set up your outdoor lighting for maximum efficiency.

*Outdoor lighting adds ambiance and security . . . but can waste energy.*

I want to enjoy my outdoor living spaces as much as anyone, and sometimes the enjoyment can't begin until after dark. Still I don't light up the night when I don't need to. Allowing the lights to burn all night when it's not necessary is a wasteful drain on our resources, not to mention our pocketbooks. It interrupts wildlife rhythms—and even bothers the sleeping rhythms of neighbors who might prefer that my yard light didn't shine into their bedroom window all night!

All of us want that modicum of safety and security that night lighting provides. Once again, we must find a compromise between what we want and what is needed. To do so, look for ways to reduce your energy consumption by limiting the amount of time lights remain on. Programmable timers are an excellent way to accomplish this. You can program the timers so that lights come on when you know you will be working or walking around your landscape at night.

> ### DID YOU KNOW THAT . . .
>
> ❀ Each 100-watt incandescent light bulb burning 10 hours a day consumes 1 kilowatt hour. In a year, that could add up to $57.80.[1]

If you prefer to illuminate a particular area all night, using a photocell unit will turn the lights off at dawn and on again at dusk without your having to think about it. Motion sensors can provide the right amount of light for short periods of time or frighten away unwanted visitors. Combining a photocell unit and motion detector will decrease your energy usage as well.

And consider replacing standard outdoor lighting with either low-voltage lighting, which uses far less electricity, or solar-powered lighting to harness the energy of the sun to make the exterior of your home safe and welcoming. Your neighbors, your energy bill, and your planet will thank you.

## THE IMPACT OF GARDENING GREEN

• Most electricity in the U.S. is produced by coal-fired power plants. So, leaving one 100-watt porch light on all night, depending on your electrical power plant's operating system, can require 357 pounds of coal and result in throwing 2 ½ pounds of sulfur dioxide into the air as well as 26 pounds of nitrogen oxides and 626 pounds of carbon dioxide.[2]

# Use low-voltage lighting in the landscape.

*Innovations in do-it-yourself lighting technology give us the look of a professional job while saving energy at the same time.*

The name gives it away. Low-voltage lighting translates into less energy used to illuminate the system. But it doesn't have to mean less satisfaction in lighting up your landscape.

Besides the aesthetic benefits, lighting a dark space is one of the most important deterrents to keeping possible intruders away, illuminating potentially dangerous areas for visiting family and friends, and generally making your property safe and secure for everyone.

Landscaping with low-voltage lighting is not only appropriate for safety issues, it also creates ambiance by accenting your garden. Lighting can draw attention to a special feature, lead you safely down a path, or provide security.

> DID YOU KNOW THAT...
>
> ❀ A string of 6 low-voltage lights uses 108 watts, compared to a single 150-watt floodlight, a 28-percent reduction in energy used.[1]

Innovations in technology and design allow for even the most project-challenged homeowner to quickly and easily install a complete system with the look of a professional job while saving energy at the same time. Low-voltage lighting kits are readily available for purchase at home improvement and lighting stores. They're sold with everything you need to get the job done.

With so many choices in low-voltage lighting, the sky's the limit on how you choose to illuminate your landscape. But still, the most common application is pathway lighting. Even the most basic kits are appropriate for this. Lights are either illuminated or projected from about ankle to knee height to light the walking path. It certainly has an aesthetic appeal, but its basic function is to provide safety when moving around our landscape at night at a cost many times less than conventional incandescent lighting.

## THE IMPACT OF GARDENING GREEN

• When you reduce energy used, depending on your electrical source you can prevent the burning of coal and the resulting emissions of toxins such as sulfur dioxide, nitrogen oxides, and carbon dioxide being released into the atmosphere.

# Use solar-powered lights for outdoor lighting.

*It's more functional than ever, and the convenience and energy efficiency can't be beat.*

What could be simpler? Easy to install with no wiring required, a solar-powered pathway or garden lights are not only a green choice, they're a convenient one.

In days gone by, solar-powered lighting wasn't necessarily a good choice for an area that needed intense illumination, but that is no longer the case. With advances in bulb development such as LED or halogen lights, a large area that needs to be brightly lit or a space where you might need to read, grill, or do other up-close work outdoors is now a reality. The solar panels on the light fixture itself simply provide the eco-friendly energy source as a super convenient alternative.

> **DID YOU KNOW THAT...**
>
> ✻ Not only do solar-powered lights not use any electricity, unlike traditional lights, they contain no mercury—one of the most toxic water pollutants around.

Solar-operated lights can be found for a number of outdoor applications, including motion-activated security lights, and entryway, wall, and accent lighting. They are an excellent way to provide functional lighting along paths, sidewalks, water features, the perimeter of a deck or patio, and more.

Choosing to go solar is the perfect application for accent lighting in the landscape, especially in areas farther away from the house where wiring complicates the issue. And, the energy savings are the best part. By harnessing the power of the sun, you are tapping into clean energy from a renewable resource. That alone makes me feel good, and you can, too.

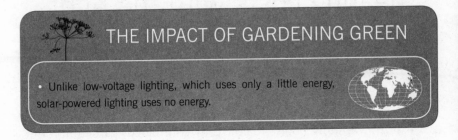

THE IMPACT OF GARDENING GREEN

• Unlike low-voltage lighting, which uses only a little energy, solar-powered lighting uses no energy.

*To cultivate a garden is
to walk with God.*

CHRISTIAN NESTELL BOVEE

# Reduce swimming pool heating costs with the right type of cover.

*While having a pool can be part of a healthy lifestyle,*
*it may not contribute to a healthy planet.*

I realize swimming pools are not really considered "gardening," but if you have a pool, it is almost always a *part* of the garden, and heating one can be a pricey proposition. But there are a number of ways to keep a pool warm and lessen the environmental impact at the same time. Here are some energy-saving ideas you might consider if a pool is in your yard, or in your future.

Depending on your climate and swimming habits, a pool cover will keep those heating costs down. According to the EPA, simply covering a pool when it is not in use is the single most effective way of reducing pool heating costs and can save 50 to 70 percent on energy use.

And those energy costs can be significant. In colder regions, a pool owner can spend more heating a pool than heating a home. Even in warm, sunny Florida, the average yearly cost for heating a residential pool is around five hundred dollars using an electric heat pump, and five hundred eighty dollars using natural gas.

The California Energy Commission says that simply covering your pool can reduce water and chemical evaporation, saving nearly a thousand gallons of water per month. Evaporation is what you want to avoid, so almost any large sheet of plastic would insulate a pool. What type of cover you choose depends somewhat on your climate. But for ultimate savings, covers made specifically for pools work best.

Where the evaporation rate is high, it is better to leave the cover on during the day, even though it will slightly block solar heat gain. In humid conditions, leaving the cover off during the day will allow for maximum heat gains with less water lost to evaporation. However, the best of both worlds incorporates specially designed solar pool covers that can keep your pool warmer by about thirty degrees, reducing or even eliminating the need for an external heater.

A popular option for keeping a pool warmer naturally is to design it with dark walls and/or bottom. This creates the aesthetically pleasing effect of a natural lagoon, and the dark color absorbs heat better.

However, some building codes will not allow dark pool sides and bottoms for safety reasons—it's hard to see a swimmer in trouble near the bottom, and it can be difficult to see harmful debris or other items that may have fallen into the pool. Be sure to consider the risks and check the codes where you live before pursuing this method.

Solar heating systems for pools are well worth looking into for saving precious resources. In 2007, Florida's governor had a solar heating system installed at the Governor's Mansion. According to the press release: "The system will produce 20 percent fewer emissions than the current natural gas system, saving approximately 22,000 pounds of carbon emissions per year. The Governor's Mansion will see a first-year energy savings of over $3,500 and a ten-year fuel savings of over $45,000."

Pools do require a lot of resources, from the water used to fill them, to the energy consumed to keep them warm beyond what the sun provides. A simple cover may be all that is needed, but it's nice to know that when you need more than just the warming rays, solar power is still the best eco-friendly option. The up-front cost might appear hefty, but costs recovered in saved energy and dollars will be recouped in just a few summers.

## THE IMPACT OF GARDENING GREEN

• By installing a pool cover, you can reduce the energy needs for heating your pool by 50 percent to 70 percent. If you use a pool cover that is translucent, you can also enjoy solar heat gain that can eliminate the need to heat your pool altogether.[4]

• Pool covers reduce the amount of make-up water you need to add to your pool by 30 to 50 percent, greatly reducing water consumption.[5]

• Pool covers also reduce the pool's chemical consumption from 35 to 60 percent, and by keeping dirt and other debris out of the pool, they greatly reduce the time needed to keep the pool clean.[6]

# Resist the temptation to burn yard waste.

*Burning even seemingly harmless yard waste emits particles that are easily taken into the lungs and releases a host of toxic chemicals.*

Because I'm so focused on composting and recycling, I never think about burning yard waste, but I see others doing it all the time. My first thought is it's such a waste of potential compost! Then I immediately think about how much unnecessary pollution is going into the atmosphere.

Burning trash, leaves, meadows, and more has been a time-honored tradition, but fewer and fewer local governments allow open burning, and for some very good reasons. It's far too easy to create a hazard that could spread quickly out of control, but it's a nasty air polluter as well.

In reality, compared to *closed burning*, which is done with an incinerator, open burning doesn't really burn the waste efficiently or completely. The evidence is there in the black smoke and particles pouring from most open fires.

> DID YOU KNOW THAT . . .
>
> ❀ Open burning of yard debris produces carbon monoxide, nitrogen oxides, and volatile organic compounds. If household trash is also burned, large amounts of toxic chemicals, especially dioxins and polycyclic aromatic hydrocarbons (PAHs), will be emitted.[1]
>
> ❀ Green plants sequester large amounts of carbon dioxide from the atmosphere when they are alive, but they release all of that stored carbon dioxide very rapidly when they are burned. Open burning of plant debris is a significant source of greenhouse gases.

Clearly the type of pollutants a fire puts into the air depends on what's being burned, but even the burning of harmless twigs and

## THE IMPACT OF GARDENING GREEN

• If you live in an area that still allows open burning of yard waste and trash, refrain from doing so and you'll make a significant contribution to the reduction of particulate pollution, toxic gases, and greenhouse gases in the atmosphere.

• Avoid the burning of yard waste, and you'll enjoy other benefits, too. Instead of burning twigs and branches, chip them and use them as mulch. They'll prevent the need for weed killers. Cut up larger pieces and create a brush pile in an out-of-the-way area of your landscape. It makes an ideal backyard wildlife habitat for birds and other small animals.

branches releases particles that are easily taken into the lungs. It also releases a host of toxic chemicals, including carbon dioxide, carbon monoxide, nitrogen oxides, and volatile organic compounds.

If household trash is included, toxins such as dioxins and polycyclic aromatic hydrocarbons, or PAHs (big words for stuff you really don't want in your lungs), will be given off, and both have been shown to be very hazardous to human health. Household trash, with its complex blend of chemicals and toxins, is best left to the professionals.

Rather than jeopardize our air quality by burning yard debris and trash at home, check with a waste management company on an economical, environmentally sound trash removal service. Better yet, compost all that you are able and only send what is necessary to the landfill.

*The man who has planted
a garden feels that he has done
something for the good of
the world.*

VITA SACKVILLE-WEST

# CHAPTER SEVEN

# GARDENING TO PROTECT THE ECOSYSTEM

If we were to step outside of our green bubble for a moment and look at the reasons we are facing such an ecological crisis today, we'd realize that biodiversity indeed contributes to many facets of our human health and the comforts of life. And although many people enjoy and benefit from activities that lead to the loss of biodiversity and cause ecological change, our actions' true cost to our planet often far exceeds the benefit to us.

Protecting ecosystems and maintaining biodiversity are so critical to keeping the earth in balance; it's hard to even comprehend the complexities of the concept in words. Just try to imagine a balanced ecosystem as a web of connections from one living organism to other living and non-living things. The web connects them, providing the necessary resources for survival, like food and shelter.

Due to the highly complex nature of ecosystem relationships, the removal or disruption of a single one of its members could throw the entire system out of balance. Unfortunately, we have yet to fully understand these complex relationships, so the exact cause and effect of disturbances is many times still unpredictable.

At least as gardeners, we can identify some of the most direct benefits to preserving and protecting these relationships. Healthy ecosystems improve the chance for plant and animal populations to recover from the threat of increasingly catastrophic and often unpredictable events such as hurricanes, fires, floods, and other natural and man-induced disasters.

Maintaining natural habitats also provides protection for breeding and migrating populations of birds, as well as offering shelter from predators. Insect pests are kept in check, reducing the need for chemical control measures. The gene pool of plants vital for food and medicine is preserved, while pollinating insects continue to sustain these ecosystems as they work and breed in their diverse habitat.

When biological diversity is degraded, so many consequences begin to manifest themselves. Soils are harmed, setting a host of events into motion. After all, it is the quality of the soil that sustains plant material, helps infiltrate and purify surface water, reduces runoff and erosion, retains nutrients and minerals, and maintains the land's productivity.

Damaged soil weakens the vegetation. And it is the natural vegetation offered by biodiversity that provides buffers to catch, retain, and stabilize water runoff, recharge groundwater, and even mitigate the effects of flood and drought.

Vegetation also helps to moderate climate conditions from small areas to vast forests, creating microclimates that can be the life-giving difference to certain organisms that make up a particular balanced ecosystem.

On the positive side, efforts to preserve ecosystems allow many pollutants—including oil, sewage, and garbage—to be broken down and absorbed or consumed through the various life forms present in a biodiverse relationship. They also recycle nutrients from the soil and the atmosphere, forming the basis of food chains used by a wide range of other life.

In spite of the many essential reasons for preserving and protecting our planet, we've seen time and again throughout these pages that eco-consciousness is often a trade-off. Once again we are faced with competing goals. For example, in our desire to increase food production (not a bad endeavor in and of itself), we must modify an ecosystem to tap its resources, leading to the natural consequences of reduction in water resources and environmental degradation.

Today, virtually all of the earth's ecosystems have been altered through human actions, and yet the interruptions seem to continue at a faster rate than ever before. As our interference persists, many plant and animal species have declined in populations and scope, and the rate of extinction has increased by at least a factor of one hundred over natural rates. Biodiversity loss has occurred more rapidly in the last fifty years then at any other time in history, and these changes are expected to continue at the same pace or even accelerate.

It should come as no surprise that the global calamity we now face comes at our own hand. Some common threats around the world include population growth, habitat conversion and sprawl, exotic and invasive species, environmental degradation, pollution, and global warming. Exploiting biodiversity for raw materials and converting natural ecosystems into monocultures for agricultural use are two of the biggest culprits. Indeed, human actions have contributed in large part to irreversible losses in habitats, species, and overall diversity of life on this planet.

But it's not all bad news, nor should we feel powerless to affect change. Efforts to help slow this downward spiral are helping; many of the actions taken to promote sustainability and conserve biodiversity have been successful in slowing its loss.

But slowing down the loss of biodiversity is not sufficient.

As more environmentally sensitive areas break down at a faster rate than ever, preservation takes on an even greater sense of urgency. Efforts to achieve significant reductions in the rate of loss and to ultimately restore balanced ecosystems will demand unprecedented actions.

So what can be done? For you and me, the most direct and significant actions must be taken at local, regional, and national levels while always being mindful that our actions will contribute to the bigger picture. Starting right at home is a simple yet important place to begin. The pages that follow will give you some tangible actions you can take to make a difference.

*With a garden, there is hope.*

GRACE FIRTH

# Promote complexity and avoid monocultures.

*You'd think popularity is a good thing, but when plants are overused, it can set them—and us—up for ecological problems.*

What do the Irish potato famine and the Dust Bowl of the 1930s have in common? You guessed it—they were the result of monocultures.

Any time we plant too much of one thing, we're setting ourselves up against Mother Nature, and for problems that can have far-reaching implications. The potato famine happened when a devastating potato blight raced through the plantings of Irish peasants. It was the reliance upon one crop, and especially *one variety* of one crop, that led to massive crop failure. Had they planted several types of potatoes or rotated them with other crops, thousands of deaths could have likely been avoided.[1]

And the Dust Bowl? This was in large part the result of repeated large-scale plantings of the same crop year after year. When we don't plant a variety of crops in alternate growing seasons, land is dormant and exposed, and populations of pests and diseases can build up to decimate the same host crop when it is replanted in subsequent seasons. In the case of the Dust Bowl, tons of soil were blown into the air after a drought killed off crops that had already been weakened.

Our own backyards and neighborhoods can become microcosms of these global events. When we plant too much of a good thing, either too close together or year after year, significant problems may result. We are creating the perfect environment for a population explosion of pests or pathogens by inviting them to latch onto a single host. In monocultures, the relative abundance of a host, combined with the absence of natural predators in sufficient numbers, can have devastating effects.

Here's a more recent example: The thornless honey locust—an excellent shade tree in many ways—was overplanted along streets and highways all over the Eastern U.S., in part because it had virtually no known pests. Today these massive plantings are being attacked by several highly damaging and opportunistic pests that have finally arrived. The abundance of trees provided ample opportunities for pests and diseases by supplying food and shelter and a resulting population explosion in the absence of natural predators.

DID YOU KNOW THAT...

❀ A monoculture is a planting of just a single species of a plant, which you'll often find in a cornfield, an apple orchard, a lawn, or a rose garden. It's the opposite of a polyculture, or mixed planting.

❀ Monocultures are highly vulnerable to devastating invasion from pests and disease. Keeping them protected requires enormous amounts of intervention, mostly from chemical controls. Because of the high numbers both of plants and attacking pests typical of monocultures, target organisms develop resistance quickly, which requires a never-ending string of ever more powerful chemical controls.

Remember the old saying that those who forget the past are doomed to repeat it? Although the conditions that caused those historical disasters are not likely to happen again, many pressing threats to biodiversity still pose significant concerns. At home, we see dangerous scenarios played out every day, right where we live. Mini-monocultures of turfgrass are a ubiquitous feature in just about every landscape in America. Few are the homes that don't have some amount of turf occupying a portion of their landscape. As lovely as a well manicured lawn can be to look at, it replaces the habitats of native plants and wildlife and food sources for birds or beneficial insects.

Another threat to biodiversity in home landscapes and beyond is the introduction of exotic and invasive species which out-compete native plants for sunlight, water, and nutrients, destroying entire ecosystems in their wake.

The balance of nature is indeed a concert of all of its inhabitants. The natural environment around us is never a monoculture on its own. When we destroy this highly sophisticated yet delicate balance by precluding diversity, ecosystems falter, and in severe cases, devastating consequences are the result. Yet when biodiversity is protected and promoted in our own yards and neighborhoods, so is the stability of the ecosystems that give us fresh water, clean air, productive soil, and healthy forests.[2]

## THE IMPACT OF GARDENING GREEN

• By growing a wide variety of plants in your garden and avoiding monocultures wherever possible, you will enjoy a healthier garden with less need to use chemical controls. This in turn will promote insect and animal biodiversity.

• On a broader scale, when we avoid monocultures and encourage biodiversity, we promote the sustainability of fresh air, clean water, and healthy soil. We perpetuate plant life that is responsible for all of our food and much of our medicine. In turn, we foster a healthy economy and preserve our quality of life and the natural beauty of our planet.

# Protect the gene pool.

*Saving heirloom or sentimental favorite seeds is
a significant way to prevent their extinction.*

America has been the great melting pot in more ways than one.
With each wave of immigrants came a wave of new plants, many in
the form of a packet of generations-old seed tucked carefully into a
pocket. Each settler planted a favorite tomato, a favorite apple, a particular type of morning glory or an especially striking sunflower, and
as a result, they added to the amazing horticultural variety in
our country.

In the middle part of the last century, however, people stopped
saving seeds from year to year. With the advent of hybridization, large
seed companies began selling seeds that didn't come from seeds saved
year after year. Hybrid varieties have many advantages to farmers and
home gardeners in terms of consistency, yields, or pest and disease resistance, but there was also a disadvantage. They had to be purchased
new each year or whenever current supplies were exhausted. This
method of seed acquisition replaced much of the traditional swapping
and passing on to the next generation of our treasured seeds.

Typically the results from planting a hybridized plant from seed
will be iffy. That snapdragon which was such a gorgeous peach-yellow
blend this year might reseed next year, but the flower color can be
dramatically different. This is not necessarily a bad thing, just something to be aware of. And don't expect that hybrid tomato seed to
produce offspring identical to its parent.

Open-pollinated varieties are different. These seeds have not been
manipulated by man. Their pollination takes place naturally through
insects, birds, wind, and other means. The seeds of open-pollinated
plants *can* produce new generations of the same plant which is how

❀ The Seed Savers Exchange estimates that more than 90 percent of the fruit and vegetable varieties grown in the United States in 1900 have since been lost.[1]

❀ All life on earth depends on plants, yet it is thought that by the end of this century, 50 percent of the world's plants will be condemned to extinction.

❀ Many modern medicines we depend on for our health are derived from plants. The common aspirin, for example, is used by 10 million people a day. It is derived from the bark of a willow tree.

we can save and plant seeds from one generation to another. So if your grandmother had some wonderful russet signet marigolds that she grew in her garden decades ago and she saved the seed each year, your parents could save and grow them, and today, so could you. Many vegetables and flowers we enjoy today are the product of open-pollination and seed saving.

If you aren't lucky enough to have a grandparent who saved seeds, check out the Seed Savers Exchange online. It's a nonprofit organization in Iowa dedicated to the preservation of heirloom seeds, where members swap and receive open-pollinated seeds to grow in order to prevent some wonderful plants from being lost.

There's another reason for saving seeds that reaches far beyond our flower or vegetable gardens. The entire diversity of plant life on our planet is shrinking rapidly. Climate change is expected to exacerbate the loss of plant diversity and increase the risk of extinction for many more species, especially those already at risk from other threats. Regions of the planet that provide much of the genetic material for our cultivated crop plants are quickly being damaged or destroyed. Many times the effects are irreversible. Unfortunately, pressures on the environment no longer allow plants to remain protected in their natural habitats. Saving their seeds is a significant way to preserve these plants from one generation to the next.

In response to this pressing issue, seed banks have been established all over the world to effectively guarantee the survival of individual plant species. Their primary mission is to collect, store, and convert the stored seeds back into plants for reintroduction or habitat rehabilitation whenever necessary. This worldwide collaboration aims to save twenty-four thousand plant species around the globe from extinction. With the proper storage methods provided by seed banks, seeds can survive for hundreds and possibly thousands of years.

By saving seeds, we save plants that make up the basis of ecosystems in which all animals, including humans, survive and grow. Since human actions are fundamentally responsible for changing the diversity of life on earth, doing what we can to protect and preserve life only seems right, even a tiny seed. It really is the little things that matter.

## THE IMPACT OF GARDENING GREEN

• Supporting seed banks financially will help fund their efforts to continue as they collaborate on their worldwide mission to collect and store twenty-four thousand species of plants from the threat of extinction. Information can be found by searching "seed bank" or "seed preservation" on the Internet.[2]

• Using, collecting, and saving seeds at home from heirloom and open-pollinated varieties will promote efforts to protect the gene pools of plants that our ancestors grew. Many offer unique benefits in form or flavor or may simply be a sentimental favorite. Without our help, they may vanish forever.

# Discourage poaching of plants from the wild.

*Gardeners should be aware that this happens all too often.*

How can anyone take a walk in a wooded area and not appreciate the beauty around them? In a healthy, moist, diverse hardwood forest, for instance, plant lovers will spot wild lilies, trilliums, bluebells, gingers, blood root, hepaticas, calochortus, native irises, and perhaps even one of the very rare lady's-slipper orchids.

Sadly there exists a small but disturbing number of nurseries that have decided to capitalize on our appreciation of wild beauties by collecting them in unscrupulous ways. They take advantage of the fact that as we observe these fascinating plants in their native habitat we naturally want to grow them ourselves—we're gardeners, after all! But instead of propagating them in a nursery from seeds, cuttings, or divisions, they dig them, pot them up, and sell them, usually at a very enticing price.

But that price is actually very high. The practice of collecting plants in the wild has been compared to that of fishing in the North Atlantic. Perhaps because of its vastness, we've viewed the ocean as a source of infinite resources. The fact is, populations of many species that inhabit it are decreasing at an unsustainable rate, resulting in many now listed as endangered and threatened with extinction. As is often the case, overexploitation and habitat destruction by humans is to blame.

And so it is with plants. Two of the key reasons cited for loss of biodiversity and ecosystems around the world are directly related to commercial exploitation and habitat destruction. Too often, when plant explorers, collectors, or other individuals remove plants from their native habitat, they are removing a critical component of the ecosystem and destroying the environment that supports it.

It is true that we depend on plant explorers to bring us new and interesting varieties. And most uphold the highest standards for protecting the fragile ecosystems they encroach upon as they hunt for new species. Sensitive to environmental concerns, these workers collect from the wild only the minimum needed for propagation. A legitimate resale market is then established as those plants are propagated from the original specimens. However, others who carelessly harvest plants from the wild to keep or sell directly contribute to the destruction of those habitats and even threaten the existence of the species.

The poster child for the eastern part of the United States is the lady's-slipper orchid, which once grew in abundance. But gardeners and a few unethical nurseries, eager to possess them, dug them up and for the most part, were unable to meet their highly-specific cultural needs. So they died, and eventually that delicate, beautiful flower found its way onto the endangered species list.

We can help combat similar scenarios by asking the nurseries where you shop about their source of woodland plants. By far, most nurseries propagate their own stock. But be suspicious of very low prices or very high inventories of certain plants, as this could be a sign they are collecting slow-growing varieties from the wild. Beware of the term *nursery-grown* because it can simply mean it is literally growing in a pot there. *Nursery-propagated* is much more reliable.

> **DID YOU KNOW THAT...**
>
> ❀ The New England Wildflower Society was formed in 1931 to combat what it saw as unrestrained plant collecting that was devastating populations of certain ferns, club mosses, and woodland wildflowers.[1]
>
> ❀ Orchid smuggling, both nationally and internationally, is an illegal commercial trade totaling $5 billion by some estimates. Besides orchids, other plants that are illegally traded include threatened or endangered cacti and carnivorous plants.[2]

Another big concern is the gathering of orchids, cacti, and tropical plants. Some species within these groups are very rare, and collecting them from their native habitats is seriously threatening their existence. If you are seeking these rare plants and find them in a nursery, check to see if it carries the Convention on International Trade in Endangered Species (CITES) certification, part of a United Nations watchdog program to protect rare species of plants and animals.[3]

Ultimately, we can make a difference in the unethical collecting of endangered flowers through the simple process of supply and demand. Markets are created for these plants when there are willing buyers; the greater the demand, the greater the motivation to supply that market . . . to a limit.

Once the supply begins to shrink, in this case because plants are being wiped out, supply goes down, demand goes up, and collectors are even more motivated to bring plants to market because buyers are willing to pay more. It's a vicious cycle that exacerbates the threat to these endangered plant species. When we take a stand and refuse to support the questionable or illegal acts of the suppliers, the market for the species dries up, giving the plants a chance to flourish again.

## THE IMPACT OF GARDENING GREEN

• If all gardeners asked about the source of native and woodland plants and refused to buy any that were suspect, vendors would have no reason to sell—or collect—plants from the wild. So ask, and don't buy if you suspect that a flower or groundcover got its start on a woodland floor.

• By refusing to support the commerce of questionable or illegal selling of plants, we directly help protect and preserve fragile habitats and ecosystems literally around the world. Biodiversity is maintained, and we do our part to protect endangered or threatened species as well.

# Do your homework before using traps for insect pests— either they don't work, or they work too well!

*But just because it's not in a bottle doesn't make it an eco-friendly option.*

In an eco-friendly garden, the more chemicals you can keep out of your landscape, the better, even organic and natural ones. So what *do* you do to control those destructive Japanese Beetles, pesky flies, and annoying mosquitoes? Do we trap, zap, or gas these creatures with a botanical-based insecticide? The answers may surprise you.

## Japanese Beetle traps

Don't get me started! You see them everywhere.

Commercially available, these traps attract the beetles with two types of baits. One mimics the scent of virgin female beetles. Not surprisingly, it's highly effective at attracting males! The other bait is a sweet-smelling, food-type lure that attracts both sexes. This combination of ingredients is such a powerful attractant that traps can draw in thousands of beetles in a day.

There is plenty of information available on the effectiveness of Japanese Beetle traps. And it's unanimous—they work! In fact they work too well. Of all the information I've ever read, I have yet to find one credible source that recommends actually using them in your garden.

Research conducted by universities, laboratories, and even commercial airports has shown that the traps attract many more beetles than are actually caught. Consequently, susceptible plants along the flight path of the beetles and in the vicinity of traps are likely to suffer much more

DID YOU KNOW THAT...

❧ Insect traps were originally developed for use in the confined space of a greenhouse (mostly for trapping whiteflies), where such traps are effective. In open areas, mosquito and Japanese Beetle traps tend to attract more of the target pests to that area than they can possibly trap and can actually make a pest problem worse.

damage than if no traps are used at all. In most landscape situations, use of Japanese Beetle traps will likely do more harm than good.

For this reason, I don't recommend them at all. However, if you experiment with traps, be sure to place them far away from the plants you are trying to protect. Better yet, encourage your neighbor to buy them instead.

## Bug zappers

If you grew up in my generation, you remember bug zappers as the sweet sound of success on a summer evening. You know the sound, and you loved it. It made for some very entertaining evenings. Of *course* they worked. That zapping, sizzle sound was confirmation of that. But, what *were* those zappers cooking anyway? It's not like you could conduct a forensic I.D. of the bugs' charred remains.

But in 1996, some researchers from the University of Delaware did just that. In a study published in the journal *Entomological News*, Timothy Frick and Douglas Tallamy collected and identified the kills from six bug zappers at various sites throughout suburban Newark, Delaware, during the summer of 1994.

Of the nearly 14,000 insects that were electrocuted and counted, only 31 (0.22 percent) were mosquitoes and biting gnats. The largest group made up 48 percent (6,670). They consisted of midges and harmless aquatic insects from nearby bodies of water. Too bad, because those insects are vital to the aquatic food chain.

Another important group caught in the traps were predators and parasites. These biological control organisms (consisting of ground beetles and parasitic wasps) are the very insects that help keep pests populations down naturally. This group accounted for 13.5 percent (1,868).

So how good are bug zappers in the eco-friendly garden, or any garden for that matter? They're terrible! By design, they are nonselective and kill many harmless and beneficial insects. The authors even extrapolated their findings and determined that four million bug zappers (four years of approximate sales in the U.S) operated for forty nights each summer, would destroy seventy-one billion non-target insects each year!

Ironically, the very insects they're designed to draw aren't even attracted to the black light within the unit. So, according to this study, the number of mosquitoes would still be the same—with or without the zapper.

## Mosquito misters

One of the newer products to hit the market are misters designed to eliminate mosquito populations around a certain perimeter from the unit. They work by periodically disbursing an organic or synthetic pesticide, usually pyrethrin or permethrin. Marketers of these systems defend the use of the organic spray version because pyrethrum is organic and natural. Yes, but it's also *non-selective*, making it a very bad option. The indiscriminant application can destroy beneficial insects, pets, and especially fish.

Another concern expressed in a letter to the U.S. Environmental Protection Agency by the American Mosquito Control Association warned that the indiscriminant use of Pyrethroids (the synthetic and very potent version of pyrethrin) by misting systems could result in widespread resistance, seriously compromising the capability to control adult mosquito populations.

Unmonitored, regular spraying of a misting system like this is exactly what *not* to put into your eco-friendly garden. A better approach is to eliminate all standing water and use safe larviciding with Bt dunks and repellents.

## Mosquito trapping with $CO_2$

On a more positive note, another technology waging war on mosquitoes includes the use of carbon dioxide ($CO_2$), a gas found to attract mosquitoes. Although studies do show measurable success in controlled and mostly enclosed environments, the question of their effectiveness in a half- or full-acre outdoor setting remains a question.

The typical device converts propane into heat and carbon dioxide, two primary mosquito attractants. Some even add octenol, a third attractant. The propane storage is usually with the typical tank you'd see attached to a gas grill. Mosquitoes are attracted to the gas, and when they reach the trap, they're captured by vacuum or adhesive.

So are these traps as effective as some manufacturers claim? That depends on a number of variables: the placement of the device (upwind of the desired protection area), constant use versus intermittent, the attractant used, and even the species of mosquito determine success rates. Ironically, even in ideal cases, studies show mosquitoes prefer the $CO_2$ of people and animals. Oh well, at least a selective and somewhat eco-friendly approach to insect pest control is a step in the right direction.

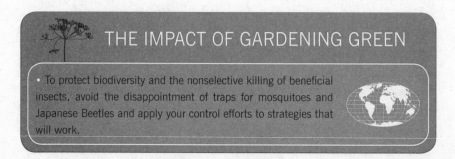

## THE IMPACT OF GARDENING GREEN

• To protect biodiversity and the nonselective killing of beneficial insects, avoid the disappointment of traps for mosquitoes and Japanese Beetles and apply your control efforts to strategies that will work.

# Build outdoor projects with environmentally responsible wood.

*Some of the most beautiful woods are harvested from threatened sources.*

The giant redwood—it's the tallest tree in the world. We revere it for its massive size and its supreme reign over the coastal forests along the western United States. For many of us, it defines what a true forest really looks and feels like. But the majestic redwoods we enjoy so much in our national forests and parks for their visual appeal are also a favorite wood used for building projects inside and outside the home. There the tree is valued for its beauty, light weight, and resistance to decay. It's redwood's ability to withstand the elements that makes it particularly attractive for use in outdoor landscapes.

> DID YOU KNOW THAT...
>
> ❀ Tropical forests harbor about ½ of all species on Earth.[1]
>
> ❀ "Deforestation, especially in tropical forests, accounts for approximately one-quarter of global greenhouse gas emissions as well as the rapid disappearance of the world's remaining natural forest habitats," says Eric Palola of the National Wildlife Federation.[2]

But this popularity as a building material has reduced redwood's total population by 40 percent in just three generations. That's more than enough to place it on The World Conservation Union's Red List of Threatened Species. Even as land is often converted to other uses after logging, the earlier population reductions are in many cases irreversible.

Since the early 1800's when redwood logging began, some 90 to 95 percent of old growth forests have been felled. The remaining stands are almost entirely in parks and reserves. These days, because of laws against old-growth logging, it's tough if not impossible to come by newly cut old-growth redwood for sale. Instead, it's likely to be redwood from younger trees, on private land and from second-growth forests.

As populations of redwoods decline, the threat to endangered species from these same environmentally important temperate rainforests goes up. And the logging process to cut and extract the wood can further harm these species and threaten their existence.

But the redwood tree is just one example. There are also endangered exotic wood species, the ones that lure us with irresistible grain patterns and interesting colors. Teak is the best known of these. Ironically, it became a popular and exclusive wood in Britain, when they recycled teak ship masts that had been crafted in foreign ports into beautiful garden furniture back home. The American and European appetite for this strong and beautiful wood has nearly eradicated it from its natural range in Southeast Asia and Central America.

Today, teak is a wood to choose with caution because of its impact on the tropical rainforests where much of it is harvested. Be aware of other rainforest woods most often used for patio and garden furniture (which includes tropical woods) such as mahogany, nyatoh, balau, jatoba (also called Brazilian cherry), parapera, kempas, iroko, and ipe.[7]

Some of the most beautiful woods for our landscapes, unfortunately, are also those whose loss can wreak the most havoc on climate change, biodiversity, and ecosystems so vital to preserving and protecting our planet. But there are ways to shop for attractive wood with sustainability in mind that will have less impact on the environment.

## Looking for the FSC label

Environmental groups such as the Sierra Club, Greenpeace, and The World Wildlife Fund endorse just one label in the marketplace—that of the Forest Stewardship Council (FSC). Its label certifies that the wood in a product has been sustainably produced. In fact, the pages of this book are printed on 100% recycled paper and the cover proudly bears the FSC certification.

The timber industry has answered with its own certification program called the Sustainable Forestry Initiative (SFI). Consumers Union (CU) doesn't give it as high marks as the FSC, but it still indicates some progress in protecting forest environments at home and abroad.

It's one thing to have worthwhile watchdog programs available such as FSC and SFI. But it's another to bring it to the level of awareness that will create the impact it needs. Currently, these labels don't yet carry the clout that comes from high consumer demand. And only the insistence from the buying public will raise the awareness of retailers and lead them to buy products from FSC or SFI sources. You can help by asking for and purchasing products with these labels.

## Looking for recycled or salvaged wood

In stores, look for recycled wood products that are certified by the SmartWood's Rediscovered Wood Program. The program utilizes wood that until its rediscovery would otherwise have been destroyed through natural decay, burning, or disposal. Inventory is derived from old buildings, fallen or removed trees, or other tree culling events. You can identify "SmartWood Rediscovered" by its label on finished products.[8]

## Looking for environmentally sound wood substitutes

There's a new wave of products made from alternative materials that lets more trees stand. The new so-called synthetic lumber made from recycled wood and plastics (sold by brand-names such as Trex® and Timbertec®) is a more forest-friendly alternative.

 THE IMPACT OF GARDENING GREEN

• Collectively we have clout! There are over 90 million gardeners in the U.S., and even more who are not gardeners but who purchase outdoor furniture for the deck and patio. By refusing to purchase any products made from tropical hardwoods, we can make a real dent in the worldwide demand for tropical hardwoods harvested by destroying rainforests around the world. Refuse to buy any wooden outdoor furniture or other products not bearing the FSC, FSI, or SmartWood Rediscovered label. Or even better, purchase outdoor furniture made from recycled wood or plastics.

# Avoid invasive non-native plants.

*The introduction or use of invasive exotic plants is listed as one of the biggest threats to biodiversity in the United States and worldwide.*

What novice gardener or uninformed weekend warrior hasn't uttered these words, "I want something that grows *fast!*" It's a natural desire to crave instant gratification in all areas of our life, even gardening. But be careful what you wish for because, in some cases, that fast grower could become your worst nightmare.

If you've ever taken a drive through the countryside of the Northern United States and seen vast open pastures carpeted with brightly colored purple loosestrife, you've seen what an invasive plant can do. If you've ever taken a drive through the South and seen entire buildings and patches of woodlands smothered by kudzu, you've seen an invasive plant in action. And in the Pacific Northwest, neon yellow Spanish broom lights up slopes, often growing so thick that nothing else can.

Invasive plants are introduced species that can thrive in areas beyond their natural range of dispersal. These plants are characteristically adaptable, aggressive, and have a high capacity to propagate. Because they evolved over eons in completely different habitats elsewhere in the world, these exotics often have few natural enemies and contribute little to the support of native wildlife. Their vigor combined with a lack of natural enemies often leads to outbreaks in populations. Invasive plants can totally overwhelm and devastate established native plants and their habitats by out-competing them for nutrients, water, and light—and because they offer so little food value to native wildlife, they are destructive of biodiversity on every level.

Despite huge government efforts to control them, invasive plants continue to spread. Aggressive weeds spread to an estimated four thousand acres (over six square miles) each day on public lands

❀ A Cornell University study estimated that invasive species (both plants and animals) cost the U.S. economy $138 billion annually. This estimate is based on known economic losses and costs of control efforts but does not include loss of biodiversity and other ecological damages.[1]

❀ Just 1 gardener planting 1 invasive plant can have a huge, negative effect. Birds can devour hundreds of seeds from just 1 plant and spread them through communities and up and down migratory routes all across the country.[2]

❀ According to the Nature Conservancy, some of the worst invasive plants nationally are those that are also very tempting plants to the gardener.[3] They include English ivy, privet, Japanese honeysuckle, purple loosestrife, pepper tree, Oriental bittersweet, bamboo, pampas grass, and salt cedar (also called tamarisk). There are many more—too many to list here.[4]

managed by the Bureau of Land Management (BLM) and the Forest Service. They are also spreading on private lands and parklands, but no one has calculated the extent of those infestations.

While some invasive species hitchhike into other countries, one of the major culprits, once again, is us. Some of the worst offenders were brought into the United States because they were so irresistible to gardeners. Japanese honeysuckle was brought to the United State in 1806, admired as an intensely fragrant ornamental groundcover. Hummingbirds and bees loved it! A great plant, right? Well that depends.

In North America, Japanese honeysuckle has few natural enemies, so it spreads wildly, taking over native plants along the way. It kills shrubs and young trees like a giant python by twisting tightly around the stems and trunks, cutting off the flow of water and nutrients through the plant. Alternately, it simply covers other plants and blocks sun from their leaves, or else its vigorous, greedy roots spread so thickly that nothing else can compete with them.[5]

The best way to stop invasives dead in their deep-rooted tracks is to first find out what's invasive in your area; check with your cooperative extension service or do some online research (www.invasive.org and www.invasivespeciesinfo.gov are excellent sources). You can also ask a trusted source at your local garden center. However, too many garden centers still sell highly invasive plants simply because we still buy them. As always, it's simply a matter of supply and demand. If you see invasive plants for sale at your nursery or garden center, please inform the manager and make them aware of the risks of promoting the sale of these environmentally destructive plants to unwitting consumers.

## THE IMPACT OF GARDENING GREEN

• Know which invasive exotic plants are problems in your area and avoid buying and planting them, and you will avoid contributing to serious destruction of the habitat needed for native plants and wildlife.

• If you already have invasive exotics growing on your property, it would be wise to get rid of them completely. Volunteering with your local native plant society for a weekend of invasive exotic plant removal somewhere on public land will help reduce invasive species from spreading even more.

# Protect standing dead trees whenever possible.

*It may look like a dead tree to you, but to eighty-five species of birds and other wildlife, it's home.*

I'm always one to preach about the importance of good sanitation in your landscape. It's a major deterrent to various pests and diseases taking up residence there from one season to the next. However, I'm about to make an exception to that very important rule. When it comes to dead trees, don't be so quick to cut them down if safety issues are not a concern. They are a vital part of an ecosystem that makes the perfect home for some woodpeckers and are a magnet for the wood-devouring insects that woodpeckers love to peck.

In fact, one way to tell that a tree is on its last legs—or maybe we should say roots— is that it's riddled with holes from where woodpeckers hammered their beaks to retrieve tasty bugs, which are usually most abundant in dead wood. Dead trees are also prime real estate for woodpeckers to make their nests. They love the hollow cavities created in dying trees.

DID YOU KNOW THAT...

❀ A century ago, redheaded woodpeckers were abundant in this country. Today, they are on the National Audubon Society's Watch List. Although the redheaded woodpecker will occupy a variety of habitats, its nesting habitat is very specific: large, dead, barkless trees. Without what we humans consider eyesores, there will be no redheaded woodpeckers.[1]

❀ Besides 19 species of woodpeckers, 66 other species of birds depend on cavities in trees for nesting—mostly the cavities created by woodpeckers and then abandoned.

❀ A significant cause of deline in the populations of most cavity-nesting birds is the removal of standing dead trees. Particularly in the habitats around our homes, standing dead trees are becoming increasingly rare.[2]

What many people don't realize is that woodpeckers are only the beginning. After they create a cavity and move on, a long string of tenants is likely to occupy that cavity—ranging from bluebirds and wrens to owls and chickadees and nuthatches. Even squirrels, chipmunks, and other mammals use these cavities as home, often enlarging them to fit.

Certainly, it is sometimes critical to remove a large dead tree if there is any possibility that people may be in harm's way, especially children who frequent the area. Dead trees may also be at risk for falling on a house, driveway, or sidewalk. Nor would you want a limb in a windstorm to take out a window or your minivan. But if it's in the back of yard or especially, if it's in a wooded spot, leave the tree alone once all safety risks have been assessed. Dying trees and branches are all part of the cycle of a natural woodland habitat. As a gardener, trying to be too clean and tidy, in this case, is working against nature.

## THE IMPACT OF GARDENING GREEN

• Leave a dead tree standing and you'll play a significant role in preserving increasingly rare, critical habitat for 85 species of cavity-nesting birds and other animals.

# Provide a variety of water sources for wildlife.

*The presence of water can mean the difference between life and death for animals in the wild.*

Have you ever wondered where wildlife goes to get the water they depend on for survival? Natural water supplies are of course the obvious first choice. Wetlands are common, but in the face of increasing drought and shrinking sources, that option is not as easy to come by anymore.

Adult animals are better equipped to handle extended periods without water, yet almost all wildlife can be found within a couple miles of a water source. As these sources become less available, animals can become weakened, and female mammals may be unable to produce milk for their young, exacerbating the problem. As limited water sources dry up, animals can be reluctant to leave their only known supply. Rather than searching for new sources, they stay put and, in many cases, die of dehydration.

At home, we may not be faced with the harsh realities of nature's survival of the fittest, but water shortages are still a reality, and so is suburban and urban wildlife. Just as man-made, supplemental water sources are sometimes provided in nature, we can easily provide supplemental

---

**DID YOU KNOW THAT. . .**

❀ Wetlands such as ponds, marshes, and bogs have never made up a huge part of the U.S., but they've always been critical, and they're on the decline. Since colonial times, the amount of acreage they take up has been cut in half, from 11 percent in 1780 to just 5 percent in 1980.[1]

❀ About ½ of the 188 animals that are federally designated as endangered or threatened are dependent on wetlands for survival. Of these, 17 are bird species or subspecies, and they are categorized as endangered or threatened.[2]

sources of water for all the creatures that may inhabit or visit our backyards.

Birds are the obvious consideration. When you create a watering spot that birds enjoy, you might be surprised at just how many of them take advantage of it. You may also be surprised to see what else shows up there! Even a simple birdbath can attract a number of birds just in the first few hours after you fill it. I must say, I have enjoyed many hours watching the birds splash and groom themselves in the small pool I set up for them just outside my office window. It is quite gratifying to know that the water I've placed for them is a safe and essential respite for my feathered friends.

## Using water to attract birds

If attracting birds to your backyard habitat is important to you, here are a few things to know that will make the experience more enjoyable for you and the birds.

**Provide shallow water.** Ever seen robins splashing in puddles after a rain? Birds love shallow water that they can easily splash in. Birdbaths serve this need, as does a shallow ledge just a few inches deep in a water garden or a shallow stream. The height of the water source also plays a role. Some birds that normally might not come to your yard will stop and visit if they can find water at ground level (this includes a stream).

Others—usually those birds that will visit a feeder, such as blackcapped chickadees, house finches, and the tufted titmouse—feel safer higher up, especially if there are shrubs or foliage around the water feature that cats might hide in. This is especially important because it's harder for birds to take flight when they're wet. For birds that prefer loftier heights, position the water two to three feet high, as with a fountain.

**The basic birdbath is still a classic.** Don't think you need a fancy water feature to attract birds. The most basic, concrete birdbath on a pedestal works great to attract those birds that prefer their water higher up.

**Include rocks and small boulders.** A flat rock, placed just in the center of a birdbath, can create a welcomed island of safety for birds to survey their surroundings from a slightly more secure position. A flat stone placed just so its top is at the water level is an ideal height.

Boulders and rocks, depending on how they are set up, also create a natural point of entry to a water garden, especially if the boulder is rough or craggy and has a good foothold.

**Provide the sound of water.** The sound of water slowly dripping is absolutely irresistible to birds. You can purchase attachments for the side of a birdbath or water feature to create that slow dripping sound. Also consider a leaf mister. This mister, which works much in the same way as a sprinkler (but uses much less water), sprays a fine mist on plant leaves for birds such as hummingbirds and warblers that prefer to bathe by rubbing against wet leaves.

And don't forget that, once frozen, these water sources might as well be dried up. In areas of the country where the water freezes, look for birdbath heaters and deicers. No matter what time of year, a fresh water supply is necessary and appreciated.

Water features on a somewhat grander scale such as a small pond or waterfall are also magnets for attracting various other forms of wildlife. Within weeks, you'll likely find raccoons, turtles, toads, frogs, hawks, owls, herons, butterflies, dragonflies, and of course more birds, creating a fascinating mini-water ecosystem. But, just as a wide variety of mammals and reptiles will find a new water source, so will other predators. These hunters are happy to have a fresh source of water, but they will also find their next meal from the wildlife that lives and forages in and around water. So it goes with nature.

## THE IMPACT OF GARDENING GREEN

• A large water garden of 10 by 20 feet will attract dozens of birds when there's ample cover nearby. When plants such as irises and rushes are growing in the water and there are other appropriate cover and food supplies, birds will feed and even nest there.

• If 218 homeowners across the country created nature-friendly water gardens of this size, together they would add an acre of watery potential habitat for birds and other wildlife.

*Not every soil can bear all things.*

VIRGIL

# Plant to support butterflies.

*Help reverse an alarming trend of butterfly endangerment.*

In the warm summer months, it's easy to tell the gardens that are the serious butterfly attractors. Where butterflies abound, it's usually not by chance. As much as we want to promote their presence in our gardens, forces such as development, pesticides, and logging have destroyed important habitats for butterflies around the world.

Although you may not be able to directly influence what happens in distant places, you can start by doing something about butterflies where you live. Your own garden can be a place that helps their populations multiply. They're attracted by specific elements, all of which can easily be added to any garden.

## Creating a butterfly-friendly garden

Butterflies need nectar throughout their life, but adults feed primarily in sunny areas. In search of nectar, they are most attracted to brightly colored flowers in hues of red, orange, yellow, purple, and pink. Flowers with flat tops make good landing pads, and short flower tubes make easier access to the nectar. Good tried and true examples of sun-loving favorite flowers include zinnia, verbena, black-eyed Susan, purple coneflower, butterfly bush, beebalm, milkweed, and lantana.

To create an even more inviting environment, provide a water source in the form of a shallow mud puddle or *muddle*. A saucer from a flowerpot or any shallow

> **DID YOU KNOW THAT…**
>
> ❀ 19 species of American butterflies are either endangered or threatened.[1]
>
> ❀ Although one of our favorite butterflies, the monarch, is not an endangered species, its annual migration is considered a "threatened phenomenon" by entomologists. Logging, development, and unwise agricultural practices have destroyed many of the best overwintering sites.[2]

container works well. By placing a flat rock within the saucer, you create a convenient spot for butterflies to land and rest as they take up water, minerals, and nutrients. Muddles are easy to make. In addition to the container and stone, add some sand, mushroom compost, and water to create a slurry mix.

Butterflies also need to warm their wings before taking flight. To accommodate them, flat stones are good for absorbing heat. Position them throughout the garden as a great place for butterflies to rest and bask in the sun's rays before their busy day begins.

Attracting butterflies is only half the pleasure. Encourage them to stay and lay eggs for a future generations by including in the garden or landscape host-specific plants that serve as food for the butterfly larvae.

Butterflies lay their eggs on host plants that will serve as the food source during the larval caterpillar stage of development. It's important to do your research and know which plants are the best hosts for each butterfly that may be in your garden. They usually have a strong preference to just one or only a few specific plants.

Some popular host plant choices include parsley, dill, fennel, Queen Anne's Lace, passion vine, milkweed, and many grasses. Again, check with your Cooperative Extension service for your state. There are also many wonderful lists online. But be sure to keep in mind, these are plants for caterpillars to eat. Some might not be the most ornamental plants in your garden. Consider putting them out of view or in more naturalized parts of your landscape.

Also consider that as the caterpillar matures, it consumes the foliage of the host plant as its only food source. Expect and anticipate this, and don't confuse the damage as a problem caused by an undesirable pest. Avoid the use of any insecticides or pesticides. This includes even the use of otherwise eco-friendly biological controls such as *Bacillus thuringiensis* (Bt).

After a few weeks of feeding on the host plants, a chrysalis will form, and the larvae will develop into the next generation of butterflies not only to adorn your garden but also to perform important pollinating duties as well.

Although there are more than seven hundred species of butterflies in North America, ranging in size from barely a half-inch to nearly ten inches, most have a short life span averaging only ten to twenty days. The more we can do to attract and keep them in our gardens, the more enjoyment we'll have from these beautiful creatures.

## THE IMPACT OF GARDENING GREEN

• Cultivating habitat for butterflies in your garden is an excellent way to supplement the habitat of threatened species and helps to ensure that other species do not decline.[3]

• Monarch butterflies lay eggs in summer. Egg numbers can vary, but 400 or so is typical. Allow just 1 milkweed plant to reseed in your garden, and you can be responsible for the reproduction of four hundred new monarchs. Assuming half of them get to adult size, that would mean 200 new monarch butterflies entering the world each summer.

# Participate in the National Wildlife Federation's Wildlife Habitat Program.

*This is an easy way for you to help raise awareness about the importance of gardening with the environment in mind.*

Perhaps you've seen them. Those small but attractive signs posted near a school yard, a backyard, or by the street. The people that display them are proud to show that they are one of the National Wildlife Federation's "Certified Wildlife Habitats." And chances are if you're an environmentally aware gardener, you're already doing many of the things in your landscape that could get it certified as a Backyard Wildlife Habitat, too.

> DID YOU KNOW THAT . . .
>
> ❀ The National Wildlife Federation recently celebrated its 70th anniversary and was able to mark it by meeting a goal of naming 70,000 yards, schools, and communities as certified Backyard Wildlife Habitats.[1]

The guidelines for certification require you to provide elements from each of the following areas:

**Food sources.** This means planting native plants or other plants that feed wildlife, such as those that produce seeds, fruits, nuts, berries, or nectar.

**Water sources.** Have in place a water feature such as a birdbath, pond, water garden, or stream.

**Cover.** Provide cover in the form of a thicket, a rock pile, or a birdhouse.

**Places to raise young**. These could be dense shrubs, vegetation, nesting boxes, or a pond.

**Sustainable gardening**. Garden in a way that assists nature, by mulching, composting, creating a rain garden, or fertilizing without chemicals.

All it takes to become certified is to fill out an application and send it along with $15 to cover costs. You'll even receive a yard sign from the National Wildlife Federation that announces your certification.

For more information, contact the National Wildlife Federation at 1-800-822-9919, visit its Web site at www.nwf.org, or email info@nwf.org.

## THE IMPACT OF GARDENING GREEN

• Establishing your property as a certified National Wildlife Federation Backyard Wildlife Habitat will go a long way toward protecting and encouraging the biodiversity of your yard and your neighborhood. In the process, you'll enjoy the beauty and animation of colorful birds, hummingbirds, and butterflies in your garden.

• If you have children, this is a great way to get them involved in environmental issues. Their Backyard Wildlife Habitat is sure to be a stepping-stone to a lifetime of ecological awareness—and there's no better way to save the planet than that!

*Over fertilized plants may be beautiful but are otherwise useless, like people whose energies are devoted so completely to their appearance that there is no other development.*

WILLIAM LONGGOOD

# CHAPTER EIGHT

# TAKING IT OVER
# THE FENCE

Writing this book has been bittersweet. I have never been more inspired to write about something than the words you've read between these pages.

When it comes to global warming, we can't turn on the radio, read the paper, watch the news, or surf the Web without the topic coming up. That's good . . . but mostly it's a shame. The reason it is in our faces so much now is because the world is finally waking up to the realization that we have a big problem and one that is not going away—at least on its own. Certainly we get the point that our world is in trouble. We barely have a chance to have coffee each morning before we hear something about global environmental issues.

You and I and everyone else who inhabits this planet are in this together, but we've all overslept. The wheels are in motion, and they're not slowing down. In fact, they're speeding up. But how do you stop a runaway train? Well, it's not quite that bad . . . yet. But it will be soon without each of us taking action. And that's why I'm glad the topic is in our face every day.

On the other hand, we can easily become numb and desensitized to such a constant barrage of information. We cannot afford to become complacent.

In some ways, the environment seems like such a nebulous concept. How can we as individuals get our arms around such a global issue? Indeed, it can be overwhelming when you think about all the time and activity involved in causing, perpetuating, and accelerating this world-wide crisis that we are now charged with stopping.

The answer to this environmental emergency lies in each of us taking action and doing what we can, one by one, starting at home. Up to this point, I've given you a number of ways in which you can begin by taking simple yet significant actions in your daily lives. But here's where that impact can have an even greater effect more quickly: Take your message to the street. Be a visible and vocal advocate for the cause we all share.

It's one thing to jump on the bandwagon of going green. It's another to know that you can do something significant and that it will impact more than your own little corner of the world. It's like the old joke: How do you eat an elephant? One bite at a time! Impacting the planet is that way. We can't change it all at once, but we can by doing it one *yard* at a time. As long as we lead by example and walk the talk, our actions will be contagious as momentum builds across the globe.

Studies show that in spite of media exposure or even saturation in this case, one of the most influential ways to effect change in conservation behavior is to be a real life example to your friends and neighbors who know and trust you. There's no better substitute than being able to lead and teach by example. No longer can we live by the expression, "Do as I say, not as I do." It is time to walk our talk, and talk we should, as much as we can. Be an advocate and active participant in making a difference, beyond the walls of your house and garden.

As gardeners, we can promote awareness by creating an eco-friendly landscape and letting our neighbors know about it, subtly or outwardly. Using environmentally responsible equipment like electric or rechargeable tools cuts down on harmful emissions and noise pollution. Refraining from the use of pesticides and chemicals protects sensitive ecosystems above and below the ground and reduces harmful pollutants that wash into our waterways.

Using water more responsibly by irrigating at the right times, using drip systems to deliver it more efficiently, and harvesting it from our roofs and impervious surfaces saves water, cuts down on runoff, and preserves a valuable resource for later use. Protecting boundaries and natural areas provides a buffer to further reduce the harmful affects of chemicals running off our property. The list goes on . . .

Beyond our garden walls and over the fence, there are so many ways to leverage your actions and your abilities to stoke the fire. Be a voice in your community and become involved through schools, churches, and civic groups. Organize habitat protection zones or cleanup days and encourage your town to sponsor curbside recycling, for example. Find a sponsor for a tree planting day or start a community or neighborhood garden.

Join special interest groups that share your goals. There are a number of them listed later in the chapter. And become politically active. The biggest leverage we can have locally and globally is to become and stay involved in our government leadership that is charged with the duty and responsibility of making our voice heard and effecting laws that protect, promote, and preserve our beliefs, our health, and the health of this planet.

Writing this book has opened my eyes to an even bigger world and helped me become more aware of the many ways we really can make a difference. I am not discouraged. More than anything, I am motivated. Our planet is in the state it's in now by the neglect and impact we have been making, mostly in the last few decades. We have greedily and irresponsibly consumed its resources, and what have we given back? Chemicals that poison the earth and pollute the air.

Now it's time to replenish the resources so they can repair and heal. By providing our human energy through our voice and, most importantly, our actions, we can begin to repay and even repair, to some extent, the resources that we have neglected, exploited, and taken for granted for way too long.

I know you're doing what you can at home to make a difference. Now it's time to take it to the next level, where your efforts can really be leveraged. The suggestions in the following pages will get you started on ways to reach out to your neighbors, your community, and beyond.

# Request that your local nursery or garden center carry eco-friendly products.

Stores by their nature want to carry what their customers like to buy. Making it known that you want them to carry environmentally friendly products just might stir them to action. But don't mention it to just any employee. Instead make sure to speak with the owner or manager, or find the name of the decision-maker responsible for product selection.

Be as precise as you can. Simply saying you want more organic or earth-friendly products is too broad. Think about exactly the kinds of products you'd like to see (use this book for reference), and make specific recommendations.

Perhaps you might like to have a better selection of certified organic or natural pest-control products and fertilizers. Or maybe it would be nice to choose MSC "certified" compost or mulch available by the truckload instead of in small plastic bags. Suggest that a more extensive native plant section be made available or agree to help organize a plastic pot recycling program.

And if your friends and family are like-minded, request that *they* ask the same questions, preferably to the same person in charge. After all, in retail, one person with a passion can be dismissed as an anomaly (or worse, a crank!). But if more people are making the effort to ask for eco-friendly alternatives, it will seem like strong customer demand. Above all, be sincere and point out the benefits of encouraging more environmental stewardship not only for you and your community but for the business as well.

Finally, remember that getting eco-friendly products on the shelf is only half the battle. Keeping them there is another. Merchants can and do respond to customer requests when they feel it is justified. But they are in business to sell product and in the law of the retail jungle, it is survival of the *most profitable!* This is especially true with shelf space often at a premium. With high costs and low margins, merchants have to be sure that any amount of space allocated to a product is earning its keep.

So when they do honor your requests, repay the favor. Support their efforts and acknowledge your appreciation by following through on your purchases, even when it means going a little out of your way or paying a little more. A few extra miles or dollars is a very small price to pay compared to the alternative.

# Educate your neighbors.

It's amazing how much learning about gardening takes place over the fence. Someone looks over to admire your most recent project or how well the roses are doing and the next thing you know, you're deep in conversation about your favorite composting or pruning methods.

These neighborly chats are also what education experts like to call "teachable moments." They're a great opportunity to slip in your plug for environmental stewardship, the benefits of a compost pile, the advantage of gasless power tools, and the attributes of native plants.

But the very best way to get your neighborhood gardening green is by shining example. Have a great yard, and be willing to share with all who will listen how you achieved it. You might even want to put up a small sign such as "My yard is eco-friendly." (Remember all those "Drug-free lawn" signs a few years back?) You will undoubtedly attract attention and draw questions from curious neighbors and passers by.

Case in point: A friend who lives in a small town in Kansas told me about a woman in the neighborhood who purchased an electric lawn mower. At first her neighbors were quite skeptical. Was it really powerful enough? Soon they began to love how quiet it was on Saturday mornings, noticing her lawn looked every bit as good as before. Two of her neighbors ended up borrowing her mower to try it out—and then bought electric mowers of their own.

Another example: I was visiting a hilly Iowa neighborhood where everyone was spending lots of time, money, and chemicals on maintaining grass on their steep front slopes. An avid gardener on the street finally decided this was enough and terraced her area, planting it entirely in perennials, groundcovers, and low-growing shrubs. Her neighbors were skeptical at first, reluctant to give up their front yard grass no matter how difficult it was to maintain. But once they were able to appreciate the yard's beauty and low maintenance, terraced front gardens started popping up all along that street. I bet many of them didn't even realize the environmental improvements they had made by reducing erosion and groundwater runoff.

### Practicing what I preach

Finally, my own personal live-by-example message is as important as anything I say or do as a professional gardener on television or in this book. In my yard, I know people are watching—not in a weird way mind you, but just that they *are* paying attention. And I'm glad for that. It also keeps me on my toes, as it should. But over the years, I have learned that although there are times where pulling out the less eco-friendly option might make the task easier, taking shortcuts can often have a price of its own.

As a gardening communicator by profession, I have the unique opportunity and privilege to reach literally millions of households each week. I'm thankful for that. But I also realize I have a responsibility to provide not only accurate but also sincere information. Anything less would be hypocritical at the very least.

Fortunately, through all my media opportunities, I am able to say what I believe. Even better, I'll never be required to say anything I don't agree with. I wouldn't have it any other way. Yet in spite of those of us in the gardening profession being perceived as genuine by the public, surveys show that there is no substitute for over-the-fence, neighborly advice.

I say it often: one of my favorite things about gardening is that no matter how much you know, there's always more to know. So no matter where you are in your gardening journey, from wet behind the ears to very green in the thumbs, you're always learning. As you learn and grow, you will be a teacher and mentor to the friends, neighbors, and even strangers who perceive you as knowing more than they do. So *carpe diem*! It's your opportunity and mine to share with anyone who will listen. Be clear in your beliefs and know why they are important, not only to you and the person you are talking to, but also to the environment.

So talk green gardening to your neighbors every chance you get. It really is a universal language!

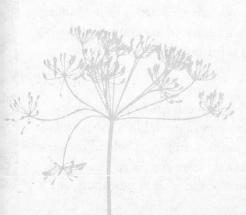

# If they're not going to use it themselves, encourage your neighbors to share compostable yard waste with you.

Want to become *really* popular with your neighbors? Ask if you can have their grass clippings, raked-up leaves, evergreen trimmings, and other branch trimmings. In my new neighborhood, I am conditioning my neighbors to deposit their bags of leaves at my house instead of leaving them in the street for the garbage truck. I also have the landscapers coming by with their shredded leaf litter collected from neighbors' yards.

But be careful what you ask for. Once neighbors know you are willing to take their leaves and grass clippings, something strange happens. In my old neighborhood, my neighbors behind and to the side relished the opportunity to unload their leaves on me. Literally hundreds of bags would appear overnight, neatly stacked up along my back fence. But it was all for the best. I put every bit of those leaves to work as shredded leaf mulch to enrich my garden beds. It took only a few seasons of those actions before people were asking me how I was able to have such great garden soil in all those beds around the yard. Now you know.

The word got out after that, and other neighbors started doing the same thing. The competition for yard waste was perfectly fine with me; I still had plenty to work with, but the best part was that now fewer leaves and grass clippings were going into the landfills and solid waste areas. They were staying home instead, eliminating the associated costs of transporting and storage. As every seasoned gardener knows and my neighbors soon found out, grass clippings and leaves make the world's best compost and mulch.

Anytime you start asking for something people thought had no value, they begin to wonder if perhaps it *does* have value—that maybe they should be keeping their yard waste and composting it themselves. After all, when they look at your landscape and see the benefits, it makes a pretty convincing argument! Keeping compostable yard waste close to home is a great way to help the planet and beautify the neighborhood at the same time.

# Start an eco-friendly garden at your local school, day care, or other facility.

Any gardener can attest to the therapeutic benefits of digging in the dirt and of the pleasure derived from nurturing its offspring. Consider developing a healing garden at a hospital, church, retirement home, or local women and children's shelter. The staff at these places is often looking for opportunities to involve its children or patrons in educational, enriching activities—and usually on a shoestring budget.

It would be especially meaningful to start a garden at your child's school. It sends an important message to children that their parents care so much about the environment, their school, and *them*, that they're willing to put in the time and effort to build a garden.

Even if you don't have school-age children, being a gardening mentor is a great way to tap into the enthusiasm for nature that nearly all children have. Instilling an appreciation for stewardship at the earliest stages of education teaches lessons that last a lifetime. And it's more than just gardening. Although that's what gets them excited, slip in history about the plants and the origins of the names, have them draw the design and measure the beds, make the plant tags and record the progress, and I'd say you've more than covered all-important reading, writing, and arithmetic requirements for the season. (You can even tap into art, language, math, English, history, and nutrition—gardening as the frame for an entire curriculum!)

Consider talking with classroom teachers about how they can work with you on developing science lessons around the theme of the garden and allow the students to come out and help. It's a great opportunity for hands-on learning.

By letting children take ownership of the garden, from seed to harvest, you instill in them a sense of pride and responsibility and a desire to learn even more. When you include vegetables and herbs and then allow children to experience what truly fresh, homegrown food tastes like, chances are very good they'll be hooked for life. And think of the relationships you'll build as you watch things grow together!

And the biggest reward of all this? When you do it all in an eco-friendly way, you teach children about environmental stewardship, biodiversity, and sustainable ecosystems. Indeed those are big words, but they will come to life in ways that even children can understand when you show them simple but real-life examples. In the eco-friendly way of gardening, you can feel good about knowing they are not exposed to chemicals and pesticides—especially when they sneak a taste of that plump red cherry tomato, fresh from the vine!

Most schools are delighted for parents to help start a garden or tend to an existing one. But don't just stop there. Talk with the principal or the head of the daycare center about green gardening, and watch them really get excited. Consider creating an organic garden that attracts butterflies, includes a compost heap, and of course produces fruits and vegetables for the children to harvest and eat. If you make sure you'll have enough support to keep the project going through the years, you'll likely have no problem getting them on board. A little recruiting on your part should unearth some willing parents who would love to give time back to the school through a gardening project.

Money is usually the biggest obstacle to developing a sustainable gardening program in schools, day cares, and other facilities. But it doesn't have to be. There are many private companies that offer grants to schools and non-profits for educationally related garden endeavors. Organizations like The National Gardening Association offer opportunities for qualified applicants to apply for financial assistance, and there are many others. Local gardening centers may also be glad to act as sponsors—just make sure that you are in charge of what kinds of products and methods you use!

The garden doesn't have to be outdoors, either. During the cold winter months, encourage teachers to set up indoor gardens in containers, start seeds indoors, or explore hydroponic gardening.

As one who enjoys providing these opportunities to children whenever I can, there is no greater joy than to see them delight in the pleasures of gardening. Moreover, it is very reassuring to know that the children are working in safe, eco-friendly conditions. For me it is all a joy, but the experience of seeing their faces as they bite into the fruits of their labor for the very first time—it's nearly indescribable. The bonus for me is knowing that these foods are likely the freshest, most nutritious, and only chemical-free vegetables and fruits they have ever eaten . . . so far.

No matter how busy we are, teaching children about gardening—green gardening—is a priceless opportunity to make memories and teach important lessons that last a lifetime. You'll be cultivating far more than just plants.

# Develop an eco-friendly garden in your neighborhood.

You've probably heard somewhere that "great fences make great neighbors." I guess if you're really into privacy, there's an argument in favor of that statement. But is that really how you want to live? I propose a new statement: "Great *gardens* make great neighbors." And honestly, it doesn't have to be great. But if your neighborhood has a vacant lot, a small park or playground, or any parcel of plantable common ground, it's a green opportunity just waiting to happen.

Stories abound about how neighborhoods across the country transformed from crime-infested war zones to a beehive of all things good when a neighborhood or community garden was installed. There's something both magical and magnetic about a garden. When neighbors come together to create a common garden, it often becomes the catalyst to stimulate social interaction, as well as neighborhood and community development. Strangers become friends, and neighborhoods come together. Quality of life improves, and neighborhoods are beautified. What better way to enhance an unadorned space while creating a place to connect people across intergenerational and multicultural boundaries.

## To consider as you create your garden

As you create a common garden, an organizing body may decide on the ground rules for the garden. Maybe the space is used as a community vegetable garden and everyone works together in one common plot. Or neighbors may be allotted individual spaces for their own personal gardening where they can plant whatever they want.

But however the garden is laid out, it is good to decide ahead of time the issues that are most important for the individual gardeners and the community as a whole. Your group may want the garden to be entirely eco-friendly. It certainly would be an environmentally responsible way to act locally to protect children and pets, neighbors, the community, and the environment from the hazards associated with nonsustainable gardening practices.

You will also need to address money issues. When it comes to funding the start-up and ongoing costs for smaller projects, individuals may chip into the pot. It is also possible that grants for such plans might be available from the city, state, or federal government or that others will subsidize your project. The city manager's office or state department of natural resources is a good starting point. Corporations that focus on gardening often set aside grant money to promote community gardening efforts. The reference librarian at your local library can help you track down possible grants.

Planting an eco-friendly garden in your neighborhood builds a sense of community like nothing else. Such gardens provide opportunities for exercise, education, therapy, relaxation, and social interaction. In addition, green space is preserved and resources are conserved. Neighborhoods can even come together through their gardens for community outreach programs like Plant a Row for the Hungry. The eco-friendly garden in your community or neighborhood is limited only by your imagination and commitment—but the benefits can reach far beyond its original boundaries.

# Get involved in tree preservation and planting in your neighborhood.

I don't believe it's possible to overemphasize the many benefits of trees or even to have too many of them. Beyond their natural beauty, they make a new neighborhood look established, provide blissful shade on hot days, screen cold winds, buffer erosion and runoff, and of course, exchange bad air for good.

So if trees are so good, why are so many cut down to establish new developments, change the landscaping, or simply to . . . well, that part I've never figured out yet. Maybe you've seen what I see: large, mature trees topped like a hat rack for *no* apparent reason. And believe me, there is *no* reason (other than safety or power line obstruction) that necessitates the senseless topping of trees.

Topping trees has been a problem for decades, and it is remarkable how widespread it is. Simply put, topping hideously deforms and can eventually kill a tree. It causes stress when much of the leaf-bearing crown is removed, which can temporarily starve the tree. As a defensive action, the starving tree responds by rapidly sending out multiple shoots from the latent buds below each cut. The new grow that ascends is only anchored in the outermost layers of the parent branch, making the tree weaker and actually more dangerous than before topping it. If you'd like more information about the topic of terrible tree topping (sorry, couldn't resist again), visit www.plantamnesty.org.

By the way, if encroaching branches are truly a problem on our roads, then the wrong tree or shrub was planted there in the first place. Often it is simply a matter of selecting plant material that is more suitable for growing under power lines. Understanding the mature height of a tree or large shrub and putting that knowledge to work is critical to preventing this abusive practice nationally.

As we lose trees that eventually die from topping, clear-cutting, or indiscriminant development, look for the opportunity to plant trees at every turn. An obvious place to start is in neighborhoods, especially new neighborhoods, where the developer has stripped the land of vegetation. If you don't have many in your community, organize a neighborhood effort to plant more. A good source for information is a local certified arborist, or contact your Cooperative Extension office to find out what trees are recommended for your area.

If you will be planting trees along a street, it's especially important to choose the right *mature*-sized tree. Too often trees are planted in an area that will not support its mature height and width. When planted near obstructions, especially power lines, an inappropriately placed tree is destined for disaster as it grows and encroaches onto those lines.

Other considerations for street plantings should include choosing trees that don't produce a lot of litter, don't have the type of root system that will crack streets and sidewalks, and aren't prone to weak branch structure (which can end up falling on cars). They should also be known for their ability to grow in the often difficult, harsh conditions street trees have to endure.

# Get involved in local parks and green spaces, and work with them to use eco-friendly management.

I hope I have convinced you that you can make a difference just by gardening your own little corner of the world a bit differently. Imagine if your garden were many or even hundreds of acres! That's the idea behind ecologically smart management of parks and other green spaces.

Most parks and green spaces have governing boards overseeing them, such as a city parks department or a county board. Often, these boards are starved for active citizens who want to be involved, so getting on the board or at least on a committee may be easier than you'd think.

These organizations usually also have a critical need for volunteers to help clear trails, tend to plantings, staff visitor's centers, and maintain campgrounds among other things. Even at this level, you have the ability to make a difference by helping perform tasks you feel are ecologically healthy, or by gently nudging community leaders to convert to practices that are more environmentally sound. This is also a good way to get to know the people in charge and make a positive impact by encouraging their commitment to environmental stewardship.

As with all pursuits, it's best to choose something either close to home or near and dear to your heart. When you're involved in something you're passionate about, there is an enthusiasm and energy to get things accomplished that otherwise may never happen. Getting involved in your local or state park will not only enhance a place you enjoy already, but it will benefit the planet as well.

# Get involved in local bird habitat programs.

I can't imagine my own backyard without birds. My feeders are teeming with activity bringing color, motion, and sweet melody to compliment the other elements of my garden. The birds are sure to please whenever they visit and are always a reliable form of entertainment.

In spite of my best efforts to be a good steward to the birds under my watch, statistics such as the following are startling:

According to the Washington-based Worldwatch Institute, human-related factors are threatening 99 percent of the most imperiled bird species and contributing to what has become the greatest wave of extinctions since the dinosaurs disappeared.[1]

According to a 2007 survey by BirdLife International, "about 22 percent of the 10,000 known bird species are seriously threatened, and of these, 179 are critically endangered with a serious possibility of imminent extinction."[2]

This is a sad statement about the health of our environment. Remember, both man and animals depend on this same habitat which we call Earth and compete for the natural resources it provides. Just like the poor canaries that were taken down into coal mine shafts as a test for toxic air, birds are still indicators of the state of our environment. Studying the relative health or decline of bird populations tells us a great deal about the effects of deforestation from logging, agriculture, urban development, and more. Unfortunately, the common result of these practices—no matter the root cause—is habitat loss and fragmentation.

Deforestation rates from 50,000 to 170,000 square kilometers per year (approximately 19,000 to 65,000 square miles) are ranked as the single greatest overall threat to birds, jeopardizing 85 percent of the world's most threatened bird species.[3]

According to www.birdlife.org, "The dramatic decline in Eurasian Skylark numbers in western Europe is indicative of the relentless intensification of agricultural practices and the non-sustainability of the European Union's Common Agricultural Policy."

BirdLife International has hypothesized that the rapid decline of raptors in Asia and elsewhere may be compared to the destructive effects of DDT on Peregrine Falcons and other birds of prey in the United States. By revisiting history, they hope to discover if a type of pesticide or poison is the cause.

You too can help by getting involved with local or national bird habitat programs that work with state and national parks to help raise funds and restore bird habitats. The Audubon Society can provide information about programs not far from where you live. Go to www.audubonpopulation.org.

There are also local volunteer opportunities to restore bird habitats and help monitor populations through the U.S. Fish and Wildlife Service. Contact your local office or visit a listing of federal government volunteer positions involving fish and wildlife at www.volunteer.gov/gov.

Some of the things you can do to protect and preserve habitats include hands-on activities such as planting trees, shrubs, and groundcovers that provide the necessities of life for birds living or passing through your area. But you can also help by getting involved politically and working with special interest groups that focus on preserving tropical rain forests and other areas far away that are so critical to migratory birds.

# Get political! Join an organization that organizes and lobbies for ecological issues.

Protecting our land, water, air, and wildlife requires citizen action. Nothing is going to change if we sit complacently and wait for others to make a difference. And together, we can make a huge difference—we can change the entire course of history, in fact.

Nowhere is that opportunity for change more apparent than in the political arena. We live in a country where laws are written for the people, by the people. Our representatives locally and nationally are just that: representatives that we put in office to be our voice and to represent our interests. It begins at the local level, taking the time to understand the issues that affect you and the environment right in your own backyard. It involves getting to know the candidates who will be your voice and letting them know the issues that are of the most concern to you. Tremendous opportunities are often overlooked to meet with candidates seeking office, understand their position on the issues, and share yours with them.

Once you find a candidate whom you support, do all that you can to help that person get elected. Grassroot efforts are still the most effective ways to accomplish many things, from electing our representatives to protecting the planet. Once your candidates are elected, stay involved. Provide support financially if you can, and through service. Be their eyes and ears. The stronger the relationship you have with those who represent you, the better opportunity you will have to be heard and supported in return.

As we move from local, regional, and state involvement, we still have elected officials who represent us in the nation's capitol.

Although direct access becomes more difficult, there are many easy ways now to have our voices heard through toll-free numbers and online access.

Web sites of many foundations and organizations for your special interest are a good way to stay informed on the issues. And of course, always consider the source of the information. As unbiased as information may seem, there is always a slant, no matter how slight. Being informed and staying current on important issues that affect our planet allows you to make informed decisions and communicate effectively with others.

Some organizations to check out online (most have special sections you can click on to find out about local volunteer opportunities) include the following: The League of Conservation Voters, The Nature Conservancy, the Sierra Club, the Audubon Society, the National Park Service, The World Wildlife Fund, Izaak Walton League of America, Scenic America (a tree preservation group), the National Wildlife Federation, The Ocean Conservancy, Friends of the Earth, the Land Trust Alliance, Republicans for Environmental Protection, The Natural Resources Defense Council, and Greenpeace.

Fellow citizens and gardeners, we should never underestimate the opportunity we have to be heard and the influence we hold even as individuals, but especially when we unite with others as one voice. The passage of even one law can have a huge impact on our planet.

Today, nothing can be taken for granted. To be sure, if we are to change the world, there is no room for complacency. Apathy has no place in this day and age as we face an ever-growing global crisis.

*He who plants a tree loves
others besides himself.*

ANONYMOUS

*There are no passengers*
*on spaceship Earth.*
*We are all crew.*

MARSHALL McLUHAN

# NOTES

## Chapter Two: Conserving Water in the Garden

**Pages 20-22**: Introduction

1. EPA, www.epa.gov/watersense/water/why.htm
2. Amy Vickers, *Handbook of Water Use and Conservation*, WaterPlow Press, 2003.
3. EPA, www.epa.gov/watersense/water/why.htm

**Pages 23-27**: Supply only the water your plants need—know when to water and how much.

1. EPA, www.epa.gov/watersense/water/why.htm
2. Amanda Dewees *Improving Landscape Irrigation Efficiency*, Austin Water Utility, Water Conservation Department, www.awwa.org/waterwiser
3. "Residential Weather-Based Irrigation Scheduling: Evidence from the Irvine 'ET Controller' Study." The Irrigation Association, www.irrigation.org

**Pages 28-29**: Water deeply and less often.

1. Interview, Tom Ash, WeatherTRAK, www.weathertrak.com
2. Interview, Tom Ash, WeatherTRAK, www.weathertrak.com

**Page 30**: Water at the right time of day.

1. The Irrigation Association, www.irrigation.org
2. Texas Cooperative Extension, www.texasextension.tamu.edu/ag_nr.html

**Page 31**: Mulch, mulch, mulch!

1. California Integrated Waste Management Board, www.ciwmb.ca.gov/Publications/Organics/44302010.pdf

**Pages 32-36**: Use rain barrels.

1. www.rainbarrelguide.com
2. Amy Vickers, *Handbook of Water Use and Conservation*, WaterPlow Press, 2003.
3. Interview, Lisa Ayres, AridSolutionsInc.com

**Pages 37-38**: Fix leaky faucets and hoses.

1. American Water Works Association, www.awwa.org/awwa/waterwiser/dripcalc.cfm

**Page 40**: Don't leave your hose running while unattended.

1. Indiana Department of Natural Resources, www.in.gov/dnr/
water/oldsite/water_availability/WaterResource/water_cons.html

**Pages 41-42**: Program your irrigation system correctly to apply the
right amount of water.

1. Amanda Dewees, *Improving Landscape Irrigation Efficiency*,
Austin Water Utility, Water Conservation Department,
www.awwa.org/waterwiser

**Pages 43-44**: Include a rain sensor in an automatic
irrigation system.

1. Bernard Cardenas-Lailhacar and Michael D Dukes, P.E., "Ex-
panding Disk Rain Sensor Performance and Potential Irrigation
Water Savings," University of Florida, www.irrigation.ifas.ufl.edu/RS/
pubs/RS%20accepted.pdf

**Pages 45-46**: Install an integrated weather monitoring system.

1. Amanda Dewees, *Improving Landscape Irrigation Efficiency*,
Austin Water Utility, Water Conservation Department, www.awwa.
org/waterwiser

2. Tom Ash, WeatherTRAK, www.weathertrak.com

3. WeatherTRAK Irrigation Systems from Hydropoint Data
Systems, Inc., www.weathertrak.com

4. City of Pelham, Alabama, www.pelhamonline.com

**Pages 47-48**: Irrigate deeply using the two-step
"cycle-and-soak" process.

1. Amy Vickers, *Handbook of Water Use and Conservation*, Water-
Plow Press, 2003.

2. Ibid.

3. Tom Ash, WeatherTRAK, www.weathertrak.com

**Page 49**: Program your irrigation system for seasonal needs.

1. City of Albuquerque, www.cabq.gov/water

2. www.ext.colostate.edu/mg/files/gardennotes/266-checkup.html

**Pages 50-53**: Maintain your irrigation system.

1. California Urban Water Conservation Council, cuwcc.org

2. Tom Ash, WeatherTRAK, www.weathertrak.com

3. Las Vegas Valley Water District, Southern Nevada Water

Authority, www.snwa.com/html/cons_waterfacts.html

**Pages 54-56**: Convert to soaker hoses or drip irrigation where feasible.

1. Amy Vickers, *Handbook of Water Use and Conservation*, Water-Plow Press, 2003.

2. Ibid.

**Pages 57-63**: Use plants that need less water—Xeriscape™.

1. Southern Nevada Water Authority, H2O University, www.h2ouniversity.org/html/6-12_facts_conservation.html

2. "Water—Use It Wisely" campaign of Phoenix, Arizona, www.wateruseitwisely.com/info4conserv/H2OwaterIcons.pdf

3. City of Albuquerque, www.cabq.gov/waterconservation

4. Michael D. Dukes and Grady L. Miller, "Residential Irrigation Efficiency Assessment Monitoring," University of Florida, Agricultural and Biological Engineering Department

5. Denver Water, www.denverwater.org/drought/fourhouses.html

## Chapter Three: Reducing Garden Chemicals to Protect Our Water

**Pages 64-66**: Introduction

1. *Pesticides Industry Sales and Usage 2000 and 2001 Market Estimates* (May 2004), www.epa.gov/oppbead1/pestsales/01pestsales/market_estimates2001.pdf

2. www.beyondpesticides.org/lawn/factsheets/facts&figures.htm

3. Ibid.

4. Ibid.

5. Ibid.

**Pages 67-69**: Protect soil flora and fauna.

1. www.epa.gov/oppfead1/Publications/catalog/greenscaping.pdf (p4)

2. *Pesticides and Water Quality: Principles, Policies, and Programs*, Purdue University, www.btny.purdue.edu/pubs/PPP/PPP-35.pdf (5/0; p13)

3. Jeff Lowenfels and Wayne Lewis, *Teaming with Microbes: A Gardener's Guide to the Soil Food Web*, Timber Press, 2006.

NOTES

**Pages 70-72**: Build healthy soil by adding organic matter.

1. Colorado Master Gardener Notes #711, www.cmg.colostate.edu/gardennotes/veg.html

2. Ibid.

**Pages 73-75**: Use compost as a soil conditioner and fertilizer.

1. EPA: Compost in Landscaping Applications 5/03 report, www.epa.gov/GreenScapes/pubs/compost.pdf

2. Ibid.

3. Ibid.

4. California Integrated Waste Management Board, www.ciwmb.ca.gov/Publications/Organics/44302010.pdf

5. Ibid.

**Pages 76-78**: Let earthworms do the work for *really* healthy soil.

1. www.organicrosecare.org/articles/worm_castings.php

2. ATTRA, Sustainable Soil Systems, www.cmg.colostate.edu/gardennotes/212.pdf

3. www.organicrosecare.org/articles/worm_castings.php

4. Jeff Lowenfels and Wayne Lewis, *Teaming with Microbes: A Gardener's Guide to the Soil Food Web*, Timber Press, 2006.

**Pages 79-82**: Use natural and organic sources of nutrients.

1. *A Gardener's Guide to Protecting Water Quality*, www.cals.ncsu.edu/agcomm/publications/Ag-612.pdf

2. *A Gardener's Guide to Protecting Water Quality*, www.cals.ncsu.edu/agcomm/publications/Ag-612.pdf

3. EPA, www.epa.gov/oppfead1/Publications/catalog/greenscaping.pdf

4. Marty Petrovic, "For A 'Green' Lawn, Focus On Mowing, Not Early Fertilizing," Department of Horticulture at Cornell University, 4/30/07, www.gardening.cornell.edu/news/lawn.html

**Pages 91-93**: Reduce chemical use by raising your tolerance for little imperfections.

1. EPA: "Pesticide Industry Sales and Usage, 2000 and 2001 Market Estimates" (2004), www.epa.gov/oppbead1/pestsales/01pestsales/market_estimates2001.pdf

2. Ibid.

340

THE **green** GARDENER'S GUIDE

3) "Pesticides and Pest Prevention Strategies for the Home, Lawn and Garden," Purdue University (5/01; p24), www.btny.purdue.edu/pubs/PPP/PPP-34.pdf

**Pages 94-95**: Catch problems early.

1. "Understanding Glyphosate to Increase Performance," Iowa State University, Purdue University, University of Wisconsin, and University of Guelph (12/06) www.ces.purdue.edu/extmedia/GWC/GWC-2.pdf

2. Cornell University, www.nysaes.cornell.edu/pubs/press/2004/060210Ullrich.html

3. Ohio State University Extension, "Natural Organic Lawn Care for Ohio," HYG-4031-04, ohioline.osu.edu/hyg-fact/4000/4031.html

**Pages 106-109**: Use beneficial insects, the predatory agents of biological control.

1. "Pesticides and Pest Prevention Strategies for the Home, Lawn and Garden," Purdue University (5/01; p24), www.btny.purdue.edu/pubs/PPP/PPP-34.pdf

**Pages 110-112**: If you're going to use an insecticide, explore biological ones first.

1. www.pesticide.org/bacillus.pdf

2. W.S. Cranshaw, *Bacillus thuringiensis*, Updated 7/31/06, www.pcmg-texas.org/bacillus_thuringiensis.pdf

3. Ibid.

**Pages 113-115**: Mulch to control weeds.

1. Cornell University, "Types and Uses of Mulch in the Landscape," www.counties.cce.cornell.edu/chemung/publications/mulch-in-landscape.pdf

**Pages 118-120**: Use other easy ways to eliminate weeds without chemicals.

1. Lawn Pesticide Facts and Figures (from Beyond Pesticides), www.beyondpesticides.org/lawn/factsheets/facts&figures.htm

2. U.S. Department of the Interior, U.S. Geological Survey. *Pesticides in the Nation's Streams and Ground Water, 1992–2001— A Summary*, March 2006, www.pubs.usgs.gov/fs/2006/3028/

3. www.ourwaterourworld.org/pub/ow/lawns101.pdf

**Pages 121-124**: Don't nuke those weeds—solarize 'em.

1. U.S. Department of the Interior, U.S. Geological Survey. *Pesticides in the Nation's Streams and Ground Water, 1992–2001— A Summary*, March 2006, www.pubs.usgs.gov/fs/2006/3028/

**Pages 125-127**: Use corn gluten as a natural pre-emergence weed control.

1. NCAP, Northwest Coalition for Alternatives to Pesticides, www.pesticide.org/factsheets.html

2. Nick Christians, "Part III: Weeds," *Iowa State University Grounds Maintenance 34(3):28-32*, March 1999.

3. www.hort.iastate.edu/gluten/pdf/how-to-use-corn-gluten-meal.pdf

**Pages 128-131**: If you need to use a chemical, follow the label.

1. www.beyondpesticides.org/lawn/factsheets/facts&figures.htm

2. www.epa.gov/oppfead1/Publications/catalog/greenscaping.pdf

**Pages 135-137**: Don't spray on windy days.

1.www.beyondpesticides.org/infoservices/pesticidesandyou/Summer%2002/backyard_mosquito_management.pdf (2002)

2. www.beyondpesticides.org/infoservices/pesticidesandyou/Summer%2004/Getting%20the%20Drift%20on%20Chemical%20Trespass.pdf. Getting the Drift on Chemical Trespass (2004)

3. Ibid.

**Pages 138-140**: Get a soil test before you add fertilizers and other amendments.

1. *A Gardener's Guide to Protecting Water Quality*, www.cals.ncsu.edu/agcomm/publications/Ag-612.pdf

2. Ibid.

3. www.gardening.cornell.edu/news/lawn.html

*For A 'Green' Lawn, Focus On Mowing, Not Early Fertilizing* (4/30/07)

**Page 148**: Store chemicals safely.

1. "What you need to know about storing a pesticide," Penn State, 2003. www.pubs.cas.psu.edu/FreePubs/pdfs/uo216.pdf

2. www.epa.gov/pesticides/regulating/store and The Penn State

Pesticide Education Program, College of Agricultural Sciences

**Pages 151-153**: Dispose of chemicals safely.

1. EPA: "Household Hazardous Waste," www.epa.gov/epaoswer/non-hw/muncpl/hhw.htm

2. EPA: "Household Hazardous Waste," www.epa.gov/epaoswer/non-hw/muncpl/hhw.htm

3. www.dcr.virginia.gov/soil_&_water/nps.shtml

4. EPA: "Clean Sweep Program" (last updated 7/24/07), www.epa.gov/pesticides/regulating/clean_summ.htm

5. EPA: "Safe Disposal of Pesticides," www.epa.gov/pesticides/regulating/disposal.htm

**Pages 154-155**: Use bagged soil and mulch that is certified.

1. EPA: "Chromated Copper Arsenate (CCA)," www.epa.gov/oppad001/reregistration/cca/mulch_text_only.htm

**Pages 156-158**: Use alternatives to CCA-treated wood.

1. American Chemistry Council 2007, www.plasticsresource.com/s_plasticsresource/sec.asp?TRACKID=&CID=128&DID=230

2. Ibid.

**Pages 159-161**: Beware of the unintended effect of de-icers in winter.

1. Purdue Extension: "Roadside De-Icing Salts and Ornamental Plants" (4/06), www.hort.purdue.edu/ext/HO-142.pdf

2. Ibid.

3. University of Nebraska—Lincoln Extension, "Winter De-icing Agents for the Homeowner," www.ianrpubs.unl.edu:80/epublic/pages/publicationD.jsp?publicationId=716

**Pages 162-163**: Avoid fuel spills when filling gasoline-powered equipment.

1. The Alliance for Proper Gasoline Handling, www.gas-care.org/Press_release.htm

2. Michigan Master Gardener newsletter for January 2007 (p4), www.msue.msu.edu/objects/content_revision/download.cfm/item_id.361553/workspace_id.28611/Master%20Gardener%20Newsletter%20January%202007.pdf/

3. The Alliance for Proper Gasoline Handling,

www.gas-care.org/Press_release.htm
4. Ibid.
5. Ibid.

## Chapter Four: Landscaping to Control Runoff

**Pages 164-166**: Introduction

1. EPA: "Nonpoint Source Pollution: The Nation's Largest Water Quality Problem," www.epa.gov/owow/nps/facts/point1.htm

2. "Cornell University: Chronicle Online," www.news.cornell.edu/stories/March06/soil.erosion.threat.ssl.html

3. Water Education Foundation, "Where does MY water come from?" www.water-ed.org/watersources/subpage.asp?rid=9&page=385

**Pages 167-169**: Protect topsoil on construction sites.

1. "Cornell University: Chronicle Online," www.news.cornell.edu/stories/March06/soil.erosion.threat.ssl.html

2. Minnesota Pollution Control Agency, "Stormwater Program for Construction Activity," www.pca.state.mn.us/water/stormwater/stormwater-c.html

3. Tualatin Soil and Water Conservation District and the Small Acreage Steering Committee; Managing Soil Erosion on Small Acreages, Small Acreage Fact sheet #13, Protecting Your Land from Erosion

**Pages 170-171**: Add organic matter to the soil for percolation and retention.

1. University of Georgia Cooperative Extension Service

2. Washington State University, Whatcom County Extension, "Compost Basics," www.whatcom.wsu.edu/ag/compost/homecom1.atm

**Pages 172-174**: Don't till—let earthworms do the job.

1. R. Lal, School of Natural Resources, Ohio State University, "Mulching Effects on Runoff, Soil Erosion and Crop Response in Alfisols in Western Nigeria."

2. ATTRA, Sustainable Soil Systems, www.cmg.colostate.edu/gardennotes/212.pdf

**Pages 175-177**: Mulch to reduce runoff.

1. Tualatin Soil and Water Conservation District and the Small Acre-

age Steering Committee; Managing Soil Erosion on Small Acreages, Small Acreage Fact sheet #13, Protecting Your Land from Erosion

2. "Cornell University: Chronicle Online," www.news.cornell.edu/stories/March06/soil.erosion.threat.ssl.html

3. R. Lal, School of Natural Resources, Ohio State University, "Mulching Effects on Runoff, Soil Erosion and Crop Response in Alfisols in Western Nigeria."

**Pages 178-179**: Plant perennials to control erosion beautifully.

1. Albuquerque Bernalillo County Water Utility Authority, www.abcwua.org/waterconservation/xeric.html

**Pages 180-181**: Plant trees and shrubs to control erosion.

1. Center for Urban Forest Research, USDA Forest Service, "Is All Your Rain Going Down the Drain?" www.cufr.ucdavis.edu/

2. Ibid.

3. Ibid.

4. Ibid.

**Pages 182-183**: Use porous paving.

1. Interview, Bruce K. Ferguson, Professor and Director, School of Environmental Design, University of Georgia

2. Ibid.

**Pages 189-191**: Use terracing and walls to slow the flow of water.

1. Natural Resource Conservation Service; Backyard Conservation Tip Sheet and Alabama Cooperative Extension Systems; Soil Management to Protect Water Quality; Structural Measures for Soil Management

**Pages 196-19??**: Plant a rain garden.

1. Interview, Kari Mackenbach, Water Resource Specialist, URS, and www.rainkc.com

2. www.landandwater.com

## Chapter Five: Turning Waste into Gardening Gold

**Pages 200-203**: Introduction

1. EPA, 2003, and www.ecocycle.org/tidbits/index.cfm

2. www.californiaprogressreport.com/2007/01/reduction_of_gr.html:

3. www.dnr.state.md.us/bay/protect/home.html

4. www.epa.gov/msw/faq.htm#7

5. www.epa.gov/epaoswer/osw/conserve/resources/msw-2005.pdf

6. www.californiaprogressreport.com/2007/01/reduction_of_
gr.html:

7. www.zerowasteamerica.org/Landfills.htm

8. Ibid.

**Pages 204-206**: Compost your garden waste.

1. www.epa.gov/epaoswer/non-hw/muncpl/facts.htm

**Pages 207-209**: Compost grass clippings as a valuable resource.

1. www.dnr.state.md.us/bay/protect/yard.html

2. www.bae.ncsu.edu/topic/vermicomposting/pubs/composting.pdf

3. Ibid.

**Pages 210-213**: Compost kitchen waste, paper, and other items to reduce landfill costs.

1. www.epa.gov/epaoswer/non-hw/muncpl/facts.htm

2. Ibid.

3. www.epa.gov/msw/faq.htm#9

**Pages 214-216**: Mulch or compost your leaves—don't send them to the landfill.

1. www.wasteage.com/mag/waste_yard_waste_4/:

2. Purdue University research report, www.agry.purdue.edu/turf/
report/1999/page24.htm

**Pages 217-219**: Use a mulching mower and grasscycle.

1. www.bae.ncsu.edu/topic/vermicomposting/pubs/composting.pdf

2. web.extension.uiuc.edu/homecompost/recycle.html

3. Ibid.

**Page 220**: Use a chipper to break down tree branches.

1. www.wasteage.com/mag/waste_yard_waste_4/:

**Pages 221-222**: Recycle those plastic pots.

1. "Beauty and the Plastic Beast," *Chicago Tribune*, June 10, 2007,
www.chicagotribune.com/news/local/nearwest/chi-0610plastic_
jpjun10,1,7562317,full.story/

2. Ibid.

3. EPA: "Agri-Plas: Recycling Plastics," www.epa.gov/epaoswer/

non-hw/green/projects/agriplas.htm

**Pages 223-224:** Think outside the pot

1. "Beauty and the Plastic Beast," *Chicago Tribune*, June 10, 2007, www.chicagotribune.com/news/local/nearwest/chi-0610plastic_ jpjun10,1,7562317,full.story/

2. Agri-Plas, Inc., www.agriplasinc.com/index_Page385.htm

**Pages 225-227:** Buy plants in pots made from biodegradable material.

1.[needs space]www.marketplace.publicradio.org/display/ web/2007/04/20/putting_more_green_into_pots/#

2. www.neseed.com/CowPots_made_from_Cow_ Manure_p/63100.htm

**Pages 228-229:** Recycle old bricks and broken concrete, windows, etc.

1. www.sfgate.com/cgi-bin/article.cgi?f=/c/a/2007/07/20/BAGC-SQV2VR1.DTL

**Pages 230-231:** Create garden art out of found objects.

1. Cracked Pots Website, www.crackedpots.org, and Portland Tribune, October 29, 2004, "Cracked Pots," www.portlandtribune.com/features/story.php?story_id=25761

## Chapter Six: Consuming Less Energy in the Landscape

**Pages 232-234:** Introduction

1. U.S. Department of Energy, Energy Information Administration, "2001 Residential Energy Consumption Survey," www.eia.doe.gov/emeu/recs/recs2001/enduse2001/enduse2001.html

2. Ibid.

3. Dr. Leonard Perry, Extension Professor, University of Vermont, and www.mindfully.org

4. Dr. Leonard Perry, Extension Professor, University of Vermont

**Pages 235-236:** Plant trees, tall shrubs, and vines to reduce your home's cooling needs.

1. U.S. Department of Energy, Energy Information Administration, "2001 Residential Energy Consumption Survey," www.eia.doe.

gov/emeu/recs/recs2001/enduse2001/enduse2001.html

2. Gordon Heisler, USFS meteorologist, "How Trees Fight Climate Change," *American Forests,* 1999, www.americanforests.org/resources/climatechange/

**Pages 237-238**: Plant an evergreen hedge or windbreak to reduce your home's heating needs.

1. M.A. (Kim) Powell, Extension Horticultural Specialist, Department of Horticultural Science, North Carolina Cooperative Extension Service, North Carolina State University, "Conserving Energy With Plants," www.ces.ncsu.edu/depts/hort/hil/hil-631.html

2. Greentags USA/Bonneville Environmental Foundation, www.greentagsusa.org

3. U.S. Department of Energy, Energy Information Administration, "2001 Residential Energy Consumption Survey," www.eia.doe.gov/emeu/recs/recs2001/enduse2001/enduse2001.html

**Pages 239-240**: Plant trees to purify the air.

1. Diane Relf, Extension Specialist, Environmental Horticulture Virginia Cooperative Extension, "Plants Actually Clean the Air!" www.ext.vt.edu/departments/envirohort/articles/misc/plntclar.html

2. The Center for Urban Forest Research, Pacific Southwest Research Station, USDA Forest Service, Davis, California

**Pages 241-243**: Install and plant a green roof to reduce cooling needs.

1. Erica Oberndorfer et al, "Green Roofs as Urban Ecosystems," *BioScience,* November 19, 2007, www.bioone.org/perlserv/?request=get-document&doi=10.1641%2FB571005#toclink1

2. EPA: "Green Roofs," www.epa.gov/hiri/strategies/greenroofs.html

3. Erica Oberndorfer et al, "Green Roofs as Urban Ecosystems," *BioScience,* November 19, 2007, www.bioone.org/perlserv/?request=get-document&doi=10.1641%2FB571005#toclink1

**Pages 244-245**: Plant a large perennial garden, prairie garden, or meadow garden.

1. Dr. Leonard Perry, Extension Professor, University of Vermont

2. Dr. Leonard Perry, Extension Professor, University of Vermont, and www.mindfully.org.

**Pages 246-247**: Use eco-friendly paving for driveways and parking areas.

1. W. James and B. Verspagen, "Thermal Enrichment of Stormwater by Urban Paving," Chapter 8 in *Advances in Modeling the Management of Stormwater Impacts*, Vol. 5. Published in *Proceedings of the Stormwater and Water Quality Management Modeling Conference*, Toronto, ON, February 22-23, 1996, www.forester.net/sw_0203_green.html

2. Lloyd Alter, "Porous Paving: Open Cell Concrete Block," www.treehugger.com/files/2006/07/porous_pavingop.php

**Pages 248-249**: Use passive solar design in a greenhouse.

1. Edward Mazria, *The Passive Solar Energy Book*, Rodale Press, 1980.

2. Washington State University Energy Extension, www.energy.wsu.edu/

**Pages 252-253**: Grow your own fruits, vegetables, herbs, and other edibles.

1. Interview, Rich Pirog of the Leopold Center for Sustainable Agriculture at Iowa State University

**Pages 254-255**: Reduce the use of fertilizers made from fossil fuels.

1. www.seekingalpha.com/article/33925-natural-gas-investors-to-benefit-from-global-ethanol-boom, and Hosein Shapouri and Andrew McAloon, U.S. Department of Agriculture, "The 2001 Net Energy Balance Of Corn-Ethanol," www.ncga.com/ethanol/pdfs/netEnergy-BalanceUpdate2004.pdf

2. Dr. Leonard Perry, Extension Professor, University of Vermont

**Pages 256-257**: Reduce the use of gasoline-powered engines.

1. Dr. Leonard Perry, Extension Professor, University of Vermont

2. Deepak Sivaraman, Angela S. Lindner, "Comparative Life Cycle Analysis of Gasoline, Battery and Electric Lawn Mowers," *Journal of Environmental Engineering Science*, 2004, 21(6): 768-785. doi:10.1089/ees.2004.21.768:

3. Dr. Leonard Perry, Extension Professor, University of Vermont, and www.mindfully.org.

4. EPA: "Lawn and Garden (Small Gasoline) Equipment,"

www.epa.gov/otaq/equip-ld.htm

**Pages 258-259**: Reduce the size of your lawn—and care for it more responsibly.

1. EPA: "Lawn and Garden (Small Gasoline) Equipment," www.epa.gov/otaq/equip-ld.htm

2. www.seekingalpha.com/article/33925-natural-gas-investors-to-benefit-from-global-ethanol-boom, and Hosein Shapouri and Andrew McAloon, U.S. Department of Agriculture, "The 2001 Net Energy Balance Of Corn-Ethanol," www.ncga.com/ethanol/pdfs/netEnergy-BalanceUpdate2004.pdf

**Pages 260-261**: Keep engines properly maintained for maximum efficiency.

1. EPA: "Your Yard and Clean Air," www.epa.gov/otaq/consumer/19-yard.pdf

2. Ibid.

3. www.bobvila.com/HowTo_Library/Maintaining_Small_Engines-Power_Tools-F2200.html

**Pages 262-263**: Replace your outdoor light bulbs with more energy-efficient types.

1. *Popular Mechanics*, "The Best Compact Fluorescent Light Bulbs," www.popularmechanics.com/home_journal/home_improvement/4215199.html

2. "EPA: If Every Home Changes 1 Bulb, $600 Million Saved," KABC, Los Angeles, November 3, 2007, www.abclocal.go.com/kabc/story?section=consumer&id=5740382

**Pages 264-265**: Set up your outdoor lighting for maximum efficiency.

1. City of Berkeley, Office of Energy & Sustainable Development, www.ci.berkeley.ca.us/sustainable/residents/TrueCosts/100Watt.html

2. www.science.howstuffworks.com/question481.htm

**Pages 266-267**: Use low-voltage lighting in the landscape.

1. San Diego Gas and Electric Utility, www.sdge.com/forms/savingenergy.pdf

**Pages 270-272**: Reduce swimming pool heating costs with the right type of cover.

1. U.S. Department of Energy, "A Consumer's Guide to Energy Efficiency and Renewable Energy," www.eere.energy.gov/consumer/ your_home/water_heating/index.cfm/mytopic=13140?print

2. Ibid.

3. Ibid.

4. Florida Solar Energy Center website/University of Central Florida

5. U.S. Department of Energy, "A Consumer's Guide to Energy Efficiency and Renewable Energy," www.eere.energy.gov/consumer/ your_home/water_heating/index.cfm/mytopic=13140?print

6. Ibid.

**Pages 273-275**: Resist the temptation to burn yard waste.

1. www.treehugger.com/files/2007/05/ask_treehugger_15.php:

## Chapter Seven: Gardening to Protect the Ecosystem

**Pages 276-279**: Introduction

1. www.countdown2010.net

2. Greenfacts, www.greenfacts.org

3. The United Nations Environment Programme; The UNEP World

4. Conservation Monitoring Centre; www.unep-wcmc.org

5. The World Conservation Union (IUCN); www.iucneurope.org

**Pages 280-282**: Promote complexity and avoid monocultures.

1. www.helpfulgardener.com

2. www.biodiversityproject.org/biodiversity.htm

**Pages 283-285**: Protect the gene pool.

1. www.newfarm.org

2. Millennium Seed Bank Project, Wakehurst Place, Ardingly, West Sussex RH17 6TN UK

**Pages 286-288**: Discourage poaching of plants from the wild.

1. www.newfs.org

2. Tanya Schevitz, "Flesh-eating plants so beguiling they lure 3 men to commit crime; Members in Bay group plead guilty to smuggling

rare plants into U.S." *The San Francisco Examiner*, April 16, 1995, p.C2.

3. www.cites.org/

**Pages 293-296**: Build outdoor projects with environmentally responsible wood.

1. www.earthobservatory.nasa.gov/Library/Deforestation/

2. Forest Stewardship Council, press release on Garden Furniture Report www.fscus.org/news/?article=503

3. Ibid.

4. www.rainforestrelief.org

5. Forest Stewardship Council, press release on Garden Furniture Report www.fscus.org/news/?article=503

6. Ibid.

7. www.rainforestrelief.org

8. www.thegreenguide.com/doc/96/wood

**Pages 297-299**: Avoid invasive non-native plants.

1. Cornell University research, www.news.cornell.edu/releases/Jan99/species_costs.html

2. www.asla.org/profpractice/Invasive_species/invasive_spp.htm:

3. www.nature.org/initiatives/invasivespecies/features/

4. www.invasivespeciesinfo.gov/plants/main.shtml

5. The Nature Conservancy, www.nature.org/wherewework/northamerica/states/northcarolina/initiatives/art12730.html

**Pages 300-301**: Protect standing dead trees whenever possible.

1. www.wnrmag.com/stories/2005/aug05/red.htm

2. www.dnr.sc.gov/news/Yr2006/dec25/dec25_snag.html

**Pages 302-305**: Provide a variety of water sources for wildlife.

1. U.S. Geological Survey, National Water Summary on Wetland Resources, Water Supply Paper 2425 www.water.usgs.gov/nwsum/WSP2425/birdhabitat.html

2. Ibid.

**Pages 306-308**: Plant to support butterflies.

1. www.prairiefrontier.com/pages/butterflies/endangered.html

2. U.S. Forest Service, www.fs.fed.us/monarchbutterfly/index.shtml

3. www.suite101.com/article.cfm/endangered_species/73391:

**Pages 309-311**: Participate in the National Wildlife Federation's Wildlife Habitat Program.

1. www.nwf.org/backyard/70000goal.cfm:

## Chapter Eight: Taking It Over the Fence

**Pages 331-332**: Get involved in local bird habitat programs.

1. Worldwatch Paper #165: "Winged Messengers: The Decline of Birds," Worldwatch Institute, March 10, 2003, www.worldwatch.org/node/1763

2. Ibid.

3. Ibid.

# LIST OF ACTIONS

## Chapter One
*Gardening to Make a Difference* 10

## Chapter Two
*Conserving Water in the Garden*
Introduction, *20*
Supply only the water your plants need—know when to water and how much. *23*
Water deeply and less often. *28*
Water at the right time of day. *30*
Mulch, mulch, mulch! *31*
Use rain barrels. *32*
Fix leaky faucets and hoses. 37
Don't use water in place of a broom or blower. *39*
Don't leave your hose running while unattended. *40*
Program your irrigation system to apply the right amount of water. *41*
Include a rain sensor in an automatic irrigation system. *43*
Install an integrated weather monitoring system. *45*
Irrigate deeply using the two-step "cycle-and-soak" process. *47*
Program your irrigation system for seasonal needs. *49*
Maintain your irrigation system. *50*
Convert to soaker hoses or drip irrigation where feasible. *54*
Use plants that need less water—Xeriscape™. *57*

## Chapter Three
*Reducing Garden Chemicals to Protect Our Water*
Introduction, *64*
Protect soil flora and fauna. *67*
Build healthy soil by adding organic matter. *70*
Use compost as a soil conditioner and fertilizer. *73*
Let earthworms do the work for *really* healthy soil. *76*
Use natural and organic sources of nutrients. *79*

Grow the right plant in the right place. *83*
Grow tough pest- and disease-resistant plants. *87*
Reduce chemical use by raising your tolerance for little imperfections. *91*
Catch problems early. *94*
Control pests with natural controls first. *96*
Practice good sanitation for a healthy garden. *101*
Water at the right time of day and keep it off the foliage. *104*
Use beneficial insects, the predatory agents of biological control. *106*
If you're going to use an insecticide, explore biological ones first. *110*
Mulch to control weeds. *113*
Use landscape fabric to control weeds. *116*
Use other easy ways to eliminate weeds without chemicals. *118*
Don't nuke those weeds—solarize 'em. *121*
Use corn gluten as a natural pre-emergence weed control. *125*
If you need to use a chemical, follow the label. *128*
Good timing is everything. *132*
Don't spray on windy days. *135*
Get a soil test before you add fertilizers and other amendments. 138
Apply fertilizers responsibly and follow the label. *141*
Keep fertilizers and other chemicals off pavement. *144*
Store chemicals safely. *148*
Dispose of chemicals safely. *151*
Use bagged soil and mulch that is certified. *154*
Use alternatives to CCA-treated wood. *156*
Beware of the unintended effect of deicers in winter. *159*
Avoid fuel spills when filling gasoline-powered equipment. *162*

## Chapter Four
### *Landscaping to Control Runoff*
Introduction, *164*
Protect topsoil on construction sites. *167*
Add organic matter to the soil for percolation and retention. *170*
Don't till—let earthworms do the job. *172*
Mulch to reduce runoff. *175*

Plant perennials to control erosion beautifully. *178*
Plant trees and shrubs to control erosion. *180*
Use porous paving. *182*
Grade for on-site drainage. *184*
Install a drainage system. 187
Use terracing and walls to slow the flow of water. *189*
Use swales to slow or capture drainage. *192*
Plant a rain garden. *194*
Create a seasonal water feature. *198*

## Chapter Five
*Turning Waste into Gardening Gold*
Introduction, *200*
Compost your garden waste. *204*
Compost grass clippings as a valuable resource. *207*
Compost kitchen waste, paper, and other items to reduce landfill costs. *210*
Mulch or compost your leaves—don't send them to the landfill. *214*
Use a mulching mower and grasscycle. *217*
Use a chipper to break down tree branches. *220*
Recycle those plastic pots. *221*
Think outside the pot by reducing the use of other garden-related plastics. *223*
Buy plants in pots made from biodegradable material. *225*
Recycle old bricks and broken concrete, windows, etc. *228*
Create garden art out of found objects. *230*

## Chapter Six
*Consuming Less Energy in the Landscape*
Introduction, *232*
Plant trees, tall shrubs, and vines to reduce your home's cooling needs. *235*
Plant an evergreen hedge or windbreak to reduce your home's heating needs. *237*
Plant trees to purify the air. *239*

Install and plant a green roof to reduce cooling needs. *241*

Plant a large perennial garden, prairie garden, or meadow garden. *244*

Use eco-friendly paving for driveways and parking areas. *246*

Use passive solar design in a greenhouse. *248*

Buy locally grown and processed garden materials. *250*

Grow your own fruits, vegetables, herbs, and other edibles. *252*

Reduce the use of fertilizers made from fossil fuels. *254*

Reduce the use of gasoline-powered engines. *256*

Reduce the size of your lawn—and care for it more responsibly. *258*

Keep engines properly maintained for maximum efficiency. *260*

Replace your outdoor light bulbs with more energy-efficient types. *262*

Set up your outdoor lighting for maximum efficiency. *264*

Use low-voltage lighting in the landscape. *266*

Use solar-powered lights for outdoor lighting. *268*

Reduce swimming pool heating costs with the right type of cover. *270*

Resist the temptation to burn yard waste. *273*

## Chapter Seven

*Gardening to Protect the Ecosystem*

Introduction, *276*

Promote complexity and avoid monocultures. *280*

Protect the gene pool. *283*

Discourage poaching of plants from the wild. *286*

Do your homework before using traps for insect pests—either they don't work, or they work too well! *289*

Build outdoor projects with environmentally responsible wood. *293*

Avoid invasive non-native plants. *297*

Protect standing dead trees whenever possible. *300*

Provide a variety of water sources for wildlife. *302*

Plant to support butterflies. *306*

Participate in the National Wildlife Federation's Wildlife Habitat Program. *309*

## Chapter Eight

*Taking It Over the Fence*

Introduction, *312*

Request that your local nursery or garden center carry eco-friendly products. *316*

Educate your neighbors. *318*

If they're not going to use it themselves, encourage your neighbors to share compostable yard waste with you. *321*

Start an eco-friendly garden at your local school, day care, or other facility. *323*

Develop an eco-friendly garden in your neighborhood. *326*

Get involved in tree preservation and planting in your neighborhood. *328*

Get involved in local parks and green spaces, and work with them to use eco-friendly management. *330*

Get involved in local bird habitat programs. *331*

Get political! Join an organization that organizes and lobbies for ecological issues. *333*

# INDEX

*Actinomycetes*, 67

Aerating, 62

    and earthworms, 76

Air quality, 18

Aquatic life, 13, 160, 166

*Bacillus thuringiensis* (Bt), 97, 110, 111, 307

Biodegradable pots, 225-227

Biodiversity, 18, 276-282, 297

    loss of, 286-288

Biological control, 106, 110, 111

Bioretention, 185

Birds

    habitat programs, 331-332

    water to attract, 303-305

Blood meal, 82

Bone meal, 82

Botanical insecticides, 100

Bt, 97, 307

Butterflies, 306-308

Buy locally, 17, 250-252

Calcium chloride, 160

Carbon neutral, 10

CCA-treated wood, 154, 156-158

Chemical(s), 13, 17, 18

    correct use of, 128-131

    de-icers, 159-161

    drift, 135-137

    impact of, 128

    reducing use of, see Chapter 3, 64-163

    safe disposal of, 151-153

    safe storage of, 148-153

Climate change, 10, 11

Cold frames, 229

Compact florescent light bulbs, 262-263

Compost, 16, 18, 62, 200-216, 220, 321-322

    as fertilizer, 73-75

    as soil conditioner, 73-75

    essential elements, 74

    how to, 74-75

    starting, 74

    structures for, 74

    tea, 36

Conserving

    water, 20-63

Corn gluten, 125-127

    application rate, 126

    proper application, 126

Deadheading, 62

Deforestation, 331-332

De-icers, 159-161

Diatomaceous earth, 99

Disease

    and garden sanitation, 101-103

    resistance, 87-90

    signs of, 101-102

    treatment of, 92-93

    triangle, 101

Dragonflies, 107

Drainage, 184-193

    French drain, 187-188

Drip irrigation, 54-56, 105

Dry stream bed, 198-199

Earthworms, 76-78, 172-174

    and fertilizer, 142

Eco-friendly, 10

    containers, 225-227

    garden(s), 83, 193, 254-255, 323-327

    landscape, 185-186

    park and green space management, 330

    paving, 246-247

    pest control, 96-100, 132-134

    products, 316-317

    weed control, 125-127

Ecological issues, 333-334

Ecosystem(s), 18

    gardening to protect, 276-310

Emissions

    from landfills, 200-203

Energy, 18

    consuming less, 232-274

    covering swimming pools, 270-271

    efficient light bulbs, 262-263

    miles, 250

    outdoor lighting, 264-265

    planting to reduce consumption, 235-238

Engines

    proper maintenance of, 260-261

Environmental

    footprint, 10

    stewardship, 12

Erosion, 167-168

    control of, 116, 175-183, 189-191

Evapotranspiration (E.T.), 24, 45-46

Fertilizer, 70

    application of, 141-147

    application rates, 142

    basics, 81

build up in soil, 142
compost as, 73-75
equipment for, 145-146
follow directions, 141-147
leaching, 143
micronutrients, 141
organic and natural alternatives, 81-82
organic vs. non-organic, 80-81
over application of, 142
prevent contamination by, 146
reduce use of, 254-255
runoff, 143
soil test, 138-140
spills, 147
Fish emulsion, 82
Fossil fuels
fertilizer made from, 254-255
French drain, 187-188
Fusarium wilt, 87
Garden
art, 230-231
eco-friendly, 83, 96-100
know conditions of, 84
rain, 194-197
sanitation for healthy, 101-103
Gardening
lasagna, 173-174
proactive vs. reactive, 94
tolerance for imperfections, 91-93
to protect ecosystem, 276-310
to support butterflies, 306-308
vegetables, 252-253
Gasoline
powered engines, 256-257
powered equipment, 162
proper handling of, 162-163
Gene pool
protecting, 283-285
Geotextile fabrics, 116
Global warming, 10
Going green, 10
Grass
clippings, 207-209
fertilization, 62, 141-143
mowing, 62
Grasscycle, 62, 207, 217-219
Greenhouse, 248-249
gases, 10
Green nutrients, 80-82
Green roof, 241-243
Ground Beetles, 107
Groundwater, 110

contamination by deicers, 159-161
Grow your own, 252-253
Grubs, see Japanese Beetles
Heat zone maps, 11
Herbicide(s)
chemical drift, 135-137
corn gluten, 125-127
safe disposal of 151-153
safe storage of, 148-150
Hoses
leaks, 37-38
soaker, 54-56, 61, 105
Humus, 81
Hydrozoning, 58
Insecticidal oil, 98
Insecticidal soap, 98
Insecticide(s),
biological, 110-112
botanical, 100
chemical drift, 137
diatomaceous earth (DE) 99
low toxicity, 110
microbial, 97
milky spore, 111
natural, 96-100
neem oil, 99
non-selective, 108
oils, 98
pyrethrin, 100
reduced need for, 116-117
safe disposal of, 151-153
safe storage of, 148-153
soaps, 98
Insect(s)
attracting beneficial, 108
beneficial, 13, 106-109
control of, 132-134, 289-292
life cycle of, 133
manual control of, 92
purchasing beneficial, 108
Integrated pest management (IPM), 18, 66, 95, 104, 144
IPM, 18, 66, 95, 104, 144
Irrigation
contribution to disease, 104
correct timing, 104-105
cycle-and-soak process, 47-48
efficient, 61
Xeriscape, 59
Irrigation system, 41-56
adjust timing, 42, 61
drip system, 54-56, 61

leaks, 50-53
maintenance, 50-53
measure output, 41
programming, 49, 50
rain sensor, 43
weather monitoring system, 45-46
Xeriscape, 61
Japanese Beetle
milky spore, 111, 133
traps, 289-290
Kitchen waste
composting, 210-213
Lacewings, 107
Lady Beetle, 107
Landfills, 200-203
Landscape
consuming less energy in, 232-274
design, 58
fabric, 116-117
lighting, 262-269
Landscaping
dry stream bed, 198-199
to control runoff, 164-199
Xeriscape, 557-63
Lawn     (s), 13
fertilization, 62
grasscycling, 217-219
mowing, 62
reduce size of, 258-259
watering, 104-105
Xeriscape, 59
Leaks, 16
fixing, 37-38
irrigation system, 50-53
Leaves
composting, 214-216
Light bulbs, 262-263
Lighting
landscape, 262-269
Maintenance
engines, 260-261
Meadow garden, 244-245
Microorganisms, 67
Milky spore, 111-112, 133-134
Monocultures, 280-282
Mowing, 13, 62
Mulch, 31, 60
certification of, 17, 154-155
choosing, 175-177
inorganic, 114
organic, 114
to control weeds, 113-115

to reduce runoff, 175-177
Xeriscape, 60
National Wildlife Federation, 309-310
Native plants, 58, 244-245
Natural nutrients, 79-82
Neem oil, 99
Nitrogen, 82, 141
Nutrients, 13, 70
earthworm castings, 76
green, 80-82
natural and organic sources of, 79-82
organic vs. non-organic, 80-81
Organic matter, 67
adding to soil, 60 70-72
for percolation and retention, 170-171
nutrients, 70
Organic
nutrients, 79-82
pest control, 96-100
Overwatering, 23, 26, 45
Paper
composting, 211-213
Parasitic wasps, 108
Passive solar design
for greenhouse, 248-249
Paving, 182-183, 246-247
Perennial garden, 244-245
Perennials
list of hardy, 85
to control erosion, 178-179
Pest control, 63
beneficial insects, 106-109
biological control, 106-109
diatomaceous earth, 99
insecticidal oil, 98
insecticidal soap, 98
insect life cycle, 132-133
microbial insecticides, 97
natural, 96-100
neem oil, 99
no-spray method, 96
resistance, 87-90
timing of, 132-143
Pesticides, 18, 129
importance of label, 129-131
safe disposal of, 151-153
safe storage of, 148-153
use of chemical, 129-131
Phosphorus, 81-82, 141
Planting
for healthy gardens, 65
green roof, 241-243

meadow garden, 244-245
perennial garden, 244-245
prairie garden, 244-245
slopes, 179
to control erosion, 178-181
to purify air, 239-240
to reduce cooling needs, 235-236
to reduce heating needs, 237-238
to support butterflies, 306-308
trees, 328-329
Plant(s)
avoid invasive non-native, 297-299
discourage poaching, 286-288
grouping of, 59
exclusion of, 101
health of, 65
hardy perennials, 85
ideal conditions, 84
integrated pest management, 66
keeping healthy, 18
native, 179
pest- and disease-resistant, 87-90
placement, 17, 65, 83-86
read the tag, 84
resistance, 87
right place for, 83-86
tough, 88
Xeriscape, 59
Plastic
recycling pots, 221-222
reduce use of, 223-224
Pollution, 12, 13, 17
Potassium, 81-82, 141
chloride, 160
Pots
biodegradable, 225-227
plastic, 221-229
Prairie garden, 244-245
Pressure-treated lumber, 156-158
Proactive gardening, 94
Pruning, 62
Pyrethrin, 100
Rain barrels, 16, 32-36
Rainfall
and runoff, 180
irrigation sensor, 43
Rain garden, 194-197
Rain gauge, 24
Rainwater
harvesting of, 32-36
Recycling, 18, 221-229
for garden art, 230-231

to build cold frames, 229
Reduce use of
fertilizer, 254-255
gasoline-powered engines, 256-257
Retaining walls, 191
Roguing, 102-103
Root-knot nematodes, 87
Runoff
French drain, 187-188
from paving, 182-183
grading to prevent, 184-186
landscaping to control, 164-199
mulch to reduce, 175-177
perennials to control, 179
rain garden to control, 194-197
shrubs to control, 180-181
terracing to slow, 189-191
trees to control, 180-181
walls to slow, 189-191
Sanitation
for healthy garden, 101-103
Seeds, 283-285
Shrubs
to control erosion, 180-181
Soaker hoses, 54-56
Sodium chloride, 160
Soil
aerating, 62
building healthy, 70-72
certification of bagged, 17, 154-155
conditioner, 73-75
drainage, 60
erosion, 116, 167-168, 175, 189-191
fertilizer, 73-75
improvement, 60
microbes, 68
moisture, 68
protection of, 67-72, 167-169
solarization of, 121-124
structure, 81
Soil food web, 13, 69, 173
Soil health, 62, 67-72
using earthworms, 76-78
test, 17, 138-140
Solarization, 121-124
Solar-powered lights, 268-269
Stormwater, 166
management, 184-186, 192-193,
194-199
Swales, 192-193
Swimming pool, 270-272
Syrphid flies, 106

Terracing, 189-191
Tobacco mosaic virus, 87
Topsoil, 167-169
Trees
    planting, 328-329
    protect dead, 300-301
    to control erosion, 180-181
    to purify air, 239-240
Turf, 59 *See also* Grass; Lawns
USDA Plant Hardiness map, 11
Vermicastings, 76
Vermicompost, 76-78
    tea, 36
Verticillium wilt, 87
VFNT, 87
Water
    amount, 41-42
    conserving, 20-63
    dry stream bed, 198-199
    harvesting of, 32-36
    judging need for, 25-27
    pollution, 164
    protecting, 64-163
    reduce need for, 57-63
    reduce use of, 18
    removing pollutants, 192-193
    retention, 14
    reuse in garden 14
    runoff, 14, 47, 57, 189-191
    sources for wildlife, 302-310
    use less, 23
    Xeriscape, 57-63
Watering, 16, 25-27
    at soil level, 54, 105
    cycle-and-soak process, 47-48
    deeply, 28-29,
    grouping plants, 59

    runoff, 47
    seasonal needs, 49
    supplemental, 23
    time of day, 104-105
    Xeriscape, 57-63
Watersheds, 110
Weather
    monitoring system, 45-46
Weed(s)
    annual, 113
    eliminate, 118-120
    hand-pulling, 114, 118
    perennial, 113, 126
    physical barrier, 116-117
    prevention, 120
    suppression of, 116
    tap-rooted, 120
Weed control
    by mowing higher, 118
    by solarization, 121-124
    with acetic acid (vinegar), 119
    with boiling water, 119
    with corn gluten, 125-127
    with flame weeders, 120
    with landscape fabric, 116-117
    with mulch, 113-115
    with plant-based ingredients, 119
Wildlife, 302-310
Windbreak, 237-238
Wood
    CCA-treated alternatives, 156-158
    use of environmentally responsible, 293-296
Xeriscape, 57-63
Yard waste
    burning, 273-274
Yellow jackets, 108

*Let us give Nature a chance;*
*she knows her business better*
*than we do.*

MICHAEL EYQUEN de MONTAIGNE

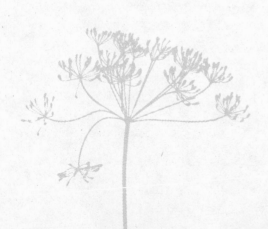

With a gift for teaching and an inspirational personality, when Joe Lamp'l shares his enthusiasm for environmental stewardship, it's contagious.

Interested in horticulture since childhood, he has gardened both personally and professionally for more than thirty years.

In 2002, he was tapped to host *Fresh from the Garden* on the DIY Network.

Joe Lamp'l

The series was unique, relying on Joe's expertise as a Master Gardener and Certified Landscape Professional, because it showed viewers how to take vegetables from seed to harvest in a single episode--all while maintaining a picture-perfect garden. After three successful seasons, the show retired.

Joe was immediately selected to host *GardenSMART* on PBS television where he currently features spectacular gardens, bringing inspiration and relevant information into the homes of viewers around the country.

In addition, Joe is a frequent guest expert on other popular national television and radio shows and is a presenter and prolific writer, penning a weekly syndicated newspaper column, magazine and Web site articles, blogs, and his previous book, *Over the Fence with joe gardener®*.

At the hub of this diverse network of eco-friendly information about gardening and sustainable outdoor lifestyles is his business and its Web site, The *joe gardener®* Company and joegardener.com, where the central focus is to provide smart, eco-friendly resources for gardeners of every level.

Joe lives and gardens in North Carolina with his wife and two young daughters.

NOTES